Commerce

25 Years 2025-2001

ISC

CHAPTERWISE QUESTION BANK

Commerce

Class 12

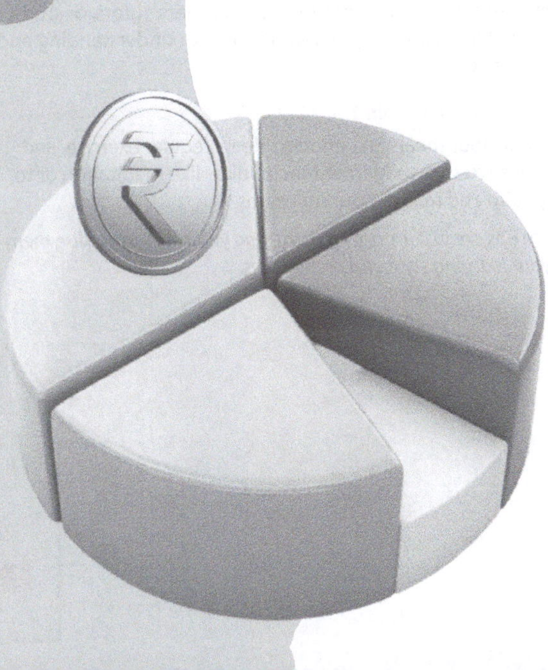

Author
Sapna Malik

arihant
SUCCESS AND NOTHING LESS

arihant
SUCCESS AND NOTHING LESS

ARIHANT PRAKASHAN
(School Division Series)

ADMINISTRATIVE & PRODUCTION OFFICES

Regd. Office
'Ramchhaya' 4577/15, Agarwal Road, Darya Ganj, New Delhi -110002
Tele: 011- 47630600, 43518550

Head Office
Kalindi, TP Nagar, Meerut (UP) - 250002, Tel: 0121-7156203, 7156204

SALES & SUPPORT OFFICES

Agra, Ahmedabad, Bengaluru, Bareilly, Chennai, Delhi, Guwahati, Hyderabad, Jaipur, Jhansi, Kolkata, Lucknow, Nagpur & Pune.

PO No : TXT-XX-XXXXXXX-X-XX

Published By Arihant Publications (India) Ltd.

For further information about the books published by Arihant, log on to www.arihantbooks.com or e-mail at info@arihantbooks.com

PRICE ₹220.00

Follow us on

Achieving 99+
Marks in Board Exams

Achieving 99+ marks in board exams is definitely an ambitious goal, but with the right approach and these 7 tips from toppers, you can definitely increase your chances of success!

Here are the 7 Topper Tips to ace your board exams:

1. Master the art of consistency

Consistency builds understanding and confidence, both crucial for excelling in exams.

2. Build a winning study strategy

Create a personalised timetable that prioritises subjects based on your strengths and weaknesses.

3. Befriend the syllabus

Focus on high-weightage topics and prioritise mastering core concepts before moving on to advanced ones.

4. Embrace active learning

Explain concepts to yourself or in study groups to solidify understanding.

5. Conquer the past

Solve Past years' papers and Sample Papers under timed conditions to practice time management and understand paper pattern.

6. Seek help, when needed!

Don't hesitate to clarify doubts with teachers, tutors, or study groups. Asking questions strengthens your understanding and prevents confusion.

7. Prioritise well-being

Eat nutritious meals, get enough sleep, regular exercise and practice stress management techniques like meditation or to stay calm and focused during exams.

These tips are just a starting point, and you can personalise them to fit your learning style and preferences.

Description of

Newly Added Features

01

Business Environment

TREND ANALYSIS 5 YEARS

		Average No. of Questions Across all Sets					
		Types of Questions	2024	2023	2020	2019	2018
TOPIC 01	Concept of Business Environment	1 Mark	1	1	—	—	—
		2 Marks	—	—	—	1	—
		3/4/5 Marks	—	—	—	—	1
TOPIC 02	Dimensions of Business Environment	1 Mark	1	2	—	—	—
		2 Marks	—	—	1	—	1
		3/4/5 Marks	2	2	1	1	—

Trend Analysis

At the start of each chapter, Trend Analysis is given to indicate the types of Questions asked from different topics of the chapter. This feature helps students to know the importance of different topics of the given chapter from exam point of view and helps them to prepare accordingly.

8. Write a short note on SWOT analysis. *ISC 2016 (4M)*

Ans SWOT is an acronym for Strengths (S), Weaknesses (W), Opportunities (O) and Threats (T).

This is a very important and useful tool for the marketer, entrepreneur or business person for analysing business environment. The SWOT analysis provides information that is helpful in matching the firm's resources and capabilities to the competitive environment in which it operates.

Value Point

For getting maximum marks, following point can be included in the answer

- Give SWOT analysis of any company to increase understanding.

Value Points

'Value Points' are given with selected questions with the purpose to help students to know the key points to be covered in the answer to get full marks.

14. Which of the following is not an internal factor of micro environment? *ISC Sem I 2021*

(a) Employees and human resources
(b) Government policy
(c) Corporate culture
(d) Mission and objectives of the company

Ans (b) Government policy

Common Mistake Most of the students overlook the word NOT and select wrong answer. So, you need to read question very carefully.

Common Mistakes

It focuses on some of the general but critical mistakes that students commit while solving the questions. This feature helps students to develop the habit of avoiding mistakes while solving questions

1. Explain any five external factors of micro environment that influence a business organisation. *ISC 2024 (5M)*

Or Briefly explain any four external factors of micro environment of business. *ISC 2019 (4M)*

Ans External factors of micro environment are the forces, individuals, groups and agencies which come into direct contact with the organisation during its operations.

Concept Enhancer External factors of micro environment may not influence all the firms in a particular industry in the same manner.

Concept Enhancer

Concept Enhancer gives the brief description of the concept, which has been used to solve the question. This feature provides revision of important concept along with practice of question solving.

Most Important Topics

from each Chapter

On the basis of analysis of last 5 Years' Board Examination Papers, we have identified Important Topics from each chapter.

Chapter Name	Important Topics	Weightage in Last 5 Years' Boards				
		2025	2024	2023	2020	2019
Business Environment	Concept of Business Environment	1M	1M	1M		2M
	Dimensions of Business Environment	1M,1M,5M	1M,3M,5M	1M,1M, 5M,3M	2M,4M	4M
Finance and Capital	Finance					
	Financial Planning and Capital Structure		4M	1M		5M
	Fixed and Working Capital	4M	1M	1M	3M,2M	3M
Long-term Sources of Finance for a Joint Stock Company	Equity and Preference Shares and Retained Earnings	1M,4M, 5M	3M,5M	1M,5M, 5M,4M	5M,5M	4M,3M,4M
	Borrowed Capital- Debentures and Loans	1M, 5M	1M		3M,4M	3M
Short-term Sources of Finance for a Joint Stock Company	Short-term Sources, Public Deposits, Financial Assistance, Trade Credit		4M	4M	2M	4M,2M
	Customer Advances, Factoring, ICD, Instalment Credit				4M	
Banking Latest Trends	E-banking		5M	1M,3M	5M	2M,4M
	Mobile Banking, Debit Card, Credit Card and ATMs	1M, 3M, 3M	1M	3M	2M	
Management : An Introduction	Management :Meaning, Objectives and Characteristics	1M	1M	4M	2M,4M	2M,3M
	Importance and Nature of Management					4M
Principles of Management	Introduction to Principles of Management	1M	1M			
	Taylor's Principles of Scientific Management	1M				5M
	Fayol's Principles of Management and Comparison	2M, 2M	4M	1M	4M	
Functions of Management	Introduction to Functions, Planning	4M	3M,4M	1M,1M,4M	5M	3M,4M
	Organising	1M, 4M	1M, 4M	3M	3M	5M
	Staffing	1M,4M	1M,4M	4M	2M,3M,5M	2M
	Directing	1M,2M	1M,1M,5M	2M,4M	2M,4M,5M	2M,5M,4M
	Controlling	2M, 4M	4M	1M,5M		5M
	Coordination	3M		1M		
Marketing Concept and Functions	Market and Marketing	1M, 4M	1M	1M,1M	2M,2M,5M	2M,3M
	Functions of Marketing	1M	1M,4M		4M	2M
Marketing Mix	Product Mix	4M, 3M	1M,1M, 2M,4M		3M	3M
	Price Mix	5M				5M
	Place Mix		1M	1M,1M,2M	2M,4M	4M
	Promotion Mix	1M	4M	1M,2M, 2M,5M	5M,3M	3M,5M
Consumer Protection	Concept of Consumer Protection			4M	3M	
	Consumer Protection Act, 2019	1M,4M	1M,4M	1M,3M		2M,4M

Dream, Believe, Achieve Insights from ISC Toppers

Follow all the 5P's

• Persistence • Passion • Perseverance • Purpose • Practice

MANYA GUPTA
ISC Topper (99.75%)

Aim for high marks, that's what I was doing. I convinced myself that if I aim for 100 I will at least get a 95. That was my logic, but I ended up getting a 100.

I studied with the help of my school and tuition classes. I didn't study daily much, but before the exams, I used to pull all-nighters and study.

ARYAAN
ISC Topper (99.75%)

Studying for 3-4 hours every day along with six hours of school helped me secure 399 out of 400 marks, scoring 99.75%.

I'm very active on all social media platforms but it has never hindered my studies. I strike a balance between hard work and fun.

The degree of toughness of any subject is merely a subjective outlook. I made sure that I incentivised myself at times when I didn't feel like sitting at my study table, especially for theoretical subjects.

I simply believe in revising the concepts which were taught at school or tuitions that very day and minimise backlogs as much as I could.

POOJA KEJRIWAL
ISC Topper (97.5%)

I believe there is no substitute to hard work. There was no fixed hours of preparation. I read a topic till the time I completely understood it. I had to be satisfied with the topic covered.

See it is important to take breaks and everyone has their own way of entertainment. I do chat with friends on social media. I think it is fine until it becomes an addiction.

There is no secret formula as such, but one should not panic and have faith in his/her preparation.

DEVANG KUMAR
ISC Topper

DIMPLE KOTHARI
ISC Topper (97.5%)

- Don't run behind marks, crave for knowledge, experience because ultimately that's gonna help you.
- Don't let peer pressure dominate you.
- If you want to obtain good marks, leave all social media-This is a myth. I was active on Instagram & WhatsApp before my examinations, and even during my examinations. It's just that you need to remember that everyone has the same 24 hours, it's how you utilize it as well as enjoy it better than others.
- Both early morning and late night studies are best ~ you need to choose what's better for you.
- Don't hesitate to ask questions. If you have any doubts, please clarify. Everyone has different learning styles and speed, so it's nothing to be ashamed of.
- Never give up.

Please Note that all the information is collected from different websites.

Contents

ISC Chapterwise Question Bank 2025-2001

Latest Syllabus

Class XII (2025-26)

There will be two papers in the subject.

Paper I Theory : 3 Hours — 80 Marks

Paper II Project Work — 20 Marks

PAPER I THEORY — 80 Marks

S.No.	UNIT	Total Weightage
1.	Business Environment	7 Marks
2.	Financing	20 Marks
3.	Management	33 Marks
4.	Marketing	20 Marks
	Total	**80 Marks**

1. Business Environment

Concept, and importance of Business Environment.

Meaning, features and importance of Business Environment; Environmental Scanning-Meaning.

Dimensions of Business Environment – Micro (Internal and External factors) and Macro (Economic, social, technological, political and legal) – meaning and components.

S.W.O.T. Analysis - A basic understanding of S.W.O.T. (Strength, Weakness, Opportunity and Threat) Analysis.

2. Financing

(i) Capital: Sources of finance for sole trader; partnership; Joint Stock Company; financial planning.

Importance of finance for business. Sources of finance for different types of business firms. Meaning, features and importance of financial planning. Factors affecting capital structure. Fixed capital - meaning, factors affecting fixed capital. Working capital – meaning, types; factors affecting working capital. Comparison between fixed and working capital.

(ii) Sources of finance for a Joint Stock Company.

(a) Different types of shares: equity, preference.

Bonus shares, rights issue, ESOP, Sweat Equity Shares, Retained earnings.

Long-term sources of funds.

Equity shares - features, advantages and disadvantages.

Preference shares - features, types, advantages and disadvantages; distinction between equity shares and preference shares.

Bonus and rights issue, ESOP and Sweat Equity Shares, Qualified Institutional Placement - meaning. Distinction between bonus shares and right shares.

Retained earnings – meaning, merits and demerits.

(b) Loan capital: debentures.

Debentures – meaning; kinds of debentures; advantages and disadvantages of debentures. Distinction between shares and debentures.

(c) Loans from commercial banks and Financial Institutions.

Loans from commercial banks and Financial Institutions - meaning, advantages and disadvantages.

(d) Short-term sources of funds.

Short-term sources of funds – different types of short-term financial assistance by Commercial Banks; public deposits, trade credit, customer advances, factoring, Inter corporate deposits and installment credit. Meaning, advantages and disadvantages of various sources of funds.

(iii) Banking - latest trends.

Online services- transfer of funds through Real Time Gross Settlement (RTGS), National Electronic Funds Transfer (NEFT), Immediate Payment Service (IMPS), issue of demand drafts online meaning and features.

Online payments, e-Banking – meaning and features, advantages and disadvantages.

Mobile Banking - SMS alerts, transfer of funds, making payments - advantages and disadvantages.

Debit Cards vs Credit Cards, ATM (Automated Teller Machine) – Meaning; Debit card and credit card: features and differences.

Digital Banking, UPI, E-wallet-Meaning only.

3. Management

(i) Management: Meaning, objectives and characteristics of management

Meaning of Management: as an activity; as a group; as a discipline; as a process. Objectives and characteristics of management.

(ii) Nature of Management – Science, Art and Profession.
Self explanatory.

(iii) Importance of Management. Levels of Management - Meaning and functions. *Self explanatory.*

(iv) Principles of Management: nature of principles; need for principles
Nature of principles of Management; need for principles of management; Taylor's 5 scientific principles of Management; Fayol's 14 principles of Management; Relevance of the Principles of Management in today's business scenario; Comparison of Taylor's and Fayol's principles.

(v) Functions of Management: Planning; Organising; Staffing; Directing; Controlling and Coordinating.

(a) Planning

Meaning, steps, importance & limitation; Types of plans; Objectives, policy, procedures, method, rule, budget, program, strategy – meaning and features.

(b) Organising

Meaning, importance, steps; Structure of organization (functional and divisional; Formal and informal organization) – Meaning, features, merits, demerits and differences between functional and divisional, formal and informal; Meaning and importance of delegation of authority; Decentralization v/s Centralization, comparison between delegation and decentralization, merits and demerits.

(c) Staffing

Meaning, steps and importance; Recruitment – Meaning and sources; Selection –Meaning and procedure; Training and development – Meaning, types of training, methods-off the job training and on the job training, difference between selection and recruitment, Training and Development-Meaning and differences between training and development.

(d) Directing

Meaning and importance; Supervision- Meaning, functions and span of control; Motivation - Meaning and Maslow's theory; Leadership- Meaning and styles of leadership - Democratic, Autocratic, Laissez-faire, Bureaucratic - meaning only. Communication - Meaning, objectives and process. Barriers to communication and overcoming barriers to communication.

(e) Controlling

Meaning, steps and importance; Relationship between Planning and Controlling; Management by Exception.

(f) Coordination

Meaning of Coordination; Coordination as an essence of Management.

4. Marketing

(i) Marketing: Concept and Functions.
Meaning and types of markets; meaning and features of marketing. Marketing concepts: traditional v/s modern - meaning and features of traditional and modern concepts of marketing. Comparison between marketing and selling. Objectives and importance of marketing; functions of marketing – meaning, features of each function of marketing.

(ii) Marketing Mix - Meaning and Elements
Product Mix - goods and services - meaning, features and types of goods; meaning, features of services; difference between product and services. Branding: meaning and merits. Labeling: meaning and merits. Packaging: meaning and features of good packaging.
Price Mix – meaning, factors determining price. Pricing strategies - Cost plus pricing, Competitive pricing, price-skimming, penetration pricing, value based pricing- meaning only.
Place Mix – meaning, channel of distribution choice of channels of distribution and physical distribution. Elements of physical distribution-meaning only.
Promotion Mix – Meaning and elements.
Elements – Advertising, sales promotion, personal selling and publicity – meaning, features, objectives and differences.

(iii) Consumer protection: rights of consumers, methods of consumer protection.
Need for consumer protection; methods of consumer protection - self-help, legislative measures and consumer associations/NGOs, Consumer Protection Act, 2019 - Meaning of consumer, rights of consumers and responsibilities of consumers.
The revised pecuniary jurisdiction according to Consumer Protection Rule 21 to be taken with reference to the Consumer Disputes Redressal Commissions (National, State and District). The Consumer Protection Act, 2023 to be taken into consideration only with reference to misleading advertisements.
Difference between Consumer Protection Act, 1986 and Consumer Protection Act, 2019.

Analysis of Pupil's Performance: ISC Commerce

Topics found difficult/confusing by candidates

TOPICS FOUND DIFFICULT BY CANDIDATES

- Question 1 (iv): Legislative Function of the Legislature
- Question 2: Decentralization of Authority
- Question 4: Capital structure
- Question 6: Relationship between planning and controlling
- Question 8: (i) Marketing Research
- Question 9: (ii) Product liability and mandatory information provided by E-Commerce
- Question 11: Identification of a Bank draft
- Question 11: (ii) Sweat equity shares.
- Question 12: Meaning of method as a type of plan
- Question 13: Features of industrial products

CONCEPTS IN WHICH CANDIDATES GOT CONFUSED

- Question 1: Informal organization was confused with grapevine, Management as a discipline with management as a science or profession.
- Question 2: The merits of decentralization were confused with merits of delegation of authority
- Question 3: Trade credit and its features
- Question 9: (i) Provision of CPA 2019
- Question 11: (i) Securities with voting rights and securities without voting rights
- Question 11: (ii) Bank draft
- Question 11: (ii) Internal choice—Sweat equity shares was confused with ESOP
- Question 12: (ii) Method as a type of plan
- Question 13: (i) Identify the type of product manufactured

SUGGESTIONS FOR CANDIDATES

- Concentrate in class for better understanding.
- Keep abreast of updates related to the subject.
- Avoid selective study.
- Instead of learning by rote, focus on understanding the concepts.
- Write sufficient explanations under each header.
- Read the question, understand it, and then answer.
- Ensure that the headings and explanations correlate with each other.
- Avoid overlapping points to prevent duplication.
- Practice case studies.
- Time management is important.
- Avoid last-minute studying.
- Revise past years' papers along with the specimen paper and CFQs to gain expertise in writing answers.
- Keep yourself updated about changes, especially regarding the latest banking trends and CPA 2019.

01

Business Environment

TREND ANALYSIS 5 YEARS

		Average No. of Questions Across all Sets					
		Types of Questions	2024	2023	2020	2019	2018
TOPIC 01	Concept of Business Environment	1 Mark	1	1	—	—	—
		2 Marks	—	—	—	1	—
		3/4/5 Marks	—	—	—	—	1
TOPIC 02	Dimensions of Business Environment	1 Mark	1	2	—	—	—
		2 Marks	—	—	1	—	1
		3/4/5 Marks	2	2	1	1	—

Concept of Business Environment

Every business enterprise operates within various internal and external forces which influence the functioning and performance of the enterprise. These forces comprise the business environment.

Meaning of Business Environment

It refers to the set of all internal and external forces, comprising of factors, individuals and institutions which significantly affect the operations of a business firm or in other word, business environment is the aggregate of all conditions, events and influences that surround and affect the business organisation.

Features of Business Environment

The main features of business environment are

(i) **Totality of external forces** It is the sum total of all factors, forces, individuals and institutions that are external to the business but also affect it.

(ii) **General and specific forces** It is affected by general as well as specific forces. General forces include social, economic, legal and political factors that affect all business enterprises, while specific forces like customers, suppliers, competitors, etc affect individual enterprises directly.

(iii) **Interrelatedness** Various elements of business environment are related and dependent on each other. A change in one causes a change in another.

(iv) **Complexity** Business environment consists of multiple elements which are frequently changing and interrelated. This makes it complex in nature.

(v) **Dynamic** Business environment keeps on changing due to frequent changes in government policy, customers' taste, demand, etc.

(vi) **Uncertainity** Dynamic nature of business environment makes it uncertain, as it becomes difficult to accurately predict changes in future.

(vii) **Relativity** Business environment differs from one region to another because of a difference in the political, legal, social and cultural factors existing in that area.

Importance of Business Environment

Understanding business environment is important because

(i) It helps a firm in getting first mover advantage by identifying opportunities and utilising them for the growth of the business.
(ii) It gives early warning signals by identifying various threats, and helps the enterprise to take appropriate measures to reduce their adverse effects on business.
(iii) It helps to increase efficiency and performance of the enterprise.
(iv) It guides in formulation of policies and strategies so as to deal effectively with changing conditions, for the benefit of the organisation.
(v) It prepares the firm to cope up with rapid changes that are occurring in the environment. If the firm is not able to adopt changes, then it may adversely affect the organisation's efficiency.
(vi) It helps in tapping useful resources, that are present in its environment such as efficient labour, natural resources, etc.
(vii) It helps the enterprise to understand customers' needs and focus on fulfilling them, in order to increase turnover and profitability.
(viii) It helps in boosting the company's image.

Dimensions of Business Environment

Business environment consists of two major dimensions

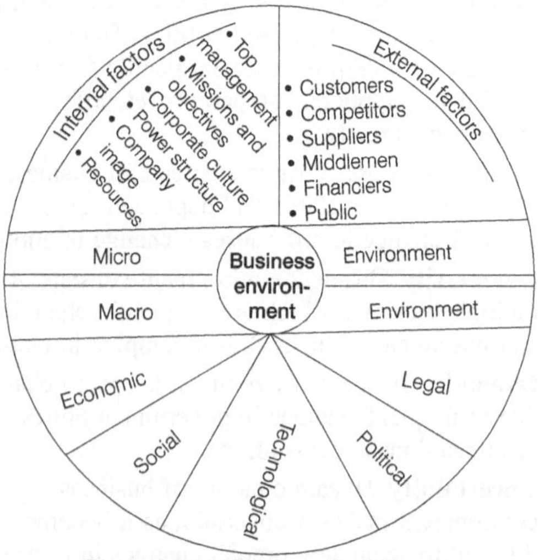

Dimensions of Business Environment

1. Micro Environment

It refers to sum total of those internal and external forces which exert direct influence on a specific/individual enterprise.

It consists of two sets of factors, as discussed below

(i) **Internal factors** These factors exist within the business firm and therefore are considered controllable and measurable.

The controllable factors include

(a) Top management, including able and qualified Board of Directors.
(b) Mission and objectives of the business, including their operational strategies, scope and development strategies.
(c) Corporate culture, which includes the attitude and value system of the management.
(d) Power structure, including relationship among the management and the employees at all levels.
(e) Company image, which influences the credibility of customers, financiers, investors, etc. towards the firm.
(f) Resources, involving human, physical, financial and natural resources possessed by an enterprise.

(ii) **External factors** The factors which influence an individual enterprise or the individuals, groups and agencies which are constantly interacting with the enterprise are part of the external factors of micro environment.

They include

(a) Customers, which may be in the form of government, households, commercial units, etc.
(b) Competitors, including direct as well as indirect competitors of an enterprise.
(c) Suppliers, who supply raw materials and other factors to the enterprise.
(d) Middlemen, like wholesalers, agents, retailers and distributors, who help in the distribution of products.
(e) Financiers, like shareholders, banks, financial institutions, etc who provide finance to the business.
(f) Public, including potential customers, media groups, government and non-government organisations, affecting the image of business in the society.

2. Macro Environment

The macro environment is the subset of general forces which may affect all business enterprises. It is indirect, generally uncontrollable and non-measurable. An enterprise attains success only if it adapts according to the changes in the macro environment.

The various components of macro environment of business are

(i) **Economic environment** It consists of economic factors that influence the business in a country. These factors include Gross National Product (GNP), corporate profits, inflation rate, employment levels, Balance of Payments (BoP), interest rates, disposable income, economic policies, infrastructure, economic planning, price mechanism, state of capital markets, level of economic growth, taxation policy and rates, etc.

(ii) **Social environment** It describes the characteristics of the society in which the organisation exists. Literacy rate, customs, value, beliefs, life style, traditions, status of women, family structures, demographic features, mobility of population, etc. are the part of the social environment changes in social characters.

The trend of change can be predicted well in advance. It is important for managers to notice the direction in which the society is moving and formulate progressive policies according to the changing social scenario.

(iii) **Political environment** It is the outcome of a combination of various ideologies advocated by different political parties. Every political party has a different attitude towards business community.

A change in power at the centre and the state affects the business community. For example, favourable government policy toward FDI has increased the number of MNCs operating in the country.

(iv) **Legal environment** It consists of legislations that are passed by the Parliament and State legislatures. This component sets the framework of law within which the business is free to operate.

Examples of legislations that specifically aims at influencing business operations include the Trademark Act, 1969, Essential Commodities Act, 1955, Standards of Weights and Measures Act, 1969 and Consumer Protection Act, 2019.

(v) **Technological environment** Technological environment covers the nature of technology available and used by an economy or industry in general.

It also includes development in technology which is likely to take place in future in various spheres like innovating new products, methods of production, techniques, plant and equipment, etc. to meet the changes in customers' needs.

SWOT Analysis

SWOT is an acronym for Strengths (S), Weaknesses (W), Opportunities (O) and Threats (T). Various techniques are used for analysing and scanning the environment. SWOT technique is one such important technique.

Strengths and weaknesses are peculiar to all enterprises and are identified and evaluated by analysing the internal environment, whereas, opportunities and threats can be identified and evaluated by understanding the external environment.

Strengths (S)

These are the inherent competencies of the organisation which help them to have an advantage over their competitors.

The enterprises strength may lie in its technical capabilities, good customer base, efficient management, efficient distribution system, good image or a strong brand.

Weaknesses (W)

These are the constraints or limitations which an enterprise faces. These pose challenges to the enterprise and place them at a disadvantageous position in front of their competitors.

The firm may face obstacles due to poor managerial policies, ineffective distribution network, obsolete machinery, lack of technical staff, shortage of funds, etc.

Opportunities (O)

Opportunities refer to the positive external trends or changes which put the firm in a favourable position and help to strengthen their foothold in the market.

These may arise due to favourable political decisions like allowing Foreign Direct Investment (FDI) in retail sector, social changes like more females working population leading to increase in demand for ready to serve food items, etc. Opportunities may also arise internally, e.g. New product/service development, etc.

Threats (T)

External environment may many times create obstacles in the functioning of the enterprise. These may be due to economic slowdown, political instability, natural calamity, technological advancements, etc. Internal environment may also pose threat due to inefficient management, strikes, inadequate finance, etc.

PYQs Previous Years' Questions

1 Mark Questions

1. An awareness of business environment enables an enterprise to take advantage of early opportunities instead of losing them to competitors.

   Which benefit of understanding the business environment is highlighted in the above statement? **ISC 2024**

   (a) Customer focus (b) Early warning signal
   (c) First mover advantage (d) Public image

Ans (c) First mover advantage

2. Organisation and development of financial market has created a surge in primary and secondary capital market.

   Which dimension of macro environment is referred to in this statement? **ISC 2024**

Ans Economic environment is referred to in this statement.

3. The changes in technology and the tastes and preferences of the consumers cannot be predicted. Which feature of the business environment is highlighted here? **ISC 2023**

   (a) Non-controllable (b) General and specific forces
   (c) Interrelatedness (d) Uncertainty

Ans (d) Uncertainty

4. State whether the following are true and false. The organisational structure and the composition of the Board of Directors, are one of the internal factors of micro environment of a business organisation.

Ans True **ISC 2023**

5. Which force exerts a direct and immediate influence on the working of a business organisation? **ISC 2023**

Ans Micro environment

6. Select and write the odd one out of the following **ISC Specimen 2023**

   (a) Different elements of business environment are closely interrelated
   (b) Business environment is rigid in nature
   (c) Business environment is difficult to predict
   (d) Social and cultural forces exercise significant influence on business

Ans (c) Business environment is difficult to predict

7. Business environment differs from country to country and region to region. Which feature of business environment is being referred to here? **ISC Specimen 2023**

Ans **Relativity** Business environment is a relative concept since it differs from country to country and even region to region.

8. With the introduction of photostate machines in the market, carbon paper industry was adversely affected. Which dimension of business environment is involved in this case? **ISC Specimen 2023, 2021**

   (a) Economic (b) Political
   (c) Technological (d) Social

Ans (c) Technological

9. Which feature of business environment shows that the environment differs from country to country? **ISC Sem I 2021**

   (a) Non-controllable
   (b) Relativity
   (c) Mutual dependence
   (d) General and specific forces

Ans (b) Relativity

10. The term environmental scanning implies **ISC Sem I 2021**

    (a) gathering data relating to the organisation and its surrounding
    (b) collecting information relating to the employees
    (c) collecting information about the shareholders
    (d) gathering information relating to customers, suppliers and public

Ans (a) gathering data relating to the organisation and its surrounding

11. Due to voltage fluctuation in some parts of India, washing machines made by multinational companies for Indian consumers have internal voltage stabilizers.

    Which importance of understanding the business environment is highlighted in this case? **ISC Sem I 2021**

    (a) Customer focus
    (b) First mover advantage
    (c) Early warning signals
    (d) Top management structure

Ans (a) Customer focus

12. In India, nuclear families have been increasing in number. Which dimension of business environment is reflected in this statement? **ISC Sem I 2021**

    (a) Social environment
    (b) Political environment
    (c) Economic environment
    (d) Legal environment

Ans (a) Social environment

13. Compact discs are becoming obsolete, due to the advent of portable MP 3 players and USB. Which dimension of business environment is evident here? *ISC Sem I 2021*

(a) Social environment (b) Technological environment
(c) Political environment (d) Legal environment

Ans (a) Social environment

14. Which of the following is not an internal factor of micro environment? *ISC Sem I 2021*

(a) Employees and human resources
(b) Government policy
(c) Corporate culture
(d) Mission and objectives of the company

Ans (b) Government policy

Common Mistake Most of the students overlook the word NOT and select wrong answer. So, you need to read question very carefully.

15. Passing of the Company's Act of 2013 is a component of *ISC Sem I 2021*

(a) legal environment (b) technological environment
(c) economic environment (d) social environment

Ans (a) legal environment

16. With reference to the elements of macro environment, choose the odd one out. *ISC Sem I 2021*

(a) Economic (b) Time
(c) Political (d) Social

Ans (b) Time

17. For a manufacturing concern, finances are part of *ISC Sem I 2021*

(a) social environment
(b) internal factors of micro environment
(c) external factors of micro environment
(d) economic environment

Ans (c) external factors of micro environment

18. During the Covid 19 pandemic, many businesses started selling goods online and flourished. For such firms, the pandemic situation was *ISC Sem I 2021*

(a) a strength (b) a weakness
(c) a threat (d) an opportunity

Ans (d) an opportunity

19. Which of the following is a threat to the firm? *ISC Sem I 2021*

(a) Entry of rivals in the market
(b) Expansion of rural market
(c) Large financial resources
(d) Strong brand portfolio

Ans (a) Entry of rivals in the market

20. With reference to strength is SWOT analysis, choose the odd one out. *ISC Sem I 2021*

(a) External environment (b) Strategic advantage
(c) Internal environment (d) Inherent capability

Ans (a) External environment

21. Which one of the following is not a feature of business environment? *ISC Sem I Specimen 2021*

(a) Uncertainty (b) Interdependence
(c) Complexing (d) Stabiling

Ans (d) Stabiling

22. Under which environmental effect were IBM and Coca Cola, forced to leave India? *ISC Sem I Specimen 2021*

(a) Political environment
(b) Legal environment
(c) Social environment (d) Economic environment

Ans (a) Political environment

23. Which environment prohibits the advertisement of alcoholic beverages? *ISC Sem I Specimen 2021*

(a) Legal environment (b) Social environment
(c) Technological environment
(d) Political environment

Ans (a) Legal environment

24. Banking sector reforms have led to better services. This is an example of which types of component of the business environment? *ISC Sem I Specimen 2021*

(a) Legal environment (b) Social environment
(c) Technological environment
(d) Political environment

Ans (c) Technological environment

25. Several techniques are used for analysing the environment. One such techniques is SWOT. The components of which are *ISC Sem I Specimen 2021*

(a) strength (b) weakness
(c) opportunities (d) time

Ans (d) time

26. With reference to SWOT analysis *ISC Sem I Specimen 2021*

(a) The internal environment can be identified by analysing weakness
(b) The internal environment can be identified by analysing opportunity
(c) The internal environment can be identified by analysing threats
(d) The internal environment can be identified by analysing opportunities and threats

Ans (a) The internal environment can be identified by analysing weakness

2 Marks Questions

1. What is meant by micro environment? ***ISC 2020***

Ans All the forces that directly and continuously influence the working of a specific enterprise are part of the micro environment. Micro environment consists of internal and external factors.

2. What is meant by the term business environment? ***ISC 2019, 2014***

Ans Business environment is the sum total of all individuals, institutions and other forces like customers, competitors, suppliers, distributors, trends, substitutes, regulations, government activities, social and cultural factors that affect the operations of a business enterprise. These forces continuously interact with the business and have a significant effect on the performance of the business.

3. Name the two dimensions of business environment. ***ISC 2018***

Ans Two dimensions of business environment are as follows

(i) Micro environment (ii) Macro environment

4. What is meant by macro environment? ***ISC Specimen 2018, 2017***

Ans Macro environment is the subset of general forces which may affect all business enterprises. It is indirect, generally uncontrollable and non-measurable. An enterprise attains success only if it adapts according to the changes in the macro environment.

5. State two components of legal environment of a business concern. ***ISC 2016***

Ans Two components of legal environment are as follows

(i) Legislation passed by the government
(ii) Court judgements

6. Enumerate the components of macro environment of a business concern. ***ISC 2015***

Ans Macro environment consists of the following

(i) Economic environment
(ii) Social environment (iii) Political environment
(iv) Legal environment
(v) Technological environment

7. What is economic and non-economic environment? ***ISC 2013***

Ans **Economic environment** It consists of economic factors that influence the business of a country. These factors include Gross National Product (GNP), corporate profits, inflation rate, employment levels, Balance of Payments (BoP), interest rates, disposable income, economic policy, price mechanism, taxation policy and rates, etc. It has a strong influence on the business enterprise.

Non-economic environment It consists of political, social, technological and legal environment.

8. What is technological environment? ***ISC 2013***

Ans Technological environment includes the state of technological advancements in a country. Scientific improvements and innovations continuously affect the business by way of developing new techniques and methods used for producing goods and services.

Technological advancements help in increasing the productivity and improving the quality of the product through innovation of new products, methods of production, techniques, plant, etc that help to modify the product according to customers' preference. Technological environment poses both opportunities and threats for the concern.

3/4/5 Marks Questions

1. Explain any five external factors of micro environment that influence a business organisation. ***ISC 2024 (5M)***

Or Briefly explain any four external factors of micro environment of business. ***ISC 2019 (4M)***

Or Explain any three external elements of micro business environment. ***ISC 2016 (3M)***

Or Briefly explain any five external factors of micro environment of business. ***ISC 2014 (5M)***

Ans External factors of micro environment are the forces, individuals, groups and agencies which come into direct contact with the organisation during its operations.

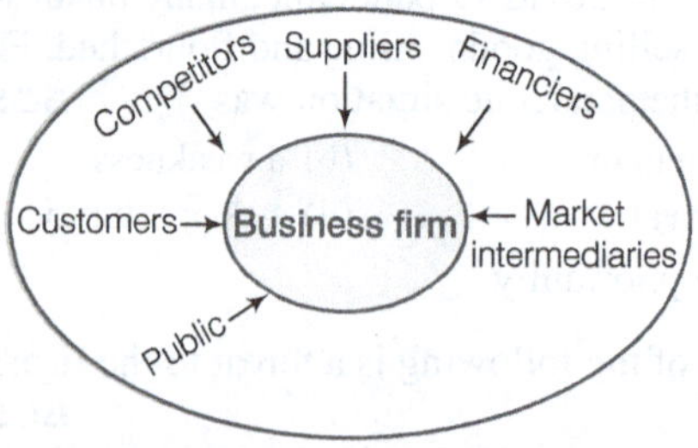

External Micro Environment

External micro environment consists of the following

(i) **Customers** They have the most direct micro economic impact on the business.

Organisations survive on the basis of meeting 'customer needs and wants' and providing benefit to their customers. A customer may be an individual or household, an organisation, institution, government agency, etc.

(ii) **Competitors** Its analysis and monitoring is crucial if an organisation has to maintain or improve its position within the market. The competition may be in direct or indirect form. Direct competition is from firms producing same products or services, e.g. Two companies manufacturing mobile sets or two restaurants offering fast food.

Indirect competition may be faced when the different alternatives are offered to satisfy the same customer need, e.g. To satisfy the need of hunger, a person may choose to eat pizza, go to a restaurant.

(iii) **Suppliers** They provide businesses with the raw materials, that they need to carry out their business activities. Suppliers influence the cost of production as raw material cost and inventory carrying cost are dependent on suppliers.

It is necessary to have close suppliers relationship and to have more than one vendor for regular supply of raw materials.

(iv) **Financiers** Shareholders, investors, creditors, debentureholders and financial institutions are the providers of funds for the company's start up and growth. Various factors like interest rates, term of loans, financial policies of financiers, etc. all affect the enterprise financial soundness.

(v) **Market intermediaries** Organisations typically rely on banks, venture capitalists and other sources to finance operations; wholesalers and retailers, transportation companies to distribute goods; and advertising, market research firms and public-relations firms to market their products. The strategy is to focus on each intermediary, as they can potentially increase or decrease customer satisfaction.

Concept Enhancer External factors of micro environment may not influence all the firms in a particular industry in the same manner.

2. State any three components of social environment. *ISC 2024 (3M)*

Or What is meant by social environment? Explain any two components of social environment. *ISC Specimen 2023 (3M)*

Or What is meant by social environment? Enumerate any three components of social environment. *ISC Specimen 2018, 17 (4M)*

Ans Social environment consists of the customs, traditions and society in which business operates.

It includes the standard of living, taste, preferences and education level of the people living in the society where the business exists.

The businessman cannot overlook the components of the social environment as these components may not have an immediate impact on the business but in the long-run, the social environment has a great impact on the business.

Three components of social environment are

(i) It is affected by literacy rates.

(ii) Life expectancy of the population affects social environment.

(iii) It is also affected by expectations of the workforce.

3. Explain any five internal factors of micro environment that influence a business organisation. *ISC 2023 (5M)*

Or Explain any three internal factors of micro environment of a business organisation. *ISC 2015 (3M)*

Ans Internal factors of micro environment of a business organisation are

(i) **Value system** The value system of an organisation means the ethical beliefs that guide the organisation in achieving its mission and objective.

The value system of a business organisation also determines its behaviour towards its employees, customers and society at large.

Internal Factors of Micro Environment

- Value system
- Organisation structure
- Corporate culture and style of functioning of top management
- Quality of human resource
- Physical resources and technological capabilities

(ii) **Organisation structure** Organisation structure means such things like composition of Board of Directors, the number of independent directors, the extent of professional management and shareholding pattern.

The nature of organisational structure has a significant influence over decision-making process in an organisation.

(iii) **Corporate culture and style of functioning of top management** Corporate culture and style of functioning of top managers is important factor for determining the internal environment of a company.

Corporate culture is generally considered as either closed and threatening or open and participatory.

(iv) **Quality of human resource** The success of a business organisation depends to a great extent on the skills, capabilities, attitudes and commitment of its employees. Employees differ with regard to these characteristics.

(v) **Physical resources and technological capabilities** Physical resources such as plant and equipment and technological capabilities of a firm determine its competitive strength which is an important factor determining its efficiency and unit cost of production.

Common Mistake Students sometimes get confused between factors of micro environment with importance of micro environment. So, students are advised to learn them under separate headings properly.

4. What is meant by technological environment? Explain any two components of technological environment. *ISC 2023 (3M)*

Ans Technological environment refers to the changes in the output, production methods, use of equipment and quality of the product. It includes force related to scientific innovations and improvements in products as well as production technology.

For example, with recent improvements in technology and computerisation, marketing and selling of products is now possible online leading to increase in sales and output of many firms.

Two components of technological environment are

(i) Better utilisation of productive resources.

(ii) Improvement in competitive strength.

5. Explain any five features of business environment. *ISC Specimen 2023 (5M)*

Or Explain any four features of business environment. *ISC 2018 (4M)*

Or Explain any three features of business environment. *ISC 2015 (3M)*

Ans The main features of business environment are as follows

(i) **Totality of external forces** It is the sum total of all factors, forces, individuals and institutions that affect business enterprises.

(ii) **General and specific forces** General forces include social, economic, legal and political factors that affect all business enterprises, while specific forces like customers, suppliers, competitors, etc affect individual enterprises directly.

Features of Business Environment
- Totality of external forces
- General and specific forces
- Interrelatedness
- Complexity
- Dynamic nature

(iii) **Interrelatedness** Various elements of business environment are related and dependent on each other. A change in one causes a change in another.

(iv) **Complexity** Business environment consists of multiple elements which are frequently changing and interrelated. This makes it complex in nature.

(v) **Dynamic nature** The business environment is dynamic in nature, i.e. it keeps on changing whether in terms of technological improvement, a shift in consumer preferences or entry of new competition in the market.

6. With reference to the various dimensions of business environment, state what is meant by polictical environment? Mention any three components of political environment. *ISC 2020 (4M)*

Ans **Political environment** It is the outcome of a combination of various ideologies advocated by different political parties.

Every political party has a different attitude towards business community.

A change in power at the centre and the state affects the business community. e.g. Favourable government policy toward FDI has increased the number of MNCs operating in the country.

Components of political environment (any three)

(i) Political stability (ii) Political ideology

(iii) The Constitution of the Country

(iv) Relations of the country with other countries

7. Explain the importance of business environment in shaping the future of a business. *ISC Specimen 2018, 17 (5M)*

Ans Importance of business environment in shaping the future of a business can be understood by the following points

(i) **Helps a firm in getting first mover advantage** Constant monitoring of the environment enables a firm to foresee opportunities and take advantage by coming out with new products/services, e.g. With increasing incomes of people in the country, a number of car companies are coming up with SUVs (Sports Utility Vehicles).

Importance of Business Environment
- Helps a firm in getting first mover advantage
- Early warning signals
- Increases efficiency and performance
- Cope up with the rapid change
- Guides in decision-making and strategy formulation

(ii) **Early warning signals** The trends, taste, preferences, demand and technology are constantly changing. The analysis of such changes can help the firm to adapt to changes.

The threats may be in form of technology change, government intervention, legal issues, changes in consumer preferences, etc, e.g. The changes from LCD to LED to HD and now 3D and curve TV by Samsung, Sony and LG becomes threat to other manufacturers. They have to adopt this technology or innovate something all together new to remain in the market.

(iii) **Increases efficiency and performance** To meet the changes in business environment constant endeavour is made to increase the efficiency and performance of the business.

(iv) **Cope up with the rapid change** The understanding and forecasting the changes in business environment will enable the firm to take steps for coping with the changes.

(v) **Guides in decision-making and strategy formulation** Environment monitoring provides relevant information for strategy formulation, e.g. Increasing health consciousness among citizens have made companies to come out with products like-Multigrain Atta, Brown Atta Bread and Multigrain Maggi, etc.

8. Write a short note on SWOT analysis. ***ISC 2016 (4M)***

Ans SWOT is an acronym for Strengths (S), Weaknesses (W), Opportunities (O) and Threats (T).

This is a very important and useful tool for the marketer, entrepreneur or business person for analysing business environment. The SWOT analysis provides information that is helpful in matching the firm's resources and capabilities to the competitive environment in which it operates.

As such, it is instrumental in strategy formulation and selection. Environmental factors internal to the firm usually can be classified as strengths or weaknesses and those external to the firm can be classified as opportunities or threats.

Strengths (S) These are the inherent competencies of the organisation which help them to have advantage over competitors.

Weaknesses (W) These are the constraints or limitations which an enterprise faces. These poses challenges to the enterprise and place them at a disadvantageous position in front of their competitors.

Opportunities (O) Opportunities refer to the positive external trends or changes which put the firm in a favourable position and help them to strengthen their foothold in the market.

Threats (T) External environment may, many a times create obstacles in the functioning of the enterprise.

These may be due to economic slowdown, political instability, natural calamity, technological advancements, etc.

SWOT Analysis Example

Strengths	**Opportunities**
• Innovative product offering • Affordable prices • Loyal current users	• Expand social media presence • Work with industry influencers
Weaknesses	**Threats**
• Not enough brand recognition • No resources spent on marketing	• Touch competition • Supply chain challengers • Touch job market

Value Point

For getting maximum marks, following point can be included in the answer

- Give SWOT analysis of any company to increase understanding.

Additional Questions

2 Marks Questions

1. Give two examples of impact of technological change on business organisations.

Ans Two examples of impact of technological change business enterprises are

(i) Emergence of internet and multimedia has increased the scope of online selling of products by firms.

(ii) Innovation of digital watches has hampered the business of traditional watches.

2. What are specific and general forces of business environment?

Ans General forces include social, economic, political, legal and economic forces that affect all business enterprises, while specific forces include customers, suppliers, competitors, etc that influence individual enterprises directly.

4/5 Marks Questions

1. How does social environment have an impact on a business firm?

Ans Social environment has a considerable impact on a business firm. The components of social environment are

(i) Attitudes towards product innovations
(ii) Occupational distribution
(iii) Lifestyle and consumer preferences
(iv) Population migration
(v) Social groups and institutions

(vi) Consumption habits (vii) Family composition
(viii) Customs, traditions, values and social trends
(ix) Literacy level

The enterprise has to continuously look for the changes happening and adapt itself to such changes, e.g. Increase in literacy level has affected the hygiene factor. People are demanding packaged products. Likewise, change in workforce structure, where more and more females are working, has created demand for ready to cook dishes, etc.

2. Explain the various components of macro environment of business.

Ans **Components of macro environment** Refer to text on page 3.

Case Based Questions

Case 1

Ms. M was successfully running a catering service for weddings. But due to the pandemic situation, the government imposed restrictions on social gatherings. This had an adverse impact on her catering business.

The future of the catering business seemed bleak. As the number of covid positive cases increased, people were isolated at home. Seeing this situation, Ms. M started a food delivery service. She supplied simple and healthy home cooked food at reasonable price.

The food was liked by her customers. Ms. M started using social media platforms to spread word about her business. She also accepted online payment, for the convenience and the safety of her customers and employees. ***ISC Sem I 2021***

(i) In the given case, due to the pandemic the future of Ms. M's catering business seemed bleak. Which feature of business environment is highlighted in this case?
(a) Uncertainty (b) Integral
(c) Universality (d) Internal forces

Ans (a) Uncertainty

(ii) Customers are a part of
(a) internal factors of micro environment
(b) economic environment
(c) external factors of micro environment
(d) macro environment

Ans (c) external factors of micro environment

(iii) Online payment which was accepted in the given case, is an outcome of
(a) legal environment
(b) technological environment
(c) economic environment
(d) social environment

Ans (b) technological environment

(iv) The quality and price of the food supplied by the entrepreneur in the given case is
(a) opportunity (b) threat
(c) weakness (d) strength

Ans (d) strength

(v) Which of the following is a component of economic environment?
(a) Political stability of the country
(b) Customs and traditions
(c) Per capita income of people
(d) Use of automation in industry

Ans (c) Per capita income of people

Case 2

Mahesh was running a sweets shop for many years. But due to the change in the consumption habits of people, he shifted to chocolate business. On the eve of Diwali, he offered chocolates in attractive packages at reasonable prices.

He anticipated huge demand and created a website chocolate.com for taking orders online. He got lot of orders online and earned huge profit by selling chocolates. ***ISC Sem I 2021***

(i) Which components of macro environment have been discussed in the above case?
(a) Political and legal
(b) Legal and economic
(c) Social and technological
(d) Economic and social

Ans (c) Social and technological

(ii) Which feature of business environment is highlighted in the above case?
(a) Diversity
(b) Dynamic
(c) Complexity
(d) Non-controllable

Ans (b) Dynamic

(iii) Under which dimension of environment, does a supplier belong?
(a) External element of micro environment
(b) Internal element of micro environment
(c) Legal environment
(d) Political environment

Ans (a) External element of micro environment

(iv) Which one of the following options highlights the importance of business environment in the above case?
(a) First mover advantage
(b) Public image
(c) Continuous learning
(d) Coping with the change

Ans (d) Coping with the change

(v) One of the external factors that constitute micro environment is
(a) top management structure
(b) corporate culture
(c) competitors
(d) mission and objectives

Ans (c) competitors

Case 3

Naman and Govind after finishing their graduation under vocational stream decided to start their own travel agency which will book Rail Tickets and Air Tickets on commission basis. They also thought of providing tickets within ten minutes through the use of internet.

They discussed the idea with their Professor Mr. Mehta who liked the idea and suggested them to first analyse the business environment which consists of investors, competitors and other forces like social, political etc. that may affect their business directly or indirectly.

He further told them about the technological improvements and shifts in consumer preferences that were taking place and hence they should be aware of the environmental trends and changes which may hinder their business performance.

He emphasised on making plans keeping in mind the threat posed by the competitors, so that they can deal with the situation effectively.

This alignment of business operations with the business environment will result in better performance.

ISC Sem I Specimen 2021

(i) Identify the component of business environment highlighted in the above para.
(a) Technological (b) Social
(c) Legal (d) Political

Ans (a) Technological

(ii) One of the features of business environment as discussed by Professor Mehta with Naman and Govind is
(a) general and specific forces
(b) dynamic
(c) diversity
(d) totality of external forces

Ans (d) totality of external forces

(iii) One point of importance of business environment as stated by Professor Mehta is
(a) first mover advantage (b) non-controllable
(c) public image (d) continuous learning

Ans (d) continuous learning

(iv) Analysis of business environment is also known as
(a) micro environment
(b) macro environment
(c) internal environment
(d) environmental scanning

Ans (d) environmental scanning

(v) One of the internal factors that constitute micro environment is
(a) top management structure
(b) customer
(c) competitor
(d) supplier

Ans (a) top management structure

CHAPTER TEST

01 Mark Questions

1. In which of the following basic categories can business environment be divided?
(a) Local and regional (b) Regional and national
(c) Internal and external (d) Financial and non-financial

2. Factors that create opportunities and threats to business units is known as ....
(a) internal environment (b) external environment
(c) micro environment
(d) macro environment

3. External factors affecting a business environment are also referred to as .... factors.
(a) controllable (b) uncontrollable
(c) relevant (d) global

4. Study of human population is called as .... environment.
(a) political (b) social
(c) demographic (d) economic

5. In terms of its effect on marketers, the increase in petrol price is mostly effected the .... environment.

6. .... are internal factors of SWOT analysis for a business.

7. What is the primary purpose of a SWOT Analysis?

8. What is 'PEST' Analysis?

9. State whether the following is true or false.
Internal factors exist within the business firm and are considered controllable.

10. **Assertion** (A) The business environment is the sum total of the external forces.

Reason (R) The different elements of the business environment are closely interrelated.

Alternatives
(a) Both Assertion (A) and Reason (R) are true and Reason (R) is the correct explanation of Assertion (A)
(b) Both Assertion (A) and Reason (R) are true, but Reason (R) is not the correct explanation of Assertion (A)
(c) Assertion (A) is true, but Reason (R) is false
(d) Assertion (A) is false, but Reason (R) is true

02 Marks Questions

11. What do you understand by the concept of 'business environment'?

12. Name the controllable factors of micro environment.

13. Explain economic environment that affect business enterprises.

14. How do 'competitors' and 'financiers' impact business firms?

03/04/05 Marks Questions

15. List three main internal factors that can act as strengths for a business enterprise.

16. What do you understand by strengths and weaknesses?

17. "Knowledge of business environment is crucial for all enterprises." Why?

18. What is business environment? Discuss any four features of business environment.

19. Explain various elements of macro environment giving examples.

20. Discuss internal and external elements of micro environment.

Answers

1. (c) Internal and external
2. (d) macro environment
3. (b) uncontrollable
4. (c) demographic
5. economic
6. Strengths and weaknesses
9. True
10. (b) Both Assertion (A) and Reason (R) are true, but Reason (R) is not the correct explanation of Assertion (A)

02

Finance and Capital

TREND ANALYSIS 5 YEARS

Average No. of Questions Across all Sets

		Types of Questions	2024	2023	2020	2019	2018
TOPIC 01	Finance	1 Mark	—	—	—	—	—
		2 Marks	—	—	—	—	—
		3/4/5 Marks	—	—	—	—	—
TOPIC 02	Financial Planning and Capital Structure	1 Mark	—	1	—	—	—
		2 Marks	—	—	—	—	—
		3/4/5 Marks	1	—	—	1	—
TOPIC 03	Fixed and Working Capital	1 Mark	1	1	—	—	—
		2 Marks	—	—	1	—	—
		3/4/5 Marks	—	—	1	1	1

Meaning and Definition of Finance

Business finance refers to the money required for carrying out business activities. Every business organisation, either big or small, needs finance to carry out their operations.

Finance is required while starting a venture, to run its daily operations and for growing and diversifying needs of the business.

According to **BO Wheeler**, "Business finance is concerned with the acquisition and utilisation of capital funds in meeting financial needs and overall objectives of a business enterprise."

Importance of Finance for Business

Finance is required for all types and sizes of business. A business can't function unless adequate funds are made available at the right time.

Importance of finance for a business is described below

(i) All business activities require finance, whether it is
  (a) to start a business
  (b) to carry out its daily operations
  (c) to expand, modernise and diversify it

(ii) The firm can take benefit of opportunities, e.g. Expand its operation or enter into new emerging fields only if adequate finance is available.

(iii) Finance is needed to meet contingencies, e.g. During recessions or when there is increase in the prices of raw material, etc.

(iv) For smooth operations of business, timely and adequate finance plays an important role.

(v) Adequate funds help the firm to timely meet its liabilities and improve its credit rating, which further helps the firm to source finance.

(vi) Finance is required to compete in the fast changing market by innovating, researching, conducting market surveys and coming up with the latest technology and products.

Sources of Finance for Different Types of Business Firms

Capital requirement differ according to nature, size and type of business, as discussed below

1. **Sources of Finance for Sole Proprietorship Firm**
   (i) Owned capital and retained earnings
   (ii) Loans from friends and relatives
   (iii) Profits re-invested in business
   (iv) Short-term finance from creditors and commercial banks
   (v) Long-term loans from specialised financial institutions, State and Central Government assistance for small scale units
2. **Sources of Finance for Partnership Firms**
   (i) Owned capital contribution by partners
   (ii) Loans by partners, friends and relatives
   (iii) Loans from commercial banks and financial institutions
   (iv) Plant and machinery on lease or hire purchase
   (v) Short-term credit from commercial banks, suppliers of raw materials and finished goods
3. **Sources of Finance for Joint Stock Company**
   (i) Issue of shares
   (ii) Issue of debentures and bonds
   (iii) Retained profits
   (iv) Inter-corporate deposits
   (v) Public deposits
   (vi) Long-term loans from commercial banks and financial institutions
   (vii) Short-term loans in the form of trade credit, loans from commercial banks, etc.

Financial Planning

It is the process of estimating the fund requirements of business and specifying the sources of funds. It involves the preparation of a financial blue print of an organisation's future operations.

While making financial plans, three important questions need to be answered

(i) How much capital is required, i.e. estimation of quantum of finance.
(ii) What methods and sources should be used for meeting financial needs, i.e. whether finance will be raised from debt or equity.
(iii) How to use the available funds in an adequate manner, i.e. proper utilisation of funds.

Objectives of Financial Planning

Financial planning strives to achieve following objectives

(i) **To ensure availability of funds whenever these are required** This includes a proper estimation of the funds required for different purposes such as for the purchase of long-term assets or to meet day-to-day expenses of business, etc. Apart from this, there is a need to estimate the time at which these funds are to be made available.

(ii) **To ensure unnecessary finance is not raised** Excess funding is almost as bad as inadequate funding. Even if there is some surplus money, good financial planning would put it to the best possible use, so that the financial resources are not left idle and don't unnecessarily add to the cost.

Features of Financial Planning

Features of financial planning are enumerated below

(i) **Forecasting** Forecasting must be used in planning the scope of operations in order to estimate the amount of fixed capital and working capital needed in the business enterprise.

(ii) **Liquidity** Liquid assets are also required to finance purchases, to pay the daily needs like paying salaries, wages and other incidental expenses.

(iii) **Based on firm's objectives** Financial planning should be done keeping in view the overall objectives of the company. It should aim to procure funds at the lowest cost so that the profitability of the business is improved.

(iv) **Optimum use of funds** Capital should not only be adequate but should also employ productive effects. A financial plan should prevent wasteful use of the capital and ensure its proper utilisation to create earning capacity in an enterprise.

(v) **Source of funds** Financial planning helps to select appropriate sources of finance having minimum cost and their ratio in the total amount.

Importance of Financial Planning

The importance of financial planning can be viewed with the help of the following points

(i) **Helps to face the eventualities** It forecasts the future business situations which helps in preparing alternative financial plans to face the eventual situations and problems of shortage of funds.

(ii) **Helps in avoiding business shocks and surprises** Proper provision regarding shortage or surplus of funds is made by anticipating future receipts and payments. Hence, it helps in avoiding business shocks and surprises.

(iii) **Helps in coordination** It helps in coordinating various business activities, such as sales, purchase, production, finance, etc.

(iv) **Helps in avoiding wastage of finance** In the absence of financial planning, wastage of financial resources may take place. This arises due to the complex nature of business operation such as excessive over or under estimation of finance for a particular business operation. Such type of wastages can be avoided through financial planning.

(v) **Maximise shareholders' returns** Through financial planning, a finance manager develops a plan constituting proper balance between debt and equity. Thus, it leads to maximising return for the equity shareholders.

(vi) **Helps in creating link between investment and financing decisions** It helps in deciding that where to invest and from where the required funds will be made available. Under financial planning, the mix of share capital and debt capital is made in such a manner that cost of capital is reduced to the minimum.

Capital Structure

It refers to the mix between owner's funds (equity) and borrowed funds (debt). After deciding the financial requirement, it is decided, how much finance is to be raised from which source and what will be the proportion of the two sources.

Source of finance can be classified into the following types

(i) **Owner's funds** It consists of equity shares, preference share capital and retained earnings.

(ii) **Borrowed funds** Funds can be borrowed in the form of loans, debentures, public deposits, etc.

Capital Gearing

The ratio of debt and equity in the capital structure is called 'capital gearing'. If the proportion of debt is higher than equity, it is called 'high gearing' or 'trading on thin equity', whereas larger proportion of equity in capital structure is called 'low gearing' or 'trading on thick equity'.

Factors Affecting Choice of Capital Structure

Various factors influencing capital structure are as follows

(i) **Position of cash flow** Size of projected cash flow must be considered before raising debt.
Cash flow must not only cover fixed cash payment obligations, but there must be sufficient cash for smooth working of the business.

(ii) **Cost of financing** It may be defined as the payment made by the company to obtain capital. Thus, interest is the cost of debentures or loan and dividend paid by the company is the cost of equity and preference share capital. The rate of dividend on preference shares is fixed which is generally lower than that of equity shares. The cost of debentures is generally lower and tax deductible.

(iii) **Risk consideration** While deciding the capital structure, risk must be analysed and considered. Risk may take the following two forms

(a) **Financial risk** It refers to a position when a company is unable to meet its fixed financial charges namely, interest payment, preference dividend and principal payment obligations. It arises when a company borrows. Use of debt increases the financial risk of a business.

(b) **Business risk** It depends upon fixed operating costs. Higher fixed operating cost means higher business risk and *vice-versa*. If a firm's operating risk is lower, its capacity to use debt is higher and *vice-versa*.

(iv) **Period and purpose** It also affect the capital structure. While equity shares are preferable to obtain long-term funds for fixed capital, preference shares and debentures are suitable for obtaining medium-term finance to fulfil the needs of modernisation and growth.

(v) **Flexibility** The capital structure should be flexible. Since, debentures and preference shares are redeemable, issue of such securities help to make the capital structure flexible. Equity shares are not redeemable and hence they make the capital structure rigid.

(vi) **Trading on equity** It refers to the use of fixed cost sources of finance such as debentures and preference share capital in the capital structure so as to increase the return on equity shares.
There are two conditions to use trading on equity favourably, which are as follows
 (a) The rate of interest on loan/debentures should be less than the rate of Return on Investment (RoI).
 (b) The interest should be deducted from profit before tax.

Note Return on Investment (RoI) refers to the earning expected from the investment. If RoI of a company is high, it can opt for trading on equity to increase the earning per share.

(vii) **Control consideration** If a company wants to retain control, especially in case of closely held companies, they opt for debt financing. Larger equity share financing dilutes their control because shareholders have voting rights and can interfere in the management.

(viii) **Capital market conditions** During boom, it is easy to finance through shares, but during recession and depression, companies have to resort to issue debentures and preference shares.

(ix) **Investors' choice** Attitudes of investors, whether they are risk takers or conservative in their approach, also help in deciding the capital structure.

(x) **Statutory requirements** The Companies Act and SEBI have laid down certain norms of debt equity ratios, which are to be adhered by all the companies while deciding upon the capital structure.

(xi) **Nature of business** Business firms that have a stable and high income, can afford to make use of greater amount of debt, in comparison to such firms whose earnings are low and irregular.

Fixed Capital (Permanent Capital)

The amount of capital investment in fixed assets is called 'fixed capital', e.g. Plant and machinery, land and building, etc. These assets are permanently used in business. Fixed capital is required for setting up the business, for growth, mordernisation and for diversification. Fixed capital is raised through long-term sources of finance like issue of shares, debentures, long-term loans and retained earnings.

Factors Affecting Fixed Capital

The various factors that affect amount of fixed capital are

(i) **Nature of business** Manufacturing enterprises require more fixed capital, while trading enterprises require less fixed capital.

(ii) **Size of the business** Large scale enterprises require more fixed capital, whereas small scale enterprises require less fixed capital.

(iii) **Nature of products** Enterprises producing capital items require more fixed capital, whereas enterprises producing consumer goods require less fixed capital.

(iv) **Method of production** Enterprises using capital intensive technique require more fixed capital than the enterprises using labour intensive technique.

(v) **Diversity of products** Enterprises engaged in manufacturing or dealing of single product require less fixed capital.
Enterprises engaged in manufacturing or dealing in multiple products require more fixed capital.

(vi) **Mode of acquiring fixed assets** Enterprises acquiring fixed assets on cash payment basis require more fixed capital, whereas enterprises acquiring fixed assets on lease/hire-purchase system require less fixed capital.

(vii) **Intangible assets** Enterprises desirous of acquiring high goodwill, patents, copyrights, etc require more fixed capital.
Enterprises not desirous of acquiring high goodwill, patents, copyrights, etc. require less fixed capital.

Working Capital (Circulating Capital)

It is that part of total capital, which is required for holding current assets. It represents the liquid funds, which are required for day-to-day operations of the firm.

It is also known as the 'Circulating Capital or Revolving Capital'. This is because the current assets are changed from one form to another in the regular operations of the business, in the following manner

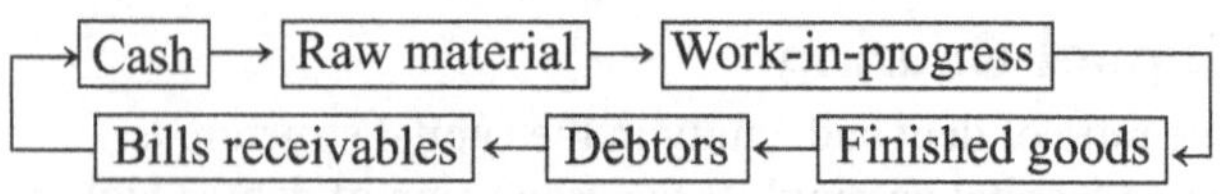

The term is used in two senses, which are given below

(i) **Gross working capital** It is the total amount of funds invested in current assets.

Gross Working Capital = Current Assets

(ii) **Net working capital** It is the excess of current assets over current liabilities.

Net Working Capital = Current Assets – Current Liabilities

Types of Working Capital

Working capital can be classified into two types, which are as follows

(i) **Permanent working capital** It is minimum amount of capital required permanently in business to maintain the regular operations of business.

It is of two kinds, which are given below

(a) **Initial working capital** It is required at the time of commencement of business.

(b) **Regular working capital** It is a part of permanent working capital, which is regularly required for continuous operations.

(ii) **Temporary working capital** It is the capital which is required in addition to permanent working capital for meeting seasonal and special needs of the business.

It is also of two types, which are given below

(a) **Seasonal working capital** It is required in the busy season for business dealing in seasonal products.

(b) **Special working capital** Extra funds required for emergencies and generally kept as reserves for reasons like increase in demand, periods of depression, natural calamities, strikes, lockouts, etc.

Factors Affecting Working Capital Requirements

The factors that affect the working capital requirements of a business are

(i) **Nature of business** Enterprises engaged in manufacturing require more working capital and enterprises engaged in trading/services require less working capital.

(ii) **Size of business** Large scale enterprises require more working capital whereas small scale enterprises require less working capital.

(iii) **Manufacturing cycle** Firms with longer manufacturing cycle require more working capital as compared to firms with shorter manufacturing cycle.

(iv) **Rapidity of turnover** Firms having rapid turnover require less working capital, whereas firms having slow turnover require more working capital.

(v) **Terms of sale and purchase** Firms operating on credit sales and cash purchase require more working capital, whereas firms operating on credit purchase and cash sales require less working capital.

(vi) **Credit policy** Firms following a liberal credit policy require more working capital than firms following a conservative credit policy.

(vii) **Operational efficiency** Firms with high operational efficiency require less working capital and the firms with low operational efficiency require more working capital.

(viii) **Goodwill** Firms enjoying a good reputation in the market require less working capital and the firms that do not enjoy a good market reputation require more working capital.

(ix) **Growth prospects** Firms having higher growth prospects require more working capital as compared to firms having less growth prospects.

(x) **Seasonal factor** Firms require more working capital during peak season, while less working capital during lean/off season.

(xi) **Cyclical fluctuations** Firms require more working capital during boom and less working capital during depression.

Difference between Fixed Capital and Working Capital

Basis	Fixed capital	Working capital
Meaning	Fixed capital are funds required to be invested in fixed assets.	For the smooth functioning of day-to-day operations, funds need to be invested in current assets. This investment is called 'working capital'.
Time period	The capital, in form of fixed assets remain in the business for longer period, i.e. more than one year.	This is short-term investment and gets converted into cash or cash equivalents within a period of one year.
Form	The capital remains fixed in one asset.	The capital, changes its form from one asset to another.
Source	It is sourced through long-term sources of finance like shares, debentures, etc.	It is generally sourced through medium-term and short-term sources like trade credit, loans from commercial banks, etc.
Examples	Examples are land and building, plant and machinery, etc.	Examples are debtors, bills receivables, etc.

PYQs Previous Years' Questions

1 Mark Questions

1. A business firm should have extra funds to meet future emergencies. Identify the type of working capital indicated here. *ISC 2024; Sem I 2021*

(a) Special (b) Seasonal
(c) Initial (d) Regular

Ans (a) Special

2. When XYZ Company acquired a toy manufacturing company, it paid a large amount for the goodwill. Which source of business funds of XYZ Company was impacted? *ISC 2023*

(a) Fixed capital
(b) Special working capital
(c) Circulating capital
(d) Gross working capital

Ans (a) Fixed capital

3. When equity shares dominate the capital structure, the capital is considered as high geared. State true or false. *ISC 2023*

Ans False. When equity shares dominate the capital structure, the capital is considered as low geared.

4. Capital structure shows *ISC Specimen 2023*

(a) debtor-creditor ratio
(b) fixed assets-current assets ratio
(c) debt-equity ratio
(d) interest coverage ratio

Ans (c) debt-equity ratio

5. Which one of the following is not counted as a current asset? *ISC Specimen 2023*

(a) Inventory (b) Cash
(c) Account receivable (d) Equipment

Ans (d) Equipment

6. Fixed capital is also known as *ISC Sem I 2021*

(a) block capital (b) gross working capital
(c) revolving capital (d) working capital

Ans (a) block capital

7. The process of retaining a part of net profits over years and reinvesting the same is *ISC Sem I Specimen 2021*

(a) public deposits
(b) retained earnings
(c) factoring
(d) capitalisation of reserves

Ans (b) retained earnings

8. A company can raise fixed capital in the form of *ISC Sem I Specimen 2021*

(a) equity shares
(b) cash credit
(c) discounting a bill of exchange
(d) bank overdraft

Ans (a) equity shares

9. Working capital has two concepts, gross and *ISC Sem I Specimen 2021*

(a) zero (b) net
(c) cumulative (d) outstanding

Ans (b) net

10. Capital needed at the commencement of business is *ISC Sem I Specimen 2021*

(a) temporary working capital
(b) permanent working capital
(c) seasonal working capital
(d) initial working capital

Ans (d) initial working capital

11. The capital which changes its form is termed as *ISC Sem I Specimen 2021*

(a) working capital (b) fixed capital
(c) seasonal capital (d) special capital

Ans (a) working capital

12. A large firm trading in biscuits will require *ISC Sem I Specimen 2021*

(a) seasonal working capital
(b) special working capital
(c) large amount of working capital
(d) small amount of working capital

Ans (d) small amount of working capital

13. Working capital is also known as *ISC Sem I Specimen 2021*

(a) net working capital (b) gross working capital
(c) revolving capital (d) block capital

Ans (c) revolving capital

14. Financial planning helps to bridge the gap between *ISC Sem I Specimen 2021*

(a) production and purchases
(b) production and sales
(c) production and advertising
(d) production and financing

Ans (b) production and sales

2 Marks Questions

1. What is net working capital? **ISC 2020**

Ans Net working capital is the excess of current assets over current liabilities.

Net Working Capital = Current Assets − Current Liabilities

2. What is the importance of finance to a business concern? **ISC Specimen 2018, 2017**

Ans Importance of finance for a business concern is described below

(i) All business activities require finance to start a business and carry out its daily operations.

(ii) The firm can take benefit of opportunities, e.g. Expand its operation or enter into new emerging field or modernise only, if adequate finance is available.

> **Common Mistake** Many times students are confused between features, importance and objective. So, there is a need to focus on difference of each.

3. Why is working capital also known as 'circulating capital'? **ISC 2016**

Ans Working capital is that part of total capital, which is required for holding current assets. It represents the liquid funds, which are required for day-to-day operations of the firm. It is also known as the 'circulating capital' or 'revolving capital'.

This is because the current assets are changed from one form to another in the regular operations of the business, in the following manner

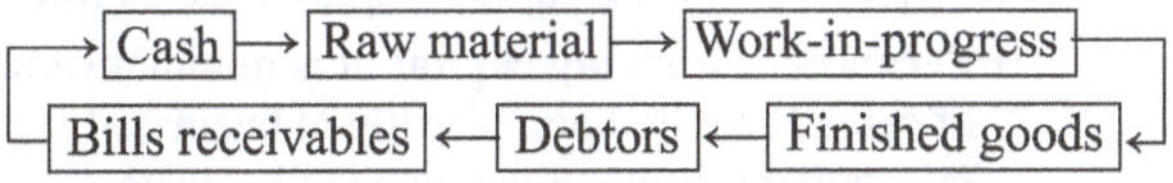

4. Explain the meaning of gross working capital. **ISC 2015**

Ans Gross working capital means the total amount of funds invested in current assets. Current assets are those assets which are converted into cash during the period of one year or during it's operating cycle.

Thus, Gross working capital = Book value of current assets

5. What is meant by capital gearing ratio? **ISC 2015**

Ans The ratio between equity (owned funds) is called capital gearing ratio or financial leverage. When the proportion of debt is high, it is called 'high gearing' or 'trading on thin equity'.

On the other hand, when equity dominates the capital structure, it is known as 'low gearing' or 'trading on thick equity'.

> **Concept Enhancer** Capital gearing ratio can also be calculated using formula
>
> $$\text{Capital Gearing Ratio} = \frac{\text{Long-term Debt} + \text{Short-term Debt} + \text{Bank Overdraft}}{\text{Shareholder's Equity}}$$

6. Distinguish between gross working capital and net working capital. **ISC 2014**

Ans Difference between gross working capital and net working capital

Basis	Gross Working Capital (GWC)	Net Working Capital (NWC)
Meaning	Total amount of funds invested in current assets is called 'gross working capital'. GWC = Book value of current assets	Net working capital is the excess of current assets over current liabilities. NWC = Current Assets − Current Liabilities
Indication	It shows the investment in current assets by both short-term and long-term sources of finance.	Net working capital shows the current assets financed through long-term sources.

7. What is meant by working capital? **ISC 2009**

Ans Working capital is a part of investments in current assets. Every business organisation needs to invest in current assets. Current assets are those investments which in normal routine of business, get converted into cash or cash equivalents within one year, e.g. Inventories, debtors, bills receivables, etc.

These short-term investments into current assets are called 'working capital'.

It is required for day-to-day operations of an enterprise. As it circulates in the business, it is also known as 'the circulating' or 'revolving capital'. Working capital is that part of total capital which is required for holding current assets over current liabilities.

8. Mention any four sources of finance for a proprietary form of business organisation. **ISC 2009**

Ans Four sources of finance for a proprietary form of business are

(i) Owner's capitals
(ii) Borrowing from friends and relatives
(iii) Loans from banks
(iv) Loans from financial institutions

9. Mention any two factors affecting the working capital requirements of an organisation. ***ISC 2006***

Ans The working capital requirements of an enterprise depends upon the following factors

(i) **Growth prospects** A growing business with increasing production and sales, needs more working capital, and *vice-versa*.

(ii) **Credit policy** A liberal credit policy results in higher amount of debtors, thereby increasing the working capital requirements. Whereas, lesser working capital is required, if conservative credit policy is followed by the organisation.

3/4/5 Marks Questions

1. The capital structure of XYZ Ltd. is highly geared. Explain any four factors that were considered by its finance manager while formulating such a capital structure for the company. ***ISC 2024 (4M)***

Or The management of Raj Ltd. has asked their finance manager to design the capital structure for the organisation. Explain any four factors that the finance manager will consider while planning the capital structure. ***ISC Specimen 2023 (4M)***

Or Explain any four factors that affect the capital structure of a company. ***ISC 2016 (4M)***

Or Briefly explain five factors to be considered while preparing a suitable capital plan. ***ISC 2014 (5M)***

Or Describe the factors that must be considered in devising a suitable capital plan for an industry. ***ISC 2005 (5M)***

Ans Refer to text on page 15 and 16.

2. Explain any three factors that you will consider while determining the working capital requirement for a business enterprise. ***ISC 2020 (3M)***

Or Discuss in brief any four factors that affect the working capital requirement of a company. ***ISC 2015 (4M)***

Or Explain any four factors which determine the working capital requirement of a business. ***ISC 2010 (4M)***

Ans The capital required by a business or venture to meet its day-to-day expenses is known as the working capital.

Factors affecting working capital requirements of a business Refer to text on page 17.

Value Point

For getting maximum marks, following point can be included in the answer

- Add definition of working capital

3. Differentiate between fixed capital and working capital. ***ISC 2019, 2014, 2005 (3M)***

Ans Refer to text on page 17.

4. What is financial planning? Explain three points of importance of financial planning for a business organisation. ***ISC 2019 (5M)***

Ans The process of estimating fund requirements of business and specifying the sources from where the funds would be arranged, is called financial planning. It is the preparation of blue-print of organisation's future operations.

Following is the importance of financial planning for a business organisation

(i) **Helps in coordination** It helps in coordinating various business activities, such as sales, purchase, production, finance etc.

(ii) **Helps in avoiding business shocks and surprises** Through financial planning, future receipts and payments are anticipated to make provision of shortage or surplus of funds. This helps in avoiding shocks and surprises in a business.

(iii) **Helps in avoiding wastage of finance** Financial planning helps in estimation of finance for a particular business operation. Therefore, the chances of wastage of finance are minimised.

Importance of Financial Planning

- Helps in coordination
- Helps in avoiding business shocks and surprises
- Helps in avoiding wastage of finance

5. Briefly explain any four types of working capital required by a business concern. ***ISC 2018 (4M)***

Ans Four types of working capital required are as follows

(i) **Permanent working capital** It is minimum amount of capital required permanently in business to maintain the regular operations of business.

(ii) **Temporary working capital** It is the capital which is required in addition to permanent working capital for meeting temporary needs of the business.

(iii) **Seasonal working capital** It is required in the busy season for business dealing in seasonal products.

(iv) **Special working capital** Capital required for emergencies and generally kept as reserves for reasons like increase in demand, periods of depression, natural calamities, strikes, lockouts, etc. is referred to as special working capital.

Common Mistake Students usually get confused in concept of working capital and types of working capital. So, student needs to understand difference between these two. Concept of working capital means gross working capital and net working capital.

6. You are the finance manager of a newly established company. The Directors have asked you to determine the amount of fixed capital requirement for the company. Explain any five factors that you will consider while determining the fixed capital requirement for the company.
ISC Specimen 2018, 2017 (5M)

Ans As a finance manager, I will consider the following five factors while determining the fixed capital requirements for my company

(i) **Nature of products** Enterprises producing capital items require more fixed capital, whereas enterprises producing consumer goods require less fixed capital.

(ii) **Method of production** Enterprises using capital intensive technique require more fixed capital than the enterprises using labour intensive technique.

(iii) **Diversity of products** Enterprises engaged in manufacturing/dealing in single product require less fixed capital. Enterprises engaged or dealing in multiple products requires more fixed capital.

Factors affecting Fixed Capital
- Nature of products
- Method of production
- Diversity of products
- Mode of acquiring fixed assets
- Intangible assets

(iv) **Mode of acquiring fixed assets** Enterprises acquiring fixed assets on cash payment basis require more fixed capital, whereas enterprises acquiring fixed assets on lease/hire-purchase system require less fixed capital.

(v) **Intangible assets** Enterprises desirous of acquiring high goodwill, patents, copyrights, etc. require more fixed capital. Enterprises not desirous of acquiring high goodwill, patents, copyrights, etc require less fixed capital.

7. What is fixed capital? Discuss any four factors affecting fixed capital requirement of a joint stock company. ***ISC 2012 (5M)***

Or Examine any four dominant factors determining the amount of fixed capital requirements for a business.
ISC 2008 (5M)

Or Briefly discuss any five factors affecting the fixed capital requirements of an organisation. ***ISC 2007 (5M)***

Ans The amount of capital investment in fixed assets is called 'fixed capital'. e.g. Plant and machinery, land and building, etc. Fixed capital requirement varies directly in-proportion of amount of fixed assets used in the business. Fixed capital is required for establishing the business, growing and expanding its market, diversifying and also for technology upgradation.

It also includes other non-current assets in which capital of the company is locked for a long period. e.g. Expenditures in research and development programmes.

For factors affecting fixed capital requirements of an organisation, refer to Q. No. 6 (3/4/5 Marks) on page 21.

Concept Enhancer Fixed capital can be raised through long-term sources of finance like issue of shares, debentures, long-term loans, etc.

Additional Questions

2 Marks Questions

1. State any two sources of finance for sole proprietorship firm and partnership firm.

Ans Two sources of finance for sole proprietorship are as follows

(i) Own capital and retained earnings.

(ii) Loan from friends and relatives.

Two sources of finance for partnership firms are as follows

(i) Own capital contribution by partners.

(ii) Loans from parnters, friends and relatives.

2. State the objectives of financial planning.

Ans Financial planning strives to achieve the following objectives

(i) **To ensure availability of funds whenever these are required** This includes a proper estimation of the funds required for different purposes such as for the purchase of long-term assets or to meet day-to-day expenses of business, etc. Apart from this, there is a need to estimate the time at which these funds are to be made available.

(ii) **To ensure unnecessary finance is not raised** Excess funding is almost as bad as inadequate funding. Even if there is some surplus money, good financial planning would put it to the best possible use, so that the financial resources are not left idle and don't unnecessarily add to the cost.

3. What is meant by capital structure?

Ans It refers to the mix between owner's funds (equity) and borrowed funds (debt). After deciding the financial requirement, it is decided, how much finance is to be raised from which source and what will be the proportion of the two sources.

4/5 Marks Questions

1. Explain the following factors affecting capital structure.
   (i) Trading on equity (ii) Capital market conditions
   (iii) Statutory requirement (iv) Investors' choice

Ans Refer to text on page 16.

2. Give the importance of finance for business by discussing any five points.

Ans Refer to text on page 13.

Case Based Question

Case 1

MM Ltd. is manufacturing small cars at its manufacturing unit in Pune. The demand of its cars is increasing at the rate of 20% annually. It is planning to set-up a new car manufacturing unit at Indore. For this the company will require approximately 1,500 crores as fixed capital and 500 crores as working capital. The company has already arranged for its working capital. ***ISC Specimen 2021***

(i) MM Ltd.'s fixed capital can be affected by
(a) size of the business (b) liberal credit policy
(c) terms of purchase and sale
(d) length of the manufacturing cycle

Ans (a) size of the business

(ii) The working capital required by MM Ltd. initially can be termed as
(a) permanent working capital
(b) variable working capital
(c) working capital
(d) initial working capital

Ans (d) initial working capital

(iii) Fixed capital is the capital used to acquire
(a) assets
(b) fixed assets
(c) current assets
(d) net assets

Ans (b) fixed assets

(iv) MM Ltd. could have raised the working capital through
(a) commercial banks
(b) loans from financial institutions
(c) issue of bonds and debentures
(d) issue of shares

Ans (a) commercial banks

(v) Working capital can be termed as the capital invested in
(a) current assets
(b) inventories
(c) cash
(d) bank

Ans (a) current assets

CHAPTER TEST

01 Mark Questions

1. Gross working capital is based on
(a) accrual concept
(b) money measurement concept
(c) going concern concept
(d) realisation concept

2. Which of the following statements is/are correct?
(a) Working capital is also known as circulating capital
(b) Large organisation needs larger working capital
(c) Shortage of working capital reduces return on investment
(d) All of the above

3. Which of the following factors affects the working capital requirement of a business unit?
(a) Nature of the business (b) Credit policy
(c) Production policy (d) All of these

4. Working capital is also known as excess of current assets over current liabilities. State true or false.

5. In general, long-term debt costs less than short-term debt. State true or false.

6. Capital structure is .... financial structure.

7. The claims by preferred shareholders on a firm's assets and income come .... those of ordinary shareholders and .... those of creditors.

8. What is financial planning?

9. What is permanent working capital?

10. **Assertion** (A) Management of working capital refers to the management of current assets and current liabilities.

Reason (R) The major thrust of course is on the management of current assets, because current liabilities arise in the context of current assets.

Alternatives
(a) Both Assertion (A) and Reason (R) are true and Reason (R) is the correct explanation of Assertion (A)
(b) Both Assertion (A) and Reason (R) are true, but Reason (R) is not the correct explanation of Assertion (A)
(c) Assertion (A) is true, but Reason (R) is false
(d) Assertion (A) is false, but Reason (R) is true

02 Marks Questions

11. What is net working capital?

12. Why is business finance required?

13. Give the definition of finance.

14. Mention any two important questions while preparing financial plans.

03/04/05 Marks Questions

15. Obtaining funds from debt and equity depend on several factors. Explain any four such factors.

16. Enumerate the various types of working capital.

17. Explain three sources of finance for joint stock company.

18. Explain, how 'risk consideration' and 'trading on equity' affect choice of capital structure.

19. Write short note on
(i) Gross working capital
(ii) Financial planning

20. Explain any five factors affecting working capital.

Answers

1. (c) going concern concept
2. (d) All of the above
3. (d) All of these
4. True
5. False
6. a part of
7. before, after
10. (a) Both Assertion (A) and Reason (R) are true and Reason (R) is the correct explanation of Assertion (A)

03

Long-term Sources of Finance for a Joint Stock Company

TREND ANALYSIS 5 YEARS

Average No. of Questions Across all Sets

		Types of Questions	2024	2023	2020	2019	2018
TOPIC 01	Equity and Preference Shares and Retained Earnings	1 Mark	—	1	—	—	—
		2 Marks	—	—	—	—	—
		3/4/5 Marks	2	3	2	3	2
TOPIC 02	Borrowed Capital-Debentures and Loans	1 Mark	1	—	—	—	—
		2 Marks	—	—	—	—	—
		3/4/5 Marks	—	—	2	1	2

TOPIC 1

Equity and Preference Shares and Retained Earnings

Meaning of Long-term Sources of Funds

Funds are required for different purposes and time period by a company. Long-term sources of finance provide finance generally for a period exceeding five years and used to obtain fixed capital for a business, which is required to purchase the fixed assets of the company.

Important Sources of Long-term Finance

The important sources of long-term finance are

(i) Equity shares (ii) Preference shares
(iii) Bonus and right issue
(iv) ESOP and sweat equity shares
(v) Retained earnings (vi) Debentures
(vii) Loans from commercial banks and financial institutions

Equity Shares

The capital raised through equity shares represents the ownership of a company. Therefore, it is known as 'ownership capital' or 'owner's funds'.

Once issued, they are not redeemed during the working life of the company. Thus, it is a source of permanent capital, which does not involve a fixed liability of payment of dividend. Dividend on equity shares is payable only in the event of profits earned by a company.

Features of Equity Shares

The features of equity shares are

(i) **Owner's fund** The equity shareholders provide fixed capital for initialising the business. Therefore they are a part of owner's fund.

(ii) **Permanent capital** The equity share capital is not redeemable during the lifetime of the company. Hence, it is a permanent capital. In case of winding up of the company, they are the last one to receive repayment of capital.

(iii) **Residual owners** Returns are uncertain as the rate of dividend is not fixed the equity shareholders receive what is left, after all other claims on the company's income and assets have been settled.

(iv) **Voting rights** Equity shareholders can participate in the company's affairs and management.

Advantages of Equity Shares

Advantages of equity shares are

1. **From the point of view of shareholder**
   (i) Shareholders enjoy voting rights in taking crucial decisions of the company.
   (ii) They have the scope of enjoying higher returns than preference shareholders.
   (iii) They enjoy capital gains, when value of the shares appreciates in the market.
   (iv) They have limited liability, i.e. upto the face value of the shares held by them in the company.
   (v) They enjoy privileges of right shares and bonus shares.
   (vi) They are not liable to pay income tax on dividends.
   (vii) They are entitled to manifold increasing returns with increase in profits.
2. **From the point of view of company**
   (i) It is a source of company's permanent capital.
   (ii) There is no charge on the assets of the company.
   (iii) It represents the company's strength, which provides credibility to borrow.
   (iv) It provides credit worthiness to the company to raise funds further.
   (v) Diffusion of risk becomes possible.
   (vi) There is no fixed obligation to pay dividend.
   (vii) A company can raise further capital through equity shares until authorised capital is reached.

Disadvantages of Equity Shares

Disadvantages of equity shares are

1. **From the point of view of shareholder**
   (i) Shareholders bear a high risk on account of repayment and dividend.
   (ii) There is uncertainty of earnings for the investors.
   (iii) It leads to oligarchic management in reality.
   (iv) It is usually not preferred by cautious investors.
   (v) Residual earnings on dividends and capital (in case of liquidation) is doubtful.
2. **From the point of view of company**
   (i) It leads to concentration of power in few hands.
   (ii) It is a costly source of funds, as the rate of dividend is not fixed.
   (iii) The company cannot avail the benefit of trading on equity.
   (iv) There is a greater degree of risk of over capitalisation.
   (v) The capital structure becomes inflexible as equity shares are irredeemable.
   (vi) Excessive formalities are involved and the process is cumbersome.
   (vii) Chances of speculation is very high.

Preference Shares

The capital raised by issue of preference shares is called preference share capital. Preference shares enjoy the following two preferential rights

(i) Preferential right to receive dividend at a pre-determined rate before dividend is paid to equity shareholders.

(ii) Preferential right to receive repayment of capital at the time of dissolution of company.

Features of Preference Shares

The features of preference shares are

(i) No voting rights are conferred to preference shareholders.

(ii) Preference in payment of dividend and capital over equity shareholders.

(iii) Fixed dividend, only in the event of profits, at the discretion of the directors.

Types of Preference Shares

There are different kinds of preference shares available, such as

(i) **Redeemable preference shares** If the amount raised through preference shares is to be paid back at the end of a specified period, then these are referred to as redeemable preference shares.

In India preference share of this category are issued with a maximum period of redemption of upto 20 years.

(ii) **Non-redeemable preference shares** If the amount raised through preference shares is not payable throughout the life of the company, then these are referred to as non-redeemable preference shares. In India, companies cannot issue this category of preference share.

(iii) **Cumulative preference shares** They enjoy the right to accumulate unpaid dividends in the future years, in case the same is not paid during a year.

(iv) **Non-cumulative preference shares** They do not enjoy the right to accumulate dividend, if it is not paid in a particular year.

(v) **Participating preference shares** They have a right to participate in the further surplus of a company's profit, after dividend at a certain rate has been paid on equity shares.

(vi) **Non-participating preference shares** They do not enjoy right of participation in the excess profits of the company.

(vii) **Convertible preference shares** They can be converted into equity shares within a specified period of time.

(viii) **Non-convertible preference shares** They cannot be converted into equity shares.

Advantages of Preference Shares

1. From the Point of View of Shareholders

(i) Shareholders get regular and stable dividends.

(ii) There is lesser risk in case of preference shares.

(iii) They get preferential right over equity share at the time of payment of dividend and capital.

(iv) Cumulative dividend is given in case of cumulative preference shares.

2. From the Point of View of Company

(i) They do not create any charge on the assets of the company.

(ii) It is a cheaper mode of finance.

(iii) They have a longer maturity period and thus provide permanent capital to the company.

(iv) Preference shareholders do not interfere in the management of the company.

(v) It appeals the conservative investors as the rate of dividend is fixed and preference is attached for its payment over equity shareholders.

(vi) It helps to enhance the credit worthiness of the company.

(vii) Redeemable preference shares provide flexibility to the capital structure.

Disadvantages of Preference Shares

1. From the Point of View of Shareholders

(i) Preference shares do not confer any voting rights to shareholders.

(ii) Redeemable preference shareholders may get redemption before enjoying the consequences of prosperity of the company.

(iii) They are not entitled to capital gains on account of prosperity.

(iv) There is no guarantee of payment of dividend.

2. From the Point of View of Company

(i) It is a costly source of finance.

(ii) It carries a permanent burden on the company as dividend is to be paid at a fixed rate.

(iii) Many legal formalities are involved in issuing preference shares.

(iv) It is less appealing for risk takers, as payment of dividend is not certain, if the company do not generate regular profits.

Difference between Equity Shares and Preference Shares

Basis	Equity shares	Preference shares
Participation in management	Full right to participate.	No right to participate.
Sequence of dividend	Dividend is paid last of all.	Preference is given in providing dividend.
Sequence of refund of capital	On winding up of the company, capital is refunded after preference shares.	Preference is given in refunding the capital.
Refund of capital during lifetime	Not possible at all.	Capital can be refunded in case of redeemable preference shares.

Basis	Equity shares	Preference shares
Permanency of dividend	Dividend is uncertain as it fluctuates with the amount of divisible profits decision of the Board of Directors.	Dividend is certain and fixed.
Unit value	Unit value is usually low.	Unit value is usually high.
Risk	It bears comparatively higher risk.	It bears compartatively lesser risk.
Nature of investors	It attracts investors who are bold enough to bear risks.	It attracts investors who are conservative.
Convertibility	They cannot be converted into preference shares.	They can be converted into equity shares.
Right issue	They have a right to further issue of shares.	They do not have a right to further issue of shares.
Arrears	They are not entitled to receive arrears of dividends.	They may be entitled to receive arrears of dividends.

Bonus Shares

When companies having large undistributed profits, issue fully paid-up shares to their existing shareholders, free of charge, in proportion to their existing share holdings then such shares are known as 'bonus shares'. Instead of distributing profits in the form of dividends, the company issues them bonus shares.

This is also known as 'capitalisation of reserves' as reserves or retained earnings are capitalised by issuing bonus shares.

However following conditions should be met before issuing bonus shares

(i) There should be adequate undistributed earnings.
(ii) It should be clearly mentioned in Articles of Association.
(iii) SEBI guidelines regarding issue of bonus shares should be met.
(iv) A resolution must be passed by the Board of Directors of the company.
(v) Approval of shareholders in the general meeting of the company should be taken if stated in the Articles.

Rights Shares or Rights Issue

When the company wants to issue further shares after the first issue to increase its share capital, it is mandatory to issue new shares first to existing equity shareholders on pro-rata basis. The shares so offered to the existing members to be issued at a discount price, are called right shares. This right to existing members is called 'pre-emptive right of the shareholders'.

Rights issue is compulsory when new issue is made

(i) At any time after the expiry of two years from the formation of the company, or
(ii) At any time after the expiry of one year from the first allotment of shares, whichever is earlier.

A company is not required to offer further shares to the existing shareholders in the following circumstances

(i) When the company issues the new shares before two years from the formation of the company or before one year from the first allotment of shares, whichever is earlier.
(ii) If it is specified in the special resolution passed by the company.
(iii) If it is specified in the ordinary resolution passed by the company and approved by the government.
(iv) If all the shareholders reject such offer of the company.

Difference between Bonus Shares and Right Shares

Basis	Bonus shares	Right shares
Meaning	Bonus shares refers to the shares issued by the company free of cost to the existing shareholders in the proportion of their holdings, out of accumulated profits and reserves.	Right shares are available to the existing shareholders equivalent to their holdings, that can be bought at a fixed price, for a definite period of time.
Price	Issued free of cost.	Issued at discounted prices.
Objective	To bring the market price per share, within a more popular range.	To raise fresh capital for the firm.
Renunciation	No such renunciation.	Shareholders may fully or partly renounce their rights.
Paid up value	Always fully paid up.	Either fully or partly paid up.
Minimum subscription	Not required	Mandatory

Employee Stock Ownership Plan/ Employee Stock Option Plan (ESOP)

An ESOP is a type of employee benefit plan, which is intended to encourage employees to acquire stock or ownership in the company by issuing them equity shares. The shares are issued to the employees at considerable discount.

Sweat Equity Shares

Sweat equity shares can be issued by a company to its employees and directors for their contribution towards the company, e.g. Providing technical knowhow, giving the right to use intellectual property, etc. Sweat equity shares are issued often at non-cash consideration or at a discount.

Sometimes, sweat equity shares are offered to a valued employee as a part of his/her remuneration package.

The company must fulfil the following conditions before the issue of sweat equity

(i) It must be of a class of shares already issued.
(ii) The company must be in operation for atleast a year.
(iii) A special resolution must be passed for such issue.
(iv) SEBI regulations must be followed for such issue.

Meaning of Retained Earnings

It means that part of trading profits which are not distributed in the form of dividends, but retained by the company for future expansion of the company. This can be also stated as **ploughing back of profits**.

These ultimately come back to the equity shareholders in the form of enhanced dividend or capital gains. Retained earnings strengthens the financial position of the company, provides a sound financial base for expansion and helps to combat difficult periods or recession.

Advantages of Retained Earnings

The main advantages of retained earnings are

1. **From the view point of company**
   (i) This method of financing does not involve much cost or legal formalities.
   (ii) There is no liability for repayment of funds.
   (iii) It helps to increase the credit worthiness of the company.
   (iv) It helps the company to face contingencies and uncertainties of business.
   (v) It helps a company to adopt a stable dividend policy.
   (vi) It does not affect control over the management of the company.
2. **From the view point of shareholders**
   (i) It enables the company to distribute dividends, even in the year of losses, providing regular income to shareholders.
   (ii) It adds to the profitability and hence increases future dividends for the shareholders.
   (iii) It provides an assurance of safe investment to the investors.
3. **From the view point of society**
   (i) It results in higher capital formation in the country.
   (ii) It facilitates in modernisation of industries, promotion of industrial growth and prosperity in the economy.
   (iii) Better services and products result in better living standard for the people.

Disadvantages of Retained Earnings

Disadvantages of retained earnings are

(i) Limited finance can be raised.
(ii) It may result in monopoly and concentration of economic power.
(iii) It is an uncertain source of finance.
(iv) It may cause dissatisfaction amongst the shareholders.
(v) It may lead to over capitalisation by excessive issue of bonus shares.
(vi) It may lead to misuse of funds.
(vii) Manipulation of prices of shares is usually done through this practice.

PYQs Previous Years' Questions

1 Mark Questions

1. ABC Company plans to capitalise its undistributed profits. Which one of the followings shares will the company issue to its existing shareholders? *ISC 2023*
   (a) Rights shares
   (b) ESOP
   (c) Sweat equity shares
   (d) Bonus shares

Ans (d) Bonus shares

2. The shares issued by a company to its directors or employees for consideration other than cash, having a lock in period of three years are called *ISC Sem I 2021*
   (a) bonus shares (b) equity shares
   (c) preference shares (d) sweat equity shares

Ans (d) sweat equity shares

3. Which type of preference shareholders are entitled to get a share in the surplus profits of the company? *ISC Sem I 2021*
   (a) Cumulative preference shares
   (b) Convertible preference shares
   (c) Participating preference shares
   (d) Redeemable preference shares

Ans (c) Participating preference shares

4. With reference to the disadvantages of equity shares as a source of finance for a joint stock company, choose the odd one out. *ISC Sem I 2021*
   (a) Manipulation of control
   (b) Permanent burden
   (c) Inflexible
   (d) Costly

Ans (b) Permanent burden

5. XYZ Public Limited company, a manufacturing company was incorporated on 1st April, 2020. It wants to raise long-term source of capital. What would it raise its funds through? *ISC Sem I Specimen 2021*
   (a) Cash credit
   (b) Discounting a bill of exchange
   (c) Bank overdraft
   (d) Shares and debentures

Ans (d) Shares and debentures

6. The shares which have a lock in period of three years are called *ISC Sem I Specimen 2021*
   (a) right shares
   (b) sweat equity shares
   (c) bonus shares
   (d) ESOP

Ans (b) sweat equity shares

7. The type of capital which is also termed as risk capital is *ISC Sem I Specimen 2021*
   (a) preference share capital
   (b) debentures
   (c) bonds
   (d) equity share capital

Ans (d) equity share capital

8. The shares which have to be paid for by the shareholders are *ISC Sem I Specimen 2021*
   (a) ESOP (b) sweat equity shares
   (c) right shares
   (d) bonus shares

Ans (c) right shares

9. The apt way of rising long-term source of finance by a joint stock company is *ISC Sem I Specimen 2021*
   (a) through issue of shares.
   (b) through issue of redeemable debentures.
   (c) through issue of redeemable preference shares.
   (d) through factoring.

Ans (a) through issue of shares.

10. With reference to bonus shares, which one of the statements given below holds true? *ISC Sem I Specimen 2021*
    (a) Bonus shares are fully paid up given to the existing shareholders.
    (b) Bonus shares are partly paid up given to the existing shareholders.
    (c) Bonus shares are fully paid shares given to the employees of the company.
    (d) Bonus shares are fully paid shares given to the existing debentureholders.

Ans (a) Bonus shares are fully paid up given to the existing shareholders.

2 Marks Questions

1. What are bonus shares? *ISC 2016*

Or Write briefly on bonus share. *ISC 2003*

Ans Bonus shares are fully paid shares issued to existing equity shareholders from the undistributed profits of the company, free of cost. Instead of distributing profits in form of dividends, the company issues them bonus shares. It is also called 'capitalisation of profits'.

Value Point

For getting maximum marks, following point can be included in the answer

- 'Fully paid', 'free of cost', 'existing shareholders', should be focussed while framing of answer by students.

2. In the context of right shares, bring out the meaning of pre-emptive rights. *ISC 2014*

Ans According to the provisions of Companies Act, 2013, whenever a company proposes to increase its subscribed capital through a further issue of shares, the shares should be first issued to the existing shareholders. However, this is done, if a issue is made

(i) at any time after the expiry of two years from the formation of the company.

(ii) at any time after the expiry of one year from the first allotment, whichever is earlier.

This right of getting issued the new shares to the existing shareholders is called 'the pre-emptive right' and 'such shares' are called 'rights shares'.

3. What is meant by cumulative preference shares? *ISC 2013*

Ans Preference shares are cumulative when dividend, if not paid in a year, accumulates and is carried forward to succeeding years. Thus, they have a right to claim dividends for years even when there were no profits.

4. Mention two drawbacks of ploughing back of profits from the shareholders' view point. *ISC 2008*

Ans Two drawbacks of ploughing back of profits from the shareholders' view point are

(i) **Dissatisfaction amongst shareholders** Excessive ploughing back may cause dissatisfaction amongst the shareholders as they would get lower dividends.

(ii) **High opportunity cost** The retained earnings are nothing, but sacrifice of profits made by equity shareholders. In other words, retained earnings are the dividend foregone by equity shareholders. This sacrifice increases the opportunity cost of retained earnings.

5. From the view point of the company, mention two disadvantages of raising money by issue of shares. *ISC 2007*

Ans Disadvantages of raising money by issue of shares from the view point of company are

(i) **High cost** The cost of shares is generally more as compared to other sources of raising finance.

(ii) **Inflexibility in capital structure** Shares cannot be paid back during the lifetime of the company. This characteristic creates inflexibility in the capital structure of the company.

6. Give two features of 'participating preference shares'. *ISC 2004*

Ans The two features of participating preference shares are given below

(i) Apart from fixed dividend, these have a right to participate in the further surplus of a company after dividend at a certain rate has been paid on the equity shares. So, in addition to the fix rate of return, they further get a share in surplus profits, therefore they are called 'participating preference shares'.

(ii) Cost of participating preference shares is higher than non-participating preference shares.

7. Why are preference shares so called? *ISC 2001*

Ans Preference shares are so called because they carry the following two preferential rights over equity shares

(i) Preferential right to receive dividend at a pre-determined rate before dividend is paid to equity shareholders.

(ii) Preferential right to receive repayment of capital at the time of dissolution of company.

3/4/5 Marks Questions

1. Ms. Rubina, a first time investor, does not understand the difference between securities with voting rights and securities without voting rights.
Give any five differences between the two types of securities to help her understand the difference. *ISC 2024 (5M)*

Or Give five differences between preference shares and equity shares. *ISC 2020 (5M)*

Or Distinguish between equity shares and preference shares. *ISC 2015, 02 (4M)*

Ans Differences between equity shares (securities with voting rights) and preference shares (securities without voting rights) are as follows

Basis	Equity shares	Preference shares
Participation in management	Full right to participate in the management of the company.	No right to participate in the management of the company.
Sequence of dividend	Dividend is paid last of all.	Preference is given in providing dividend.
Sequence of refund of capital	On winding up of the company, capital is refunded after preference shares.	Preference is given in refunding the capital.
Refund of capital during lifetime	Not possible at all.	Capital can be refunded in case of redeemable preference shares.
Permanency of dividend	Dividend is uncertain as it fluctuates with the amount of divisible profits decision of the Board of Directors.	Dividend is certain and fixed.

Value Points

For getting maximum marks, following points can be included in the answer

- Difference should be given with basis of difference
- The difference given must correlate to each other.

2. Write a short note on sweat equity shares. **ISC 2024 (3M)**

Or What are sweat equity shares? **ISC 2014 (3M)**

Ans Sweat equity shares can be issued by a company to its employees and directors for their contribution towards the company, e.g. Providing technical knowhow, giving the right to use intellectual property, etc. Sweat equity shares are issued often at non-cash consideration or at a discount. It helps to motivate the efficient employees and manager and retain them in the company.

However, such issue cannot be made before one year from the commencement of business.

Common Mistake Majority of the candidates get confused between sweat equity shares and bonus shares. Main purpose of issue of sweat equity shares is not clear. Some candidates mention that sweat equity shares are issued to the shareholders but these shares are issued to employees and directors.

3. What are retained earnings? Explain any four disadvantages of retained earnings. **ISC 2023, 20 (5M)**

Or What is retained earnings? Explain any two of its merits and two of its demerits. **ISC 2015 (5M)**

Or Write short note on 'ploughing back of profits'. **ISC 2013 (4M)**

Ans Retained earnings means that part of trading profits which is not distributed in the form of dividends, but is retained by directors for future expansion of the company. This can also be stated as 'ploughing back of profits'. These ultimately come back to the equity shareholders in the form of enhanced dividend or capital gains.

Retained earnings provide the following advantages

(i) Company does not have to spend any amount to obtain it.

(ii) The amount lying in the general reserve protects the company from the bad scenario or from ups and downs.

(iii) A company can adopt the policy of stable dividend on the strength of general reserves.

(iv) Expansion plans of the company can be executed easily because of the presence of such reserves.

However there may be following demerits

(i) Frequent capitalisation of profits may result in over capitalisation.

(ii) It may be used to manipulate share prices on the stock exchange.

(iii) It may lead to creation of monopolies and concentration of wealth.

(iv) It may lead to misuse of funds.

4. What are preference shares? Give any four types of preference shares. **ISC 2023 (5M)**

Or Discuss any four types of preference shares. **ISC 2019 (4M)**

Ans **Preference shares** Refer to text on page 25.

Types of preference shares are (any four)

(i) **Redeemable preference shares** If the amount raised through preference shares is to be paid back at the end of a specified period, then these are referred to as redeemable preference shares. In India preference share of this category are issued with a maximum period of redemption of upto 20 years.

(ii) **Non-redeemable preference shares** If the amount raised through preference shares is not payable throughout the life of the company, then these are referred to as non-redeemable preference shares. In India, companies cannot issue this category of preference share.

Types of Preference Shares

- Redeemable preference shares
- Non-redeemable preference shares
- Cumulative preference shares
- Non-cumulative preference shares

(iii) **Cumulative preference shares** In case of these shares, if dividends are not paid in any particular year, then they are carried forward to the next year and go on accumulating till the time they remain unpaid.

Such arrears of dividend become payable out of the profit of subsequent years and must be paid before the payment of dividend on any other class of shares.

(iv) **Non-cumulative preference shares** The holder of such shares get a fixed amount of dividend out of profits of each year.

Due to any reason, if dividend is not declared in any year, such shareholders get nothing nor they can claim for unpaid amount.

5. Ratan Ltd. needs to raise funds from the financial market and hence, considers issuing equity shares. State any four reasons to explain why this source of raising funds is considered by the company. **ISC 2023 (4M)**

Or

Explain the advantages of equity shares, as a source of finance. **ISC 2018 (4M)**

Or

What are equity shares? Explain any three advantages of issuing equity shares from the point of view of company. **ISC 2014 (4M)**

Ans Equity shares are ordinary shares which carry no preferential rights in payment of dividend and capital repayment. Equity shares represent the ownership of a company. Merits of equity shares are

(i) **Long-term and permanent capital** It is considered as a good source of long-term finance. A company is not required to payback the equity capital during its lifetime. Thus, they are also known as the permanent source of capital.

(ii) **No fixed burden** Payment of dividend to the equity shareholders is not compulsory. Therefore, there is no burden on the company. In this respect, they provide a cushion of safety against unfavourable development.

(iii) **Credit worthiness** Issuance of equity share capital creates no charge on the assets of the company. A company can raise further finance on the security of its fixed assets.

(iv) **Flexibility** A company can raise further capital through equity shares until authorised capital is reached.

Common Mistake Many times students are not able to understand question accordingly and try to give advantages as per shareholders point of view. Students need to focus on advantages of equity shareholder's capital from the view point of company.

6. Explain any three disadvantages of issuing equity shares, from the company's point of view. **ISC 2019 (3M)**

Ans Disadvantages of issuing equity shares from company's point of view

(i) **No benefit of trading on equity** If all the funds are raised through equity shares, the company will not be able to take advantage of trading on equity.

(ii) **Costly** The cost of raising funds through issue of equity shares is high. A lot of money is to be spent on underwriting commission, brokerage and other expenses.

(iii) **Over capitalisation** The funds raised through equity shares are not returned during the lifetime of the company.

Sometimes, more capital is raised than required which results in over capitalisation. It reduces earning per share.

Concept Enhancer Issue of equity shares leads to concentration of power in few hands and rate of dividend is also not fixed.

7. Write a short note on the ESOP. **ISC 2019 (4M)**

Ans It means the option given to the directors, officers or employees of a company which gives such directors, officers or employees, the benefit of right to purchase the shares of the company at a future date at a pre-determined price.

This is a voluntary scheme on the part of the company to give its employees a sense of belonging. The allottes of such share cannot sell their shares for a minimum period of one year from the date of allotment. This period is known as lock in period or vesting period.

8. Discuss three advantages of ploughing back of profit from the company's point of view. **ISC 2018 (4M)**

Or

Discuss any four advantages of ploughing back of profits from the company's point of view. **ISC 2011 (4M)**

Or

What are the two advantages of 'ploughing back' of profits? **ISC 2003**

Ans Four advantages of ploughing back of profit from the company's point of view are

(i) **No ownership dilution** Relying on retained earnings eliminates the fear of ownership dilution and loss of control by the existing shareholders and offers a greater degree of operational freedom.

Advantages of Ploughing Back of Profit
- No ownership dilution
- Positive connotation
- Ready availability
- Cheaper than external equity
- Safe investment

(ii) **Positive connotation** Retained earnings carry positive connotation as compared to equity issue as far as stock market is concerned.
This results in appreciating the value of shares in the stock market.

(iii) **Ready availability** Being an internal source, these earnings are readily available to the management and considered as a permanent source of funds.

(iv) **Cheaper than external equity** Retained earnings are cheaper than external equity because the floatation costs, brokerage costs, underwriting commission and other issue expenses are eliminated.

(v) **Safe investment** Retained earnings make the company financially sound. So, there is no danger of the shareholders' funds being lost.

9. Explain three disadvantages of preference shares from the investors' point of view. ***ISC Specimen 2018, 17 (3M)***

Ans Three disadvantages of preference shares from the invertors' point of view are explained below

(i) **Preference shares do not carry voting rights** One of the disadvantages of preference shares is that they do not confer voting rights on their holders. As such, they have no say in the management of the company.

(ii) **Preference shares carry a fix rate of return** The holders of preference shares are entitled to only a specified fix rate of return. They are not allowed to participate in extraordinary profits earned by the company.

(iii) **No guarantee of payment of dividend** There is no guarantee for payment of dividend to preference shareholders. Dividend is paid to them only in case of profits, at the discretion of Board of Directors.

10. Write any four features of equity shares. ***ISC 2016 (4M)***

Ans Four features of equity shares are as follows

(i) **Owner's fund** The equity shareholders are the primary risk bearers as they provide fixed capital needed to start the business.

(ii) **Permanent capital** The equity share capital is not redeemable during the life of the company. In case of winding up of the company, they are the last one to receive repayment of capital.

(iii) **Residual owners** Returns are uncertain as the rate of dividend is not fixed and they receive what is left, after all other claims on the company's income and assets have been settled.

(iv) **Voting rights** Equity shareholders can participate in the company's affairs and management by exercising their right to vote.

11. What is a participating preference share? ***ISC 2016, 12 (3M)***

Or Why are participating preference shares so called? ***ISC 2008 (4M)***

Or What is meant by participating preference shares? ***ISC 2001***

Ans Participating preference shares are those shares which have a right to participate in the further surplus of profits of the company's, after dividend at a certain rate has been paid to the equity shareholders.

In other words, apart from the fixed dividend, they have a right to receive surplus dividend from profit left after the payment of all kinds of dividends. Therefore, they are called 'participating preference shares'.

12. State three merits and demerits of raising finance through the issue of equity shares. ***ISC 2008 (5M)***

Ans Merits of equity shares are

(i) **Long-term and permanent capital** It is considered as a good source of long-term finance. A company is not required to payback the equity capital during its lifetime. Thus, it is regarded as a permanent source of capital.

(ii) **No fixed burden** Payment of dividend to the equity shareholders is not compulsory. Therefore, there is no burden on the company in this respect. They provide a cushion of safety against unfavourable development.

(iii) **Credit worthiness** Issuance of equity share capital creates no charge on the assets of the company. A company can raise further finance on the security of its fixed assets.

Demerits of equity shares are

(i) **Dilution in control** Each sale of equity share dilutes the voting power of the existing equity shareholders by extending the voting or controlling power to the new shareholders.

(ii) **Trading on equity not possible** If equity shares alone are issued, the company cannot trade on equity.

(iii) **Over capitalisation** Excessive issue of equity shares may result in over capitalisation. Dividend per share is low in that condition, which adversely affects the psychology of the investors.

13. Discuss five merits of retained earnings. *ISC 2007 (5M)*

Ans Merits of retained earnings are as follows

(i) This method of financing does not involve much cost or legal formalities.

(ii) There is no liability for repayment of funds.

(iii) It helps to increase the credit worthiness of the company.

(iv) It helps the company to face contingencies and uncertainties of business.

(v) It helps a company to adopt a stable dividend policy.

14. What are preference shares? Explain the advantages of issuing these shares. *ISC 2006 (5M)*

Ans Preference shares are those shares to which preference is attached in terms of

(i) Payment of dividend (ii) Return of capital

This means the preference shareholders are entitled to receive dividend before the equity shareholders and in case of liquidation, they have a precedence of payment of capital over equity shareholders.

Advantages of issuing preference shares are (any four)

(i) **Absence of charge on assets** Issue of preference shares does not involve any mortgage or charge on the assets of the company. Thus, fixed assets are free and can be used for raising loans in future.

(ii) **Capital structure flexibility** By means of issuing redeemable preference shares, flexibility in the company's capital structure can be maintained because redeemable preference shares can be redeemed under the terms of issue.

Advantages of Preference Shares

- Absence of charge on assets
- Capital structure flexibility
- No interference in management
- Cheaper mode of finance
- Appeals the conservative investors

(iii) **No interference in management** As preference shareholders don't have voting rights, they don't interfere in the management of the company.

(iv) **Cheaper mode of finance** Financing through preference shares is cheaper as compared to financing through equity shares.

(v) **Appeals the conservative investors** Preference shares enjoy preferential rights in payment of dividend, which is fixed. This feature makes this investment appealing to the cautious investors.

15. What are the advantages of raising capital by issuing shares? *ISC 2004 (5M)*

Ans Raising capital through issue of shares benefits both the company and investors in following ways

(i) Advantages to the company

(a) **Long-term and permanent capital** It is considered as a good source of long-term finance. A company is not required to payback the equity capital during its lifetime. Thus, these are also known as the permanent sources of capital.

(b) **No fixed burden** Payment of dividend to the equity shareholders is not compulsory. Therefore, there is no burden on the company. In this respect, they provide a pillow of safety against unfavourable development.

(c) **Credit worthiness** Issuance of equity share capital creates no charge on the assets of the company. A company can raise further finance on the security of its fixed assets.

(ii) Advantages for the shareholders

(a) **More income** Equity shareholders are the residual claimant of the profits after meeting all the fixed commitments.

The company may add to the profits by trading on equity. Thus, equity capital may get dividend at high rate during boom period.

(b) **Right to participate in the control and management** Equity shareholders have voting rights and elect competent persons as directors to control and manage the affairs of the company.

(c) **Suitable for enterprising investors** Equity shares are suitable for those investors who are willing to assume risk for higher returns.

16. Difference between cumulative preference shares and non-cumulative preference shares. *ISC 2003 (3M)*

Ans. Difference between cumulative preference shares and non-cumulative preference shares

Basis	Cumulative preference shares	Non-cumulative preference shares
Accumulation of dividend	If dividend is not paid in a particular year, it accumulates, to become payable out of profits in subsequent years.	Dividend does not accumulates, if not paid in any year.
Preference of dividend payment	Whenever the dividend is paid, accumulated preference dividend is paid first, then paying dividend on equity shares.	Accumulated dividend is not applicable in the case.
Status	Unless specified, all preference shares are cumulative preference shares .	To be non-cumulative, it has to be specifically mentioned about its non accumula-tion.

Additional Questions

2 Marks Questions

1. What is the meaning of long-term sources of funds?

Ans Funds are required for different purposes and time period by a company. Long-term sources of finance provide finance generally for a period exceeding five years and used to obtain fixed capital for a business, which is required to purchase the fixed assets of the company.

2. State any four sources of long-term sources of funds.

Ans The important sources of long-term finance are

(i) Equity shares (ii) Preference shares
(iii) Retained earnings (iv) Debentures

3. State any two features of preference shares.

Ans The features of preference shares are

(i) No voting rights are conferred to preference shareholders.

(ii) Preference in payment of dividend and capital over equity shareholders.

(iii) Fixed dividend, only in the event of profits, at the discretion of the directors.

4. What is meant by right shares?

Ans When the company wants to issue further shares after the first issue to increase its share capital, it is mandatory to issue new shares first to existing equity shareholders on pro-rata basis. The shares so offered to the existing members to be issued at a discount price, are called 'right shares'.

3/4/5 Marks Questions

1. Give the advantages and disadvantages of preference shares from the point of view of company.

Ans Refer to text on page 26.

2. State the conditions to be fulfilled before issue of bonus shares.

Ans Refer to text on page 27.

TOPIC 2

Borrowed Capital-Debentures and Loans

Debentures

It is an important instrument for raising long-term debt capital. These serve as an acknowledgement for the company that it has borrowed a certain amount of money. In general, it refers to the loan to the company by the debentureholders on which they receive a fixed rate of interest. The holders of debentures are known as 'the creditors of the company'.

Features of Debentures

The prominent features of debentures are

(i) Debenture represent borrowed funds.
(ii) It carries a fixed rate of interest, to be paid regularly.
(iii) They do not carry voting rights and right to participate in the company's management.
(iv) These are repayable after a specific time period.
(v) They create a charge on the assets of the company.

Kinds of Debentures

There are different kinds of debentures. Some prominent ones are discussed below

(i) **Mortgage/Secured debentures** They create a charge on the assets of the company, by mortgaging the assets of the company for payment of interest and the principal amount.
(ii) **Naked/Unsecured debentures** They do not create any charge or security on the assets of the company.
(iii) **Registered debentures** They are duly recorded in the register of debentureholders maintained by the company. Interest is only paid to the registered debentureholders.
(iv) **Bearer debentures** They are transferred only through a regular instrument of transfer. In other words, they are the debentures transferable on mere delivery. These debentures are not recorded in the books of the company.
(v) **Redeemable debentures** These are callable debentures and payable on or before their maturity.
(vi) **Irredeemable debentures** These are also called as 'perpetual debentures' and 'repayable' only at the time of winding up of a company.
(vii) **Convertible debentures** In such debentures, debentureholders are given an option of converting them into equity shares after a specified period. They are issued to allow the debentureholders to participate in future prosperity of a company.
(viii) **Non-convertible debentures** These debentures do not carry right of convertibility into equity shares.

Advantages of Debentures

Advantages of debentures are as follows

1. From the View Point of Company

(i) There is a possibility of trading on equity.
(ii) It is a cheaper source of finance.
(iii) It does not dilute control over the management of the company.
(iv) The company gets relief from income tax, as interest is a tax deductible expense.
(v) It is a flexible source of finance.
(vi) It helps to attract cautious investors.
(vii) It is suitable in case of stable earnings.

2. From the View Point of Debentureholders

(i) It provides a fixed return to the investors.
(ii) It involves less risk for the investors.
(iii) Prices remain stable, thus, reducing risk of loss.

Disadvantages of Debentures

Disadvantages of debentures are as follows

1. From the View Point of Company

(i) It creates a charge on assets of the company.
(ii) There is a permanent burden of interest payment on the company.
(iii) It causes a reduction in dividends to the shareholders.
(iv) Credit worthiness of the company is adversely affected.

2. From the View Point of Debentureholders

(i) No voting rights are offered to debentureholders.
(ii) Unit price of debentures is usually high.
(iii) It is less attractive to enterprising investors.

Difference between Shares and Debentures

Basis	Shares	Debentures
Status of holders	Shares represent owner's fund and shareholders are part owners of the company.	They are borrowed funds and thus debentureholders are only the creditors of the company.
Voting rights	Shareholders enjoy voting rights and thus can take part in management of company's affairs.	Debentureholders don't enjoy voting rights and thus cannot interfere in company's management.
Reward of investment	Shareholders earn dividends, which is not fixed and depends upon the earnings of the company.	Debentures carry a fixed rate of interest payment irrespective of company's earnings.
Risk to holders	Shareholders assume high risk as their return is uncertain and not fixed.	Debentureholders assume low risk, because interest rate and payment is fixed.
Redemption	Not redeemable or refundable during the lifetime of the company and only become repayable at the time of winding up. There is an exception in case of redeemable preference shares.	Debentures are repaid according to the terms of their issue and normally paid before the winding up of the company.
Convertibility	Shares are not convertible.	Debentures are convertible into equity shares after a specified time in case of convertible debentures.

Loans from Commercial Banks

Commercial banks advance money to the business firms generally for meeting their short-term and medium-term requirements. Banks also extend loans for purchasing fixed assets. Such loans are known as 'term' loans as they are to be paid back over a number of years ranging up to five years or more.

Loan is granted by the bank for some specific purpose such as purchase of plant and machinery. The repayment is made by the borrower in instalments as per the agreement between the bank and the borrower. Interest is charged at a fixed rate by banks on the amount of borrowings.

Advantages of Loans from Commercial Banks

Advantages of loans from commercial banks are

(i) Banks provide timely assistance to business by providing funds as and when needed by it.

(ii) Secrecy of business can be maintained as the information supplied to the bank by the borrowers is kept confidential.

(iii) Formalities such as issue of prospectus and underwriting are not required for raising loans from a bank. It is therefore, considered as an easier source of funds.

(iv) Loan from a bank is a flexible source of finance as the loan amount can be increased according to business needs and can be repaid in advance when funds are not needed.

Disadvantages of Loans from Commercial Banks

Disadvantages of loans from commercial banks are

(i) Funds are generally available for short periods and its extension or renewal is uncertain and difficult.

(ii) Banks make detailed investigation of the company's affairs, financial structure, etc. This makes the procedure of obtaining funds slightly difficult.

(iii) In some cases, difficult terms and conditions are imposed by banks for the grant of loan.

Loans from Financial Institutions

A large number of financial institutions have been established in India with the primary objective of providing long-term financial assistance to industrial enterprises. These institutions are also known as 'development financial institutions'.

These institutions provide financial assistance for investment projects, expansion or modernisation of plants. IFCI, SFCs, ICICI, IDBI, UTI, etc are the prominent institutions working for the development of industries, promoting economic growth on a nation-wide basis.

Advantages of Loans from Financial Institutions

Advantages of loans from financial institutions are

(i) They provide long-term loans to enterprises.

(ii) They provide managerial and technical advice to business enterprises.

(iii) Obtaining loans from financial institutions raises the goodwill in the capital market.
(iv) It helps to provide funds during depression.
(v) It helps to accelerate the pace of industrial growth.
(vi) It provides underwriting facilities to companies.
(vii) It offers credit at low rate of interest and easy terms of repayment.
(viii) Special support is given to small scale sector by financial institutions.

Disadvantages of Loans from Financial Institutions

Disadvantages of loans from financial institutions are

(i) It involves excessive formalities and lengthy procedure.
(ii) It puts certain restrictions on the company's ability to raise funds and control over the management.
(iii) It restricts power of the companies to raise funds from debt further.
(iv) It is difficult to avail loans from such institutions.

PYQs Previous Years' Questions

1 Mark Questions

1. A debenture issued by a company by creating a fixed or a floating charge on the company's assets is known as *ISC 2024*

(a) non-convertible debenture
(b) mortgage debenture
(c) redeemable debenture
(d) unsecured debenture

Ans (b) mortgage debenture

2. Unsecured long-term source of loan raised by a company can be termed as *ISC Sem I 2021*

(a) naked debentures
(b) bearer debentures
(c) registered debentures
(d) irredeemable debentures

Ans (a) naked debentures

3. With reference to the types of debentures, choose the odd one out. *ISC Sem I 2021*

(a) Redeemable debentures
(b) Convertible debentures
(c) Secured debentures
(d) Cumulative debentures

Ans (d) Cumulative debentures

4. The difference between shares and debentures is *ISC Sem I 2021*

(a) debentureholders are paid interest and shareholders are paid dividend.
(b) debentures are issued without any charge on assets, but shares are always issued against certain assets.
(c) debentureholders are the owners whereas shareholders are creditors of a company.
(d) debentures carry voting rights but shares do not.

Ans (a) debentureholders are paid interest and shareholders are paid dividend.

5. With reference to the advantages of registered debentures, to the debentureholders, choose the odd one out. *ISC Sem I 2021*

(a) Regular returns
(b) Voting rights
(c) Safety of investment
(d) Fixed returns

Ans (b) Voting rights

6. An advantage of borrowing funds from financial institution is *ISC Sem I 2021*

(a) assets may have to be kept as security against loans taken
(b) they may interfere in the management of the borrowing companies
(c) availability of funds at a low rate of interest
(d) thorough investigation of the borrowing company

Ans (c) availability of funds at a low rate of interest

7. Bearer debentures *ISC Sem I Specimen, 2021*

(a) can be converted into equity shares
(b) cannot be converted into equity shares
(c) cannot be transferred without notice to the company
(d) can be transferred by mere delivery

Ans (a) can be converted into equity shares

8. A type of debenture which is converted into equity shares at some future date is a *ISC Sem I Specimen 2021*

(a) bearer debenture
(b) registered debenture
(c) convertible debenture
(d) redeemable debenture

Ans (c) convertible debenture

2 Marks Questions

1. Differentiate between bearer debentures and registered debentures. **ISC 2014, 04**

Ans Difference between bearer debentures and registered debentures (any two)

Basis	Bearer debentures	Registered debentures
Registration	They are not recorded in the register of debentureholders.	They are recorded in the register of debentureholders.
Transfer	They can be transferred by mere delivery and no formal notice or intimation is required to be given to the company.	They can be transferred only by transfer deed or intimation to the company.
Interest	Interest is paid on the production of coupons attached to such debentures.	Interest accrues only to registered debentureholders.

Concept Enhancer Registered debentures have their owner's information with issuing entity while Bearer debentures do not have their owner's information with issuing entity.

2. Mention two specific advantages to a company from the issue of debentures. **ISC 2008**

Ans Two specific advantages of debentures to a company are

(i) **Suitable in case of stable earnings** The issue of debentures is suitable in the situation when the sales and earnings are relatively stable.

(ii) **Does not dilute control** Debentures do not carry voting rights. Thus, financing through debentures does not dilute the control of equity shareholders on the management of the company.

3. Mention two disadvantages of debentures from the company's point of view. **ISC 2002**

Ans Disadvantages of debentures from the company's point of view

(i) **Charge on assets** The assets of a company are mortgaged against the issue of debentures.

(ii) **Permanent burden of interest** The company has to pay interest to the debentureholders irrespective of financial condition, loss or any other contingency.

4. What are convertible debentures? **ISC 2000**

Ans In such debentures, debentureholders are given an option of converting their debentures into equity shares after a specified period.

Convertible debentures give a privilege to the debentureholders to change their status from creditors to owners of the company. These are also issued for attracting the conservative investors, who do not want to take immediate risk.

3/4/5 Marks Questions

1. What are debentures? Explain any four advantages of raising funds through the issue of debentures. **ISC Specimen 2023 (5M)**

Ans These are important instruments for raising long-term debt capital. These serve as an acknowledgement for the company that it has borrowed certain amount of money. In general, it refers to the loan to the company by the debentureholders, on which they receive a fixed rate of interest.

According to **Section 2(30) of the Companies Act, 2013**, "Debentures include debenture stock, bonds and any other securities of a company, whether constituting a charge on the assets of a company or not." The holders of debentures are regarded as the creditors of the company.

Advantages Refer to text on page 36.

2. State any five differences between shares and debentures. **ISC Specimen 2023, 2000 (5M)**

Or Give three differences between shares and debentures. **ISC 2019, 05 (3M)**

Or State any six differences between a share and a debenture. **ISC 2009 (5M)**

Ans Refer to text on page 37.

3. Explain any three advantages of raising finance through financial institutions. **ISC Specimen 2023 (3M)**

Ans Advantages of loans from financial institutions are

(i) They provide long-term loans to enterprises.

(ii) They provide managerial and technical advice to business enterprises.

(iii) Obtaining loans from financial institutions raises the goodwill in the capital market.

Concept Enhancer These financial institutions are also known as development financial institutions and helps to accelerate the pace of industrial growth.

4. Explain any three advantages of debentures from the debentureholder's point of view. ***ISC 2020 (3M)***

Ans Advantages of debentures from debentureholder's point of view are (any three)

(i) **Fixed and regular return** The debentureholder's are paid a fixed rate of return at regular interval irrespective of profits.

(ii) **Security of investment** Debentures are usually secured by a change on the assets of the company. This ensures safety of investment in debentures, as their repayment is assured.

(iii) **Appeal to cautious investors** Debenture is a good option for those investors who are cautions and orthodox. Safety of investment and fixed rate of return attract such investors.

(iv) **Stable prices** Price of investment in debentures is always fixed and stable. Debentures are not speculated as shares.

Advantages of Debentures to its Holders

- Fixed and regular return
- Security of investment
- Appeal to cautious investors
- Stable prices

5. Explain four advantages of raising funds from commercial banks. ***ISC 2020, Specimen 2018 (4M)***

Ans Four advantages of raising funds from commercial banks are

(i) Banks provide timely assistance to business by providing funds as and when needed by it.

(ii) Secrecy of business can be maintained as the information supplied to the bank by the borrowers is kept confidential.

(iii) Formalities such as issue of prospectus and underwriting are not required for raising loans from a bank. It is therefore, considered as an easier source of funds.

(iv) Loan from a bank is a flexible source of finance as the loan amount can be increased according to business needs and can be repaid in advance when funds are not needed.

6. Explain any three disadvantages of borrowing funds from specialised financial institutions. ***ISC 2018 (3M)***

Ans Disadvantages of loans from financial institutions are

(i) It involves excessive formalities and lengthy procedure.

(ii) It puts certain restrictions on the company's ability to raise funds and control over the management.

(iii) It restricts power of the companies to raise funds from debt further.

7. Explain any five types of debentures though which a company can collect borrowed capital from the public. ***ISC 2018 (5M)***

Or Explain any four types of debentures through which a Public Limited Company can collect its borrowed capital from the public. ***ISC 2015 (4M)***

Or Define debentures. Describe any four types of debentures. ***ISC 2013 (5M)***

Or Describe any four kinds of debentures. ***ISC 2006 (4M)***

Ans Refer to text on page 36.

8. Write a note on secured debentures. ***ISC Specimen 2018, 2017 (4M)***

Ans Debenture is an important instrument for raising long-term debt capital. It serves as an acknowledgment for the company that it has borrowed a certain amount of money.

Debentures are of different types. One of the categories of debenture is Mortgage/Secured debentures They create a charge on the assets of the company, thereby mortgaging the assets of the company for payment of interest and the principal amount. The charge created can be fixed or floating.

Fixed charge is created against fixed assets and floating charge is created against current assets.

9. Explain the meaning of debentures. State any four disadvantages of debentures. ***ISC 2016 (5M)***

Ans **Debentures** Refer to Q. No. 1 (3/4/5 Marks) on page 39.

The disadvantages of issuing a debenture for the company are as follows

(i) It creates a charge on assets of the company.

(ii) There is a permanent burden of interest payment on the company.

(iii) It causes a reduction in dividends payable to the shareholders.

(iv) Credit worthiness of the company is adversely affected.

10. Explain any four merits of borrowing funds from financial institutions. ***ISC 2015 (4M)***

Or Explain any four advantages of obtaining funds from financial institutions. ***ISC 2013 (4M)***

Or What are special financial institutions? Discuss any four advantages of obtaining funds from such institutions. ***ISC 2010 (5M)***

Ans A large number of financial institutions have been established in India with the primary objective of providing long-term financial assistance to industrial enterprises. These institutions are also known as development financial institutions.

These institutions provide financial assistance for investment projects, expansion or modernisation of plants. IFCI, SFCs, ICICI, IDBI, UTI, etc are the prominent institutions working for the development of industries, promoting economic growth on a nation-wide basis.

Advantages of loans from financial institutions

Four advantages of loans from financial institutions are

(i) **Provide long-term funds** Financial institutions provide long-term finance, that are not provided by the commercial bank.

(ii) **Assist through technical advice** These institutions not only provide funds but also imparts technical advice to business firms.

(iii) **Raise the goodwill in capital market** This will also help in raising the position as well as the goodwill of the borrowing company in the capital market.

(iv) **Provide funds in depression** These institutions can provide the funds during the period of depression also.

11. What is a debenture? Explain any two advantages and two disadvantages of debentures from the view point of a company. *ISC 2010 (5M)*

Ans **Meaning of Debenture** According to **Section 2(30) of Companies Act, 2013,** "Debentures include debentures stock, bonds and any other securities of a company, whether constituting a charge on the assets of a company or not."

Advantages of debentures from the point of view of company

(i) **Possibility of trading on equity** Debenture-holders are paid fixed rate of interest. After payment of interest, remaining profit is available to the shareholders.

As the earnings of the company increase dividend received by shareholders also increase but the interest paid to debentureholders is fixed. This ultimately increases the Earning Per Share (EPS) of the shareholders.

(ii) **Cheaper source of finance** They are less costly source of finance as compared to shares. The risk assumed by the debentureholders is low due to fixed rate of return and this leads to a lower rate of return. Tax deductibility of interest makes it still cheaper.

Disadvantages of debentures from the view point of company

(i) **Fixed burden on company** Debentures put a permanent burden on the earnings of a company. There is a greater risk when earnings of the company fluctuate.

(ii) **Repayment in case of financial difficulties** In case of redeemable debentures, the company has to make provisions for repayment on the specified date, even during periods of financial difficulty.

12. Distinguish between redeemable and irredeemable debentures. *ISC 2002 (3M)*

Ans Difference between redeemable and irredeemable debentures

Basis	Redeemable debentures	Irredeemable debentures
Term	Redeemable debentures are issued for a fixed term.	They don't have a fixed term and are called 'perpetual debentures' as they are part of permanent capital of the company.
Refund/ Repayment	They are redeemable (paid back) after the expiry of a certain specified period.	Such debentures are paid back only at the time of liquidation of the company.

Additional Questions

2 Marks Questions

1. State any two features of debentures.

Ans The prominent features of debentures are

(i) Debenture represent borrowed funds.

(ii) It carries a fixed rate of interest, to be paid regularly.

2. Write a short note on 'Loans from financial institutions'.

Ans The government has established a number of financial institutions all over the country to provide finance to business organisations. These institutions are established by the Central as well as State Governments.

In addition to providing financial assistance, these institutions also conduct market surveys and provide technical assistance and managerial services to people who run the enterprises. They also provide both owned capital and loan capital for long and medium-term capital requirements.

3. What are the limitations of loans from commercial banks?

Ans Limitations of loans from commercial banks are

(i) Funds are generally available for short period and its extension or renewal is uncertain and difficult.

(ii) Banks make detailed investigation of the company's affairs, financial structure, etc. This makes the procedure of obtaining funds slightly difficult.

(iii) In some cases, difficult terms and conditions are imposed by banks for the grant of loan.

4 Marks Question

1. What are the disadvantages of issuing debentures?

Ans Refer to text on page 36.

Case Based Question

Case 1

SD Industries Ltd. has equity share capital worth ₹ 600 crores. It also raised ₹ 300 crores through an issue of redeemable debentures. Its retained earnings amount to ₹ 500 crores. The management of the company plans to invest in modernisation of plant and replacement of machinery. The management of SD Industries Ltd. wants to utilise its funds in the best possible manner. ***ISC Sem I 2021***

(i) Which of the following is an advantage gained by SD Industries Ltd. by issuing equity share capital?

(a) Dividend is payable only if there are adequate profits
(b) It is a costly source of capital
(c) Shareholders may interfere in management
(d) Possibility of over capitalisation

Ans (a) Dividend is payable only if there are adequate profits

(ii) Which one of the following is a suitable source of capital for modernisation of plant and replacement of machinery?

(a) Public deposits
(b) Retained earnings
(c) Trade credit
(d) Inter-corporate deposits

Ans (b) Retained earnings

(iii) Which of the following is a benefit that the company will get by raising finance through debentures?

(a) Mortgage of assets
(b) No interference in management
(c) Reduction in credit standing
(d) Interest has to paid irrespective of profit or loss

Ans (b) No interference in management

(iv) Which one of the following is an internal source of finance for the company?

(a) Debentures
(b) Retained earnings
(c) Preference shares
(d) Bank loans

Ans (b) Retained earnings

(v) Which one of the following types of debentures are repayable on or before the maturity date?

(a) Convertible debentures
(b) Registered debentures
(c) Irredeemable debentures
(d) Redeemable debentures

Ans (d) Redeemable debentures

CHAPTER TEST

01 Mark Questions

1. Redeemable preference shares can be redeemed out of
(a) the sale proceeds of investments
(b) the proceeds of a fresh issue of shares
(c) securities premium reserve
(d) the proceeds of issue of debentures

2. Which of the following cannot be used for redemption of preference shares?
(a) General reserve (b) Revenue reserve
(c) Capital reserve (d) None of these

3. Right shares are not offered to the existing equity shareholders if
(a) the company in general meeting has so decided by a special resolution.
(b) decided by an ordinary resolution and same has been approved by the central government.
(c) right shares are offered to existing shareholders only.
(d) Both (a) and (b)

4. Bonus issue is made out of free reserves or securities premium collected in cash only. State true or false.

5. No bonus issue shall be made within 12 months of any public or right issue. State true or false.

6. Under the provisions of the Companies Act, the company can issue ……… .

7. Retained earnings are also known as …… of the company after paying dividends.

8. What is ESOP?

9. What are sweat equity shares?

10. **Assertion** (A) In a balance sheet, the sum of retained earnings and common stock are known as common equity.

Reason (R) Common equity is nothing but just a poughing back of profit in business.

Alternatives
(a) Both Assertion (A) and Reason (R) are true and Reason (R) is the correct explanation of Assertion (A)
(b) Both Assertion (A) and Reason (R) are true, but Reason (R) is not the correct explanation of Assertion (A)
(c) Both Assertion (A) and Reason (R) are true
(d) Both Assertion (A) and Reason (R) are false

02 Marks Questions

11. What is the advantages of participating preference shares over other preference shares?

12. What are the pre-emptive rights of shareholders?

13. Why is the issue of debentures called 'borrowed fund'?

14. State two advantages of obtaining loans from financial institutions.

03/04/05 Marks Questions

15. Write short notes on
(i) Sweat equity shares
(ii) Bonus shares

16. What is a debenture? Explain two disadvantages, each from the view point of debentureholder and the company.

17. By issuing debentures, company has certain advantages. Discuss these advantages with a special reference to 'trading on equity'.

18. What is 'Ploughing back of profits'? Explain the advantages of retained earning to the company, shareholders and the society.

19. Explain the features of preference shares. Also, discuss two advantages of preference shares from the view point of shareholders.

Answers

1. (b) the proceeds of a fresh issue of shares
2. (c) Capital reserve
3. (d) Both (a) and (b)
4. True
5. True
6. preference shares and equity shares
7. cumulative earnings
10. (b) Both Assertion (A) and Reason (R) are true, but Reason (R) is not the correct explanation of Assertion (A)

04

Short-term Sources of Finance for a Joint Stock Company

TREND ANALYSIS 5 YEARS

		Average No. of Questions Across all Sets					
		Types of Questions	2024	2023	2020	2019	2018
TOPIC 01	Short-term Sources, Public Deposits, Financial Assistance, Trade Credit	1 Mark	—	—	—	—	—
		2 Marks	—	—	—	1	—
		3/4/5 Marks	1	1	1	1	1
TOPIC 02	Customer Advances, Factoring, ICD, Instalment Credit	1 Mark	—	—	—	—	—
		2 Marks	—	—	—	—	1
		3/4/5 Marks	—	—	1	—	—

Meaning of Short-term Sources of Funds

Short-term capital is the capital which is required by a business firm only for a period of less than one year. Short-term finance is required for meeting various variable, seasonal and day-to-day working needs of the enterprise. It is necessary to run the business efficiently and smoothly.

Sources of Short-term Finance

Sources of short-term finance are

(i) Public deposits (also a source of medium-term finance)
(ii) Financial assistance by commercial banks
(iii) Trade credit
(iv) Customer advances
(v) Factoring
(vi) Inter-corporate deposits
(vii) Instalment credit

Public Deposits

The deposits that are raised by organisations directly from the public are known as 'public deposits'. Rates of interest offered on public deposits are usually higher than that offered on bank deposits. The amount raised from public deposits is generally used by the company for meeting the requirement of working capital. It can take care of both medium and short-term financial requirements.

Advantages of Public Deposits

Advantages of public deposits are as follows

(i) The procedure of obtaining deposits is simple and does not contain restrictive conditions, as in case of a loan agreement.
(ii) Public deposits do not usually create any charge on the assets of the company and hence, the assets can be used as security for raising loans from other sources.

(iii) The control of the company is not diluted as the depositors do not have voting rights.
(iv) High returns are offered to investors.
(v) It helps to achieve elasticity in capital structure, by borrowing or repaying, to solve the problem of undercapitalisation or overcapitalisation.
(vi) Benefit of trading on equity can be derived as the rate of interest on deposits is fixed.

Disadvantages of Public Deposits

Disadvantages of public deposits are

(i) New companies generally find it difficult to raise funds through public deposits, due to lack of goodwill.
(ii) It is an unreliable source of finance, as the public may not respond always when the company needs money.
(iii) Collection of public deposits may prove difficult, particularly when the size of deposits required are large.
(iv) It is unsuitable for long-term financing needs.
(v) Misuse of funds may be possible.
(vi) There is a high degree of risk as investors do not have any security for their investments.
(vii) It restricts the growth of capital markets.

Financial Assistance by Commercial Banks

Commercial banks provide funds for different purposes and for different time periods to firms of all sizes by way of cash credits, overdrafts, term loans, purchase/discounting of bills and issue of letter of credit. The rate of interest charged by banks depends on various factors such as the characteristics of the firm and the level of interest rates in the economy.

The loan is repaid either in lumpsum or in instalments. The borrower is required to provide some security or create a charge on the assets of the firm, only then a loan is sanctioned by a commercial bank.

Advantages of Financial Assistance by Commercial Banks

Following are the advantages of financial assistance by commercial banks

(i) Banks provide timely assistance to business by providing funds, as and when needed by it.
(ii) Secrecy of business can be maintained, as the information supplied to the bank by the borrowers is kept confidential.
(iii) Formalities such as issue of prospectus and underwriting are not required for raising loans from a bank.
(iv) Loan from a bank is a flexible source of finance, as the loan amount can be increased according to business needs and can be repaid in advance, when funds are not needed.
(v) There is no interference of banks in the management and control of the business.

Disadvantages of Financial Assistance by Commercial Banks

Following are the disadvantages of financial assistance by commercial banks

(i) Funds are generally available for short periods and its extension or renewal is uncertain and difficult.
(ii) Banks make detailed investigation of the company's affairs, financial structure, etc. This makes the procedure of obtaining funds slightly difficult.
(iii) In some cases, difficult terms and conditions are imposed by banks for the grant of loan and the rates of interest are usually high.
(iv) Loans are granted only against approved security provided by the borrower.

Trade Credit

Trade credit facilitates the purchase of suppliers without immediate payment. Such credit appears in the records of the buyer of goods as sundry creditors or accounts payable. It is granted to those customers, who have reasonable amount of financial standing and goodwill in the market.

Trade credit is generally extended for a period ranging from 15 days to 3 months. The volume and period of credit extended, depends on factors such as reputation of the purchasing firm, financial position of the seller, volume of purchases, past record of payment and degree of competition in the market.

Advantages of Trade Credit

Following are the advantages of trade credit

(i) Trade credit is a convenient and continuous source of funds.
(ii) It may be readily available, when the credit worthiness of the customers is known to the seller.
(iii) It helps to promote the sales of an organisation.
(iv) It does not create any charge on the assets of the firm while providing funds.
(v) It is more economical than bank loans, as no interest is payable on trade credit.
(vi) It does not involve any legal formalities or a formal process.

Disadvantages of Trade Credit

Following are the disadvantages of trade credit

(i) A firm may indulge in overtrading due to the credit available.

(ii) Only limited amount of funds can be raised through this source.

(iii) It is generally a costly source of funds as compared to others, due to high prices charged by the seller.

(iv) Risk of bad debts is very high.

Customer Advances

Advances from customers also act as sources of short-term finance. It is really useful in businesses, where it has become a trend to receive advances from customers. It is generally, provided in products which involve a waiting period for delivery, e.g. Automobiles.

Advantages of Customer Advances

Following are the advantages of customer advances

(i) It works as a source of working capital for firms.

(ii) It is a cost free source of finance.

Disadvantages of Customer Advances

Customer advances have following disadvantages

(i) It is only applicable for durable and short supply products.

(ii) It is not a reliable source of finance.

Factoring

Factoring is a financial service under which the 'factor' renders service of bills receivables financing. Under this organisation's receivables on account of sale of goods or services are sold to the 'factor' at a certain discount. The factor becomes responsible for all credit control and debt collection from the buyer.

These are two methods of factoring

(i) **Recourse** Under this, the client is not protected against the risks of bad debts.

(ii) **Non-recourse** The factor assumes entire credit risk and is responsible for bad debts.

Advantages of Factoring

The following advantages of factoring are

(i) It is a cheaper source than other means like bank credit.

(ii) Regular cash flow is maintained.

(iii) It does not create a charge on the assets of the firm.

Disadvantages of Factoring

The following disadvantages of factoring are

(i) It becomes costly, if invoices are of smaller amounts.

(ii) The factor is a third party to a customer, who may not feel comfortable while dealing with the factor.

(iii) Factors charge higher interest rate than the usual rate of interest, in the form of discounting of bill.

Inter-Corporate Deposit (ICD)

It is a deposit made by one company with another company for a short-term, say upto six months. It is generally an unsecured debt and is arranged by a broker. It is a popular source of short-term finance, as it is convenient to obtain and free from all legal formalities.

Following are the various types of ICDs

(i) Call deposits.

(ii) Three months deposit.

(iii) Six months deposit.

Advantages of ICD

Advantages of inter-corporate deposits are

(i) It helps to solve the problem of short-term capital needs.

(ii) No legal formalities are involved in obtaining the funds.

(iii) They are preferred, as it is an easy source of finance for reputed companies.

Disadvantages of ICD

Disadvantages of inter-corporate deposits are

(i) They are short-term and unsecured deposits.

(ii) They bear a high rate of interest, as compared to bank and other markets.

(iii) They are risky deposits from the point of view of lenders.

(iv) They have no organised market.

Instalment Credit

It refers to the facility of buying assets like machinery, equipments and other durable goods on credit. The buyer has to pay a part of the price at the time of delivery of the asset and the rest is distributed in a number of instalments. The supplier charges interest on the balance payment, which is included in the instalments due.

Similar arrangements can also be done by hire purchase facility. The only difference is that in hire purchase, the ownership of the asset remains with the seller until all the instalments are paid by the buyer.

Advantages of Instalment Credit

Advantages of instalment credit are

(i) It helps in making use of the asset without making full payment.

(ii) It helps to maintain a regular cash flow and can be used for fulfilling other financial needs of the business.

Disadvantages of Instalment Credit

Disadvantages of instalment credit are

(i) A high rate of interest is to be paid.

(ii) The ownership of asset remains with the seller under hire purchase until all the instalments are paid by the buyer.

PYQs Previous Years' Questions

1 Mark Questions

1. The credit extended by one business firm to another incidental to sale or purchase of goods and services is called **ISC Sem I 2021**

(a) factoring (b) instalment credit
(c) customer advance (d) trade credit

Ans (d) trade credit

2. Deposits made by the public with non-banking companies are termed as **ISC Sem I 2021**

(a) equity capital
(b) preference share capital
(c) public deposits (d) ESOP

Ans (c) public deposits

3. Raising finance through sale of book debts is called **ISC Sem I 2021**

(a) cash credit (b) trade credit
(c) discounting of bills (d) factoring

Ans (d) factoring

4. Which of the following is not a source of bank credit? **ISC Sem I 2021**

(a) Cash credit (b) Retained earnings
(c) Loans and advances (d) Discounting of bills

Ans (b) Retained earnings

5. A current account holder can avail ……… facility. **ISC Sem I 2021**

(a) cash credit (b) bank draft
(c) overdraft (d) factoring

Ans (c) overdraft

6. XYZ Co Ltd. is in urgent need of short-term funds, it borrows from Tehlot Public Ltd. funds for six months. This short-term way of raising finance is known as **ISC Sem I Specimen 2021**

(a) inter-corporate deposits (b) public deposits
(c) factoring (d) instalment credit

Ans (b) public deposits

7. Deposits made by the public in non-banking companies are termed as **ISC Sem I Specimen 2021**

(a) public deposits (b) fixed deposits
(c) retained earnings (d) savings deposits

Ans (b) fixed deposits

2 Marks Questions

1. State any four short-term sources of finance for a joint stock company. **ISC 2019, 08**

Ans Four sources of short-term finance for a joint stock company are

(i) Public deposits (ii) Trade credit
(iii) Financial assistance by commercial banks
(iv) Inter-corporate deposits

2. What is meant by factoring? **ISC 2018**

Or What is factoring? **ISC 2014**

Ans Factoring is a financial service under which the 'factor' renders service of 'bills receivables' financing. Under this, the organisation's receivables, on account of sale of goods or services are sold to the 'factor' at a certain discount. Now, the factor becomes responsible for all credit control and debt collection from the buyer. Some examples of organisations that provide these services are SBI Factors and Commercial Services Ltd, Can Bank Factors Ltd, etc.

3. Give two merits of inter-corporate deposits. **ISC 2017**

Ans Two merits of inter-corporate deposits are

(i) They help to solve the problem of short-term capital needs of a company.

(ii) No legal formalities are involved in obtaining the funds through this mode.

Concept Enhancer
- Inter-corporate deposit is made when a company is having surplus fund.
- It is made for short-term, say upto 6 months.

4. Enumerate the main forms in which financial assistance from a commercial bank may be available. *ISC 2014*

Ans Financial assistance may be available from a commercial bank in the following forms

(i) Overdrafts (ii) Cash credits

(iii) Discounting of bills

(iv) Loans and advances

5. What is meant by discounting of bill? *ISC 2013*

Ans Commercial banks provide short-term finance to business concerns by discounting their bills of exchange, promissory notes and hundies.

The bank charges commission for the service by paying less than the face value of the bills of exchange.

Bad debt if any, has to be borne by the holder of the instrument, who remains liable to the bank in case of dishonour of bills of exchange.

6. Give two advantages of public deposits from the point of view of a company. *ISC 2012, 03*

Ans Advantages of public deposits from the point of view of company

(i) The procedure of obtaining deposits is simple and does not contain restrictive conditions as in case of a loan agreement.

(ii) Public deposits do not create charge on the assets of the company.

7. How is cash credit different from loans? *ISC 2011*

Ans Difference between loans and cash credit

Basis	Loans	Cash credit
Meaning	Banks provide funds for different purposes and for different time periods to firms. A lumpsum amount is paid.	It is a revolving credit arrangement, whereby, the bank places the specified amount to the credit of the borrower's bank account. The borrower withdraws money as and when required.
Interest charged	Interest is charged on the total amount of loan.	Interest is charged on the amount actually withdrawn by the borrower.

Value Point

For getting maximum marks, following point can be included in the answer

- Difference should always be given in tabular form with basis of difference.

8. What is meant by trade credit? *ISC 2009*

Ans Trade credit is the credit extended by one trader to another for the purchase of goods and services. It facilitates the purchase of suppliers without immediate payment and is commonly used by business organisations as a source of short-term financing.

Trade credit appears in the records of the buyer of goods as 'sundry creditors' or 'accounts payable'.

It is granted prudently to those customers, who have a reasonable amount of financial standing and goodwill in the market. The volume and period of credit extended depends on factors such as reputation of the purchasing firm, financial position of the seller, volume of purchases, past record of payment and degree of competition in the market.

9. Distinguish between overdraft and loan. *ISC 2006*

Ans Difference between overdraft and loan (any two)

Basis	Overdraft	Loan
Meaning	It is a temporary arrangement under which, a depositor is allowed to draw by cheque more than the amount to his credit upto a specified limit.	It is a lumpsum advance of funds for various financial needs of the customer.
Term of facility	It is availed for a short-term.	It may be for short-term, medium-term and long-term.
Use of funds	It fulfils the working capital needs of the firm.	It fulfils medium-term and long-term needs of the firm.
Interest	Interests is charged on actual withdrawal of funds.	Interest is charged on the whole amount of advance.

3/4/5 Marks Questions

1. JSW Co. purchased goods on credit from SDW Co. and paid the amount after two months. Name the short-term source of finance used by the buyer and state any three features of this source. *ISC 2024 (4M)*

Ans The short-term source of finance used by the JSW Co. is 'trade credit'.

Features of trade credit are as follows

(i) It facilitates the purchase of supplies without immediate payment.

(ii) It is a short-term source of finance.

(iii) It is granted to those customers, who have reasonable amount of financial standing and goodwill.

2. Explain any two advantages and any two disadvantages of public deposits. *ISC 2023 (4M)*

Or

What are public deposits? Briefly explain any two merits of public deposits. *ISC 2019 (4M)*

Ans Public deposits refers to the deposits that are raised by business organisations directly from the public. By way of public deposits a company raises loans from the public for a fixed period of time at a fixed rate of interest.

Any person who is interested in depositing money in an organisation can do so, by filling up the prescribed form. Public deposits take care of both short-term and medium-term financial requirements of the company.

Merits of public deposit are as follows (any two)

(i) **Simple process** The procedure of obtaining deposits is simple.

(ii) **Does not create charge on assets** Public deposits do not usually create any charge on the assets of the company.

(iii) **Control** As the depositors do not have voting rights, the control of the company is not diluted.

Demerits of public deposits are as follows (any two)

(i) **Difficult to obtain funds** New companies generally find it difficult to raise funds through public deposits.

(ii) **Unreliable source** It is an unreliable source of finance, as the public may not respond when the company needs money.

(iii) **Collection is difficult** Collection of public deposits may prove difficult, when the size of deposits required is large.

3. Explain trade credit and factoring as sources of finance for a business enterprise. *ISC Specimen 2023*

Ans **Trade credit** Trade credit is the credit extended by one trader to another for the purchase of goods and services. It facilitates the purchase of suppliers without immediate payment and is commonly used by business organisations as a source of short-term financing.

Factoring Refer to Q. No. 2 (2 Marks) on page 47.

Common Mistake Many students are not able to understand clear meaning of "factoring" and book debt is ignored. They state that factoring is finance available for purchase of bad debts instead of book debts. Factoring provides finance through purchase of account receivables.

4. Give two advantages of trade credit, as a source of short-term finance. *ISC 2020*

Or What is meant by trade credit? Mention two advantages of trade credit as a short-term source of finance. *ISC 2015 (3M)*

Ans **Trade credit** Refer to Q. No. 3 (3/4/5 Marks) on page 49.

The two advantages of trade credit as a short-term source of finance are as follows

(i) Trade credit is a convenient and continuous source of funds.

(ii) Trade credit may be readily available, when the credit worthiness of the customers is known to the seller.

5. Write a short note on instalment credit as a source of short-term funds for business. *ISC 2020 (4M)*

Ans It refers to the facility of buying assets like machinery, equipments and other durable goods on credit.

The buyer has to pay a part of the price at the time of delivery of the asset and the rest is distributed in a number of instalments. The supplier charges interest on the balance payment, which is included in the instalments due.

Similar arrangements can also be done by hire purchase facility. The only difference is that in hire purchase, the ownership of the asset remains with the seller until all the instalments are paid by the buyer.

Merits of instalment credit are

(i) It helps in making use of the asset without making full payment.

(ii) It helps to maintain a regular cash flow and can be used for fulfilling other financial needs of the business.

Demerits of instalment credit are

(i) A high rate of interest is to be paid.

(ii) The ownership of asset remains with the seller until all the instalments are paid by the buyer.

6. What are the different types of short-term financial assistance provided by the commercial banks to business houses? *ISC 2018 (4M)*

Ans The following are the different types of short-term financial assistance provided by the commercial banks to business house

(i) **Cash credit** It is a revolving credit arrangement wherein, the bank allows the borrower to borrow money upto the specified limit. The bank places the specified amount to the credit of the borrower's bank account. The borrower withdraws money, as and when required.

He can deposit back money whenever, he has surplus funds. Interest is charged only on the amount actually withdrawn by the borrower. Cash credit limit is decided by the bank on the basis of the borrower's assets and personal reputation. This banking service is very useful for business firms.

(ii) **Bank overdraft** It is a temporary arrangement under which a depositor is allowed to draw by cheque more than the amount to his credit upto a specified limit. Overdraft is granted, when the borrower has a current account with the bank. This facility is provided against the security of some assets or on the personal guarantee of the borrower. A higher rate of interest is charged on bank overdrafts. But interest is charged on the exact amount overdrawn by the current account holder.

Types of Short-term Financial Assistance
- Cash credit
- Bank overdraft
- Discounting of bills of exchange
- Loans and advances

The excess amount withdrawn from the current account has to be deposited within the prescribed period (usually a few days). Overdraft facility is very useful for business firms for meeting their short-term needs for funds.

(iii) **Discounting of bills of exchange** Commercial banks provide short-term finance to business concerns by discounting their bills of exchange, promissory notes and hundies. The bank charges commission for the service by paying less than the face value of the bills of exchange. Bad debt, if any, has to be borne by the holder of the instrument, who remains liable to the bank in case of dishonour of bill of exchange.

(iv) **Loans and advances** Banks advance loans to the customers in lumpsum which are required to be repaid back in monthly instalments over a stipulated time period. Loans are advanced on security of assets.

7. Explain four advantages of raising funds from commercial banks. *ISC 2017 (4M)*

Ans Four advantages of raising funds from commercial banks are

(i) Banks provide timely assistance to business by providing funds as and when needed by it.

(ii) Secrecy of business can be maintained as the information supplied to the bank by the borrowers is kept confidential.

(iii) Formalities such as issue of prospectus and underwriting are not required for raising loans from a bank. It is therefore, considered as an easier source of funds.

(iv) Loan from a bank is a flexible source of finance as the loan amount can be increased according to business needs and can be repaid in advance when funds are not needed.

8. Write a short note on bank overdraft. *ISC 2016 (4M)*

Ans Refer to Q. No. 6 point (ii) (3/4/5 Marks) on page 50.

9. Briefly explain any three demerits of public deposits. *ISC 2016, 10 (3M)*

Or

Mention any two drawbacks of public deposits as a source of finance. *ISC 2010*

Ans Refer to Q. No. 2 (3/4/5 Marks) on page 49.

10. Briefly explain any two sources of short-term finance. *ISC 2016*

Or

Explain any four sources of working capital of a company. *ISC 2011 (6M)*

Ans Four sources of working capital of the company are

(i) **Trade credit** It facilitates the purchase of supplies without immediate payment. It is granted to those customers, who have reasonable amount of financial standing and goodwill. Generally trade credit is extended for a period ranging from 15 days to 3 months.

Sources of Working Capital
- Trade credit
- Advances from customers
- Bank overdraft
- Cash credit

The volume and period of credit extended, depends on factors such as reputation of the purchasing firm, financial position of the seller, volume of purchases, past record of payment and degree of competition in the market.

(ii) **Advances from customers** Customers make advance payment for buying a goods or a service. It is generally, provided in products which involve a waiting period for delivery, e.g. Automobiles. It is a cost free source of finance.

It is only applicable for durable and short supply products and is not a reliable source of finance.

(iii) **Bank overdraft** It is a temporary arrangement under which a depositor is allowed to draw by cheque more than the amount to his credit upto a specified limit.

Overdraft is granted, when the borrower has a current account with the bank. This facility is provided against the security of some assets or on the personal guarantee of the borrower. A higher rate of interest is charged on bank overdrafts. But interest is charged on the exact amount overdrawn by the current account holder.

(iv) **Cash credit** It is a revolving credit arrangement wherein, the bank allows the borrower to borrow money upto the specified limit. The bank places the specified amount to the credit of the borrower's bank account.

The borrower withdraws money, as and when required. He can deposit back money whenever, he has surplus funds. Interest is charged only on the amount actually withdrawn by the borrower.

Cash credit limit is decided by the bank on the basis of the borrower's assets and personal reputation. This banking service is very useful for business firms.

11. What is a bank? Explain any four modes of lending by commercial banks. *ISC 2014, 07*

Ans A bank is an institution that collects money from those, who have it and lends to those, who need it.

According to Indian Banking Regulation Act, 1949, 'Banking' means accepting deposits of money from the public for the purpose of lending or investments of deposits of money from the public, repayable on demand or otherwise and withdrawable by cheque, draft, order, etc.

Four modes of lending by commercial banks Refer to Q. No. 6 (3/4/5 Marks) on page 49 and 50.

12. Write short note on cash credit. *ISC 2009 (4M)*

Or What is meant by cash credit? *ISC 2004 (4M)*

Ans Refer to Q. No. 6 point (i) (3/4/5 Marks) on page 49 and 50.

CHAPTER TEST

01 Mark Questions

1. Public deposits are the deposits that are raised directly from
(a) the public (b) the owners
(c) the directors (d) the auditors

2. ……… is an example of short-term finance.
(a) Trade credit (b) Debenture
(c) Share (d) None of these

3. Which of the following is the type of trade credit?
(a) Open account (b) Bills of exchange
(c) Promissory note (d) All of these

4. Trade credit is a system of barter or exchange of credit instead of cash. State true or false.

5. Factoring is selling accounts payable or account receivable for cash. State true or false.

6. Credit protection is available in ……… .

7. Short-term financing is most common for financing of …… .

8. What is inter-corporate deposit?

9. What is instalment credit?

10. **Assertion** (A) The terms of deposit are same for all credit arrangements.

Reason (R) Credit arrangements are very complex process, so to remove the complexities same terms of deposits are used.

Alternatives

(a) Both Assertion (A) and Reason (R) are true and Reason (R) is the correct explanation of Assertion (A)
(b) Both Assertion (A) and Reason (R) are true, but Reason (R) is not the correct explanation of Assertion (A)
(c) Both Assertion (A) and Reason (R) are true
(d) Both Assertion (A) and Reason (R) are false

02 Marks Questions

11. What do you understand by the term 'trade credit'?

12. How does customer advances help the companies?

13. Distinguish between overdraft and cash credit.

14. State two advantages of availing credit from commercial banks.

03/04/05 Marks Questions

15. Explain two merits and two demerits of public deposits.

16. What are the sources of short-term finance? Explain any four of them.

17. Write short notes on
(i) Trade credit
(ii) Factoring

18. What is a bank? What are the disadvantages of availing credit from commercial banks?

19. How can inter-corporate deposits help the companies mutually? Explain any two benefits of inter-corporate deposits.

Answers

1. (a) the public *2.* (a) Trade credit
3. (d) All of these
4. False
5. False
6. without recourse factoring
7. current asset
10. (d) Both Assertion (A) and Reason (R) are false

05

Banking Latest Trends

TREND ANALYSIS 5 YEARS

	Types of Questions	Average No. of Questions Across all Sets				
		2024	2023	2020	2019	2018
TOPIC 01 E-banking	1 Mark	—	1	—	—	—
	2 Marks	—	—	—	1	1
	3/4/5 Marks	1	1	1	1	1
TOPIC 02 Mobile Banking, Debit Card, Credit Card and ATMs	1 Mark	1	—	—	—	—
	2 Marks	—	—	1	—	1
	3/4/5 Marks	—	1	—	—	—

Latest Trends in Banking

Rapid growth in information technology has revolutionised the banking services. Further development of e-commerce has also paved the way for e-banking.

Banks have reached the door steps of the customers and they have been saved from hassles and facilitated by 'any time banking facilities'. Some of the latest trends in banking are discussed ahead.

E-banking

Electronic banking is a service provided by many banks, in which a customer is allowed to conduct banking transactions over the internet, using a personal computer, mobile telephone or handheld computer (PDA).

E-banking offers the following services

(i) Electronic Funds Transfer System (EFTS)
(ii) Automated Teller Machines (ATM)
(iii) Credit Cards
(iv) Point of Sales (payment through debit cards)

Features of E-banking

Features of e-banking are as follows

(i) E-banking checks balance and transfers of funds across accounts.
(ii) Helps to review and access the online record of your day-to-day banking transactions.
(iii) Pay bills day and night.
(iv) Receive text or e-mail alerts informing you when some transation is done into account.
(v) Facilitates to trade in stocks and shares in upto 13 global stock exchanges.

Advantages of E-banking to Customers

Advantages of e-banking to customers are

(i) E-banking provides 24 hours, 365 days a year services to the customers of the bank.
(ii) It lowers the transaction cost.
(iii) It inculcates a sense of financial discipline and promotes transparency.
(iv) Customers can make the transactions from office, home or while travelling via cellular phones.
(v) Customer security and satisfaction is enhanced.

Advantages of E-banking to Bank

Advantages of e-banking to bank are

(i) E-banking provides competitive advantages to the banks.

(ii) It provides unlimited network to the bank and is not limited to any one branch.

(iii) It also helps in reducing the burden of bank by establishing a centralised database system.

Disadvantages of E-banking

E-banking suffers from the following demerits

(i) Lack of customer support creates disappointment among the customers.

(ii) There is no face to face contact between customer and banking officer.

(iii) There are many issues faced by the consumers like payment not reflected, payment failed and other technical issues.

(iv) There is a long procedure to access e-banking.

(v) The banks need to conduct training and development programmes for employees which require huge investment.

Real Time Gross Settlement (RTGS)

It is a fund transfer system, under which transfer of funds takes place from one bank to another on a **real time** and **gross** basis. Settlement on 'real time' means there is no waiting period, in payment transaction. The transaction is settled as soon as it is processed.

'Gross settlement' means the transaction is made on one to one basis without bunching or netting with any other transaction. It is considered as the fastest possible system for transfer of money through the banking system.

Features of RTGS

Features of RTGS are given below

(i) One can send the remittance by sitting at his work place or home, within 2 hours of receiving the message.

(ii) If facilitates availability of funds in your account.

(iii) RTGS is being used for remittance of over ₹ 2 lakh. It is considered as the most popular mode of remittance of funds.

(iv) Bank branches having Core Banking Solution (CBS) facility can only provide RTGS services to its customers.

(v) Bank charges commission in outward transactions, whereas no charges are levied on inward transactions.

National Electronic Funds Transfer (NEFT)

Since November, 2005, NEFT has seen an exponential growth. It is a countrywide system by which an individual, firm or company can electronically transfer funds from any bank branch to another individual, firm or company having an account with any other bank branch in the country. The funds transfer takes place on a net basis.

Features of NEFT

Features of NEFT are described below

(i) NEFT functions on net settlement basis and is different from RTGS, which functions on gross settlement basis.

(ii) NEFT is an electronic payment system that uses a secure mode of transferring funds from one bank branch to another bank branch.

(iii) It uses the Public Key Infrastructure (PKI) technology to ensure end-to-end security and rides on the Indian Financial Network (INFINET).

(iv) Fund transfer generally takes place on the same day, depending upon the time of requesting such funds transfer.

(v) No minimum or maximum amount is stipulated for NEFT transactions.

(vi) Only NEFT enabled branches can undertake NEFT funds transfers.

(vii) Foreign remittances cannot be received through NEFT.

(viii) Bank generally take some processing charges, however no charges are taken from the receiver.

(ix) An individual, firm or company can make use of NEFT system, even without having a bank account by depositing cash at a NEFT enabled bank branch.

Immediate Payment Service (IMPS)

IMPS is a real time electronic fund transfer method. Money is credited instantly to the payee or beneficiary's account through IMPS and it can be done at any time on a 24×7 basis, on all 365 days.

This service is facilitated by National Payment Corporation of India (NPCI). Interbank transfers can be initiated through IMPS via multiple channels such as mobile banking, internet banking, etc. The charges of IMPS may vary from bank to bank.

IMPS has become a most preferred mode of transferring funds for a wide population due to it's 24×7, 365 days availability which makes it highly flexible and dependable.

Features of IMPS

Features of IMPS are as follows

(i) It allows instant fund transfer.
(ii) It is available 24 × 7 throughout the year even on bank holidays.
(iii) Both the parties, the payer and the payee are notified instantly when the amount is debited from one account and credited to another account.
(iv) It is carried out over encrypted servers, making the transfer of funds safe and secure.
(v) It is versatile as it can be carried out both for person to person and person to merchant, i.e. making payments for online shopping, merchant payments, etc.
(vi) It saves time and effort as it does not require to fill up lengthy forms with secret information. One can transfer funds using just the beneficiary account number and IFSC code.
(vii) IMPS charges for fund transfer goes from a minimum ₹ 2.50 to maximum ₹ 25. Though the charges for NEFT are similar but it does not transfer funds in real time.

Online Demand Draft

A demand draft or bank draft is a financial instrument to remit money from one place to another. Anybody can avail this facility by paying the amount in the bank which also includes the commission charged by bank.

It is a secure instrument as there is no danger of dishonour because it is made after the payment is received against its issue. It is payable to the person named in it or to his order.

Now demand draft can be made online by requesting the bank online. The amount for which demand draft is made is debited from the applicant's account alongwith the specified amount of commission.

Features of Online Demand Draft

The following features of online demand draft are

(i) It is a safe and convenient way to transfer money from one place to another.
(ii) Commission is charged by the issuing bank.
(iii) It does not carry the risk of dishonour and default in payment.

Online Payments

An online payment is an electronic exchange of currency for purchase of goods or services. Online payments are facilitated by 'payment gateways' or 'payment service providers'.

Collecting money through the internet means accepting online payment.

The most common payment forms available online are credit card, debit card, e-wallet, bank transfer, smart cards, etc. Some of the examples of payments that can be made online are

(i) Payment of salaries, wages by organisations through the use of EFT (Electronic Fund Transfer).
(ii) Payments can be made for online shopping through net banking transfer or payment through debit card or credit card option.
(iii) Insurance premium can be paid online.
(iv) Bills payments like electricity bill, water bill, telephone bill, etc can be paid online.
(v) Other payments like school fee, club membership fee can be paid online.

Features of Online Payments

Features of online payments are as follows

(i) It provides a number of payment methods.
(ii) It asks for essential information only.
(iii) It provides reassurance on security and privacy.
(iv) It is an integrated payment processor.
(v) It has been proved a cost-efficient way.
(vi) A seamless, comfortable start-to-end experience always appeals to the customers.

Advantages of Online Payments

Advantages of online payments are

(i) Online payments are less time consuming as with one click, transaction is processed.
(ii) It reduces the dependency on cash.
(iii) Various bills, fees can be paid through online payments. Also, shopping can be done through online payments conveniently.

Disadvantages of Online Payments

Disadvantages of online payments are

(i) There are generally many restrictions on amount while making online payments.
(ii) If certain safety measures are not followed, then there are chances of account being hacked and further robbery.
(iii) Many online payment systems prevail due to which there may arise a problem, if the two accounts involved use different systems.

Mobile Banking

Mobile phone is used as a message carrier between the bank and its customers. Through mobile banking, banks may alert customers about their new schemes and products. Banks also provide account and credit card balance information to its customers. Mobile banking has also become an important source for customers to address their grievances.

The scope of mobile banking is expanding with the introduction of many mobile wallets, digital payment apps, UPI and own apps of banks. The bank provides an app on the store. It lets you make transactions anywhere and anytime.

The following services can be availed through the mobile banking application

(i) Funds transfer (within and outside the bank).

(ii) Immediate Payment Services.

(iii) Enquiry services (Balance enquiry/mini statement).

(iv) Demat account services.

(v) Requests (Cheque book request).

(vi) Bill pay (Utility bills, credit cards, insurance premium, donations, subscriptions).

(vii) Top up/recharge (Mobile/DTH/Mobicash wallet Top up).

(viii) M-commerce (Merchant payments, SBI life insurance premium).

SMS Alert Facility

Mobile banking services can also be availed through SMS alerts on customer's registered mobile numbers.

The following SMS alerts are given to customers

(i) **Transaction alert** Whenever the account of the customer is debited or credited the customer receives a message regarding this.

(ii) **Cheque payment status** Bank sends message if the cheque has been cleared, bounced or paid from a customers account.

(iii) **Balance alert** High balance or low balance alert is generated in case of minimum or maximum predetermined balance limit is crossed.

(iv) **Standing instruction alerts** When standing instructions regarding payments are executed, SMS alert is generated.

Transfer of Funds through Mobile Banking

Now a days, one can send and receive money through Interbank Mobile Payment Services (IMPS) of mobile banking.

One can transfer money to their friend or relatives if they have accounts in any of these banks like Union Bank of India, Axis Bank, ICICI Bank, YES Bank, HDFC Bank, Lakshmi Vilas Bank, Bank of India, etc. The process of transferring funds is described below

(i) Register at the bank's ATM to get Mobile Money ID (MMID). Swipe your debit card and enter your ATM Pin. Select Mobile Registration, then enter your mobile number and confirm.You will get the Mobile Money ID (MMID) over SMS for your primary account and Mobile Personal Identification Number (MPIN).

(ii) After registering for mobile banking services and getting mobile money ID, get the mobile number and mobile money ID of the person whom you want to send the money. (Both the sender and receiver should have mobile money ID).

Login to your mobile banking account and go to fund transfer through IMPS mobile to mobile transfer.

Enter the mobile number and MMID and amount and enter your MPIN for mobile banking. If every thing is correctly done, they will receive the money immediately.

Note Transfer of funds can also be done by downloading an application on your mobile and linking your savings account with your mobile number and application.

Making Payments through Mobile Banking

Whether the regular utility bills, premiums or payment of systematic investment plan amount of mutual funds are to be paid, it can be done through mobile banking.

The steps are

(i) Register for mobile banking (discussed before).

(ii) Type IMPS followed by merchant mobile number (whom the payment has to be made).

(iii) Enter MMID, the amount and MPIN.

(iv) Confirm and the transaction will be executed.

Advantages of Mobile Banking

Advantages of mobile banking are as follows

(i) Banks can inform customers about new schemes and policies through mobile banking. Also, banks inform customers about their transactions through mobile banking.

(ii) Transfer of funds from one bank account to another is made easy with the help of mobile banking.

(iii) It reduces the demand for hard cash.

Disadvantages of Mobile Banking

Disadvantages of mobile banking are as follows

(i) Many formalities are required to be fulfilled when the system is being started.

(ii) It is not useful for those who are not very well versed in operating mobile.

(iii) Without high speed internet, it is not possible to operate mobile banking.

Debit Card

It is a card issued to a customer in lieu of his money deposited in bank. Using it, customer can make immediate payment of purchased goods and services.

Features of Debit Card

The main features of debit card are

(i) It is a plastic card bearing bank's name, validity period, customer's name, identity number, CVV number and signature.

(ii) The card facilitates cash withdrawal from ATM and transfer of money for the purchases made by the customer. The customer swipes the card through a machine and cash is transferred from his/her savings bank account to the seller's/vendor's account.

(iii) The card is also used for online payments of electric bills, telephone bills, etc.

(iv) The payment and withdrawal amount is restricted to the balance in savings account of the holder. No overdraft facility is available to the debit card holder.

(v) No interest is charged on availing such facility.

Credit Card

It is a card issued by banks to those customers who enjoy a good reputation. It is a sort of overdraft facility and it is not necessary that a customer should have money in the bank to get a credit card. Customers can buy goods and obtain services by using it and keep on depositing the money used in the bank according to the agreement.

Features of Credit Card

The main features of credit card are

(i) It is a plastic card with bank's name, customer's name, validity period and signature engraved on it.

(ii) It allows cash withdrawals from across the ATM counters, without having any deposit into the bank.

(iii) It is used for purchasing goods and services on credit.

(iv) A nominal transaction fee is charged for every cash withdrawal.

(v) It allows overdraft facility.

(vi) Interest is charged if payments are not made within the specified period.

Difference between Debit Card and Credit Card

Basis	Debit card	Credit card
Meaning	With a debit card, one's money will get deducted to make purchase directly from his or her bank account.	With a credit card, one can take a loan to make purchases and can pay back later.
Payment	The cardholder has to pay before using the card.	The cardholder has to pay after using the card.
Interest	No interest is charged.	One has to pay back the exact amount by its due date, otherwise interest will be charged.
Limit	There is no actual limit as the bank account balance will let a cardholder use the money.	There is a pre-set card limit, until that limit the card can be used.
Fees and charges	Annual fees is applicable.	Credit cards have multiple fees applicable like annual charge, interest, etc.
Rewards	Typically, the rewards one get are minimal.	Customers get to enjoy cashback and reward points which can be redeemed.

Automated Teller Machines (ATMs)

It is a 24 hour operated automatic machine, which helps in withdrawing and depositing money. It is done by inserting card and entering Personal Identification Number (PIN).

Modern banking has increased its services by Multipurpose ATMs, which are used as an interactive link between the bank and its customers. Services like balance enquiry, cheque book request, funds transfer, cheque deposit can be availed apart from cash withdrawal by customers using ATM Kiosks.

Features of ATM

Features of ATM are as follows

(i) ATM is not bounded to only dispense cash but also provides other facilities like fund transfer, balance enquiry, etc.

(ii) It is designed in such a way that a layman can also use it.

(iii) ATM is multilingual which makes it easily usable.

(iv) It is available at convenient locations.

(v) It does not require any documentation.

PYQs Previous Years' Questions

1 Mark Questions

1. With reference to credit card, which one of the following statements is incorrect? *ISC 2024*

(a) The cardholder makes payments after using the card
(b) Some incentives/gifts are made available to the cardholders
(c) The cardholder has to deposit some money in advance with the issuer bank
(d) In certain cases, the cardholder has to pay an annual fee for the credit card

Ans (c) The cardholder has to deposit some money in advance with the issuer bank

2. Rita wants to transfer her first salary to her mother's bank account through RTGS. What is the minimum amount that she can transfer through RTGS? *ISC 2023, Specimen 2023*

(a) ₹ 50,000
(b) ₹ 2,00,000
(c) ₹ 1,00,000
(d) ₹ 20,000

Ans (b) ₹ 2,00,000

3. A trader wants to make an electronic transfer of funds through NEFT. He does not have a bank account. What is the maximum amount he can transfer? *ISC Specimen 2023, Sem I Specimen 2021*

(a) ₹ 55,000 (b) ₹ 50,000
(c) ₹ 45,000 (d) ₹ 48,000

Ans (b) ₹ 50,000

4. The electronic transfer of funds done in batches is *ISC Sem I 2021*

(a) E-banking (b) EFTS
(c) NEFT (d) RTGS

Ans (c) NEFT

5. NEFT transactions cannot be used to receive ………… remittance. *ISC Sem I 2021*

(a) intra-state (b) inter-state
(c) foreign (d) local

Ans (c) foreign

6. With reference to fund transfer through RTGS, which of the following statements is correct? *ISC Sem I 2021*

(a) Upper ceiling amount for an RTGS transaction is five lakhs
(b) RTGS does not take place on gross basis
(c) RTGS facility is provided only by CBS enabled bank branches
(d) The RTGS transaction is revocable

Ans (c) RTGS facility is provided only by CBS enabled bank branches

7. Under CBS system, a customer becomes *ISC Sem I 2021*

(a) customer of the branch of the bank
(b) customer of the bank
(c) customer of the business
(d) customer of the market

Ans (b) customer of the bank

8. IMPS stands for *ISC Sem I 2021*

(a) Immediate Money Paid Service
(b) Immediate Payment Service
(c) Indian Monetary Payment Service
(d) Indian Money Payment Service

Ans (b) Immediate Payment Service

9. A service used by bank to send a notification or an alert to the customer is *ISC Sem I 2021*

(a) IMPS (b) NEFT (c) RTGS (d) SMS

Ans (d) SMS

10. With reference to the facility of money transfer, choose the odd one out. *ISC Sem I 2021*

(a) RTGS (b) NEFT
(c) SMS (d) IMPS

Ans (c) SMS

11. Which card issued by the bank does not enjoy a credit facility? *ISC Sem I Specimen 2021*

(a) Debit card (b) Cash credit
(c) Credit card (d) Kisan card

Ans (a) Debit card

12. The full form of ATM is *ISC Sem I Specimen 2021*

(a) Automated Teller Machine
(b) Automatic Teller Machine
(c) All India Tellers Machine
(d) Automatic Toll Machinery

Ans (b) Automatic Teller Machine

13. A bank informs its account holders regarding any transaction which has taken place from their account through *ISC Sem I Specimen 2021*

(a) an SMS (b) a CBS
(c) KYC (d) ATM

Ans (a) an SMS

14. The most appropriate statement with reference to the electronic fund transfer through NEFT is

ISC Sem I Specimen 2021

(a) the fund transfer in NEFT takes place on real time, without any waiting period
(b) the fund transfer in NEFT takes place in batches
(c) the NEFT transfer takes place from one person to another
(d) the NEFT transfer takes place on gross settlement basis

Ans (b) the fund transfer in NEFT takes place in batches

2 Marks Questions

1. State any two features of credit card.

ISC Specimen 2023, 20

Ans Two features of credit card are (any two)

(i) It is used for purchasing goods and services on credit.
(ii) It allows overdraft facility.
(iii) It is a plastic card with bank's name, customer's name, validity period and signature engraved on it.
(iv) A nominal transaction fee is charged for every cash withdrawal.

2. Expand the following terms

(i) RTGS (ii) NEFT *ISC 2018*

Ans (i) Real Time Gross Settlement
(ii) National Electronic Fund Transfer

3. What is a debit card? *ISC 2018*

Ans It is a card issued to a customer in lieu of his money deposited in bank. Using it, customer can make immediate payment of purchased goods and services. It is a plastic card bearing bank's name, validity period, customer's name, identity number, CVV number and signature.

4. What is a demand draft? *ISC Specimen 2018, 17*

Ans A demand draft is a financial instrument to remit money from one place to another place. Anybody can avail this facility by paying the amount in the bank which also includes the commission charged by bank.

It is a secure instrument as there is no danger of dishonour because it is made after the payment is received against its issue.

It is payable to the person named in it or to his order. Now demand draft can be made online. The amount for which demand draft is made is debited from the applicant's account alongwith the specified amount of commission.

Common Mistake Students are usually confused in demand draft, bank draft and bank overdraft. Each of the said terms are different from each other, students need to focus on accurate meaning of each term.

5. Explain the following

(i) SMS alerts (ii) ATM *ISC Specimen 2018, 17*

Ans (i) **SMS alerts** The bank offers SMS alert services to its customers by sending SMS related to transactions conducted in their account at their registered mobile number.

Following SMS alerts are given to the customers

(a) Transaction alert, when the account is debited or credited.
(b) Cheque status alert is provided.
(c) Account balance alert is generated by the bank.
(d) Payment/Receipt on account of standing instructions

(ii) **ATM** Automated Teller Machine (ATM) is a 24 hour operated automatic machine, which helps in withdrawing and depositing money. It is done by inserting card and entering Personal Identification Number (PIN).

Modern banking has increased its services by multipurpose ATMs, which are used as an interactive link between the bank and its customers.

Services like balance enquiry, cheque book request, funds transfer, cheque deposit can be availed apart from cash withdrawal by customers using ATM kiosks.

Common Mistake Most of the candidates answer this part unsatisfactorily. Some candidates give an example about SMS relating to friends and relatives instead of the bank.

A number of candidates write 'Automated teller machine' as 'Automatic teller machine'.

6. What is mobile banking? State any two banking services available on mobile phones. *ISC 2015*

Ans Mobile banking means banking through mobile phone. Through this technology, banks may alert customers about their new schemes and products.

Mobile banking has also become an important source for customers to address their grievances.

Two common services provided on mobile phones are

(i) Funds transfer (within and outside the bank).
(ii) Immediate payment services.

7. Distinguish between NEFT and RTGS. *ISC 2015*

Ans Difference between NEFT and RTGS

Basis	NEFT	RTGS
Time taken	Transaction is done in batches, thus takes time.	It is real time fund transfer and the funds are transferred instantly.
Minimum transaction value	No minimum value.	Minimum amount of fund transfer value is ₹ 2 lakh.

8. Explain the meaning of SMS alert. *ISC 2014*

Ans Refer to Q. No. 5 (2 Marks) on page 59.

3/4/5 Marks Questions

1. Rajiv's daughter has secured a seat in a Law college. The college has asked for the payment of admission fee through the financial instrument payable on demand.

Identify and explain the financial instrument indicated above. Can it be issued online? List any two of its features. *ISC 2024 (5M)*

Ans The financial instrument indicated here is demand draft.

For meaning of demand draft, refer to Q.No. 4 (2 Marks) on page 59.

Yes, it can be issued online by requesting the bank online. The amount for which demand draft is issued, is debited from the applicant's account alongwith the specified amount of commission.

Features of online demand draft are

(i) It is safe and convenient way to transfer money from one place to another.

(ii) It does not carry the risk of dishonour and default in payment.

***2.** Expand UPI and briefly discuss its meaning. *ISC 2024 (3M)*

Ans UPI stands for Unified Payment Interface.

It is a popular mobile payment method that allows you to transfer funds from one bank account to the other, instantly and free of charge. Ever since its inception, UPI has made financial transactions much easier for account holders.

3. State any three advantages of e-banking to customer. *ISC 2023*

Or Mention any two advantages of e-banking to the customers. *ISC 2019*

Ans Advantages of e-banking to customers are

(i) It lowers transaction cost.

(ii) It facilitates 24 hours, 365 days a year service to customers of bank.

(iii) Through e-banking, customer can operate his account while sitting in his office or home.

Concept Enhancer E-banking provides enhanced customer security and inculcates a sense of financial discipline and promotes transparency.

4. State any three differences between a debit card and a credit card. *ISC 2023*

Ans Difference between debit card and credit card

Basis	Debit card	Credit card
Meaning	It is a card issued to a customer in lieu of money deposited in the bank.	It is a card issued by bank to those customers who enjoy a good reputation.
Overdraft facility	No overdraft facility is available to debit cardholder.	Overdraft facility is available to credit cardholder.
Interest	Interest is not charged on availing such facility.	Interest is charged, if payments are not made within the specified period.

5. What is meant by RTGS? Give any three features of RTGS. *ISC 2020 (5M)*

Or What is meant by RTGS? Give any two features of RTGS. *ISC Specimen 2018, 17 (4M)*

Ans Real Time Gross Settlement (RTGS) is a fund transfer system, under which transfer of funds takes place from one bank to another on a real time and gross basis.

Settlement on 'real time' means there is no waiting period, in payment transaction. The transaction is settled as soon as it processed.

'Gross settlement' means the transaction is made on one to one basis without bunching or netting with any other transaction. It is considered as the fastest possible system for transfer of money through the banking system.

Features of RTGS are given below

(i) One can send the remittance by sitting at his workplace or home.

(ii) It facilitates availability of funds in your account.

(iii) RTGS transactions are processed individually and continuously rather than in batches.

Concept Enhancer RTGS is used for high value transactions, i.e. the minimum amount of transaction that can be made through RTGS ₹ 2 lakh.

Topic not included in latest syllabus.

6. What is meant by NEFT? Give any two features of NEFT. *ISC 2019 (4M)*

Or List any four features of NEFT. *ISC 2014 (4M)*

Ans NEFT (National Electronic Fund Transfer) refers to a system of transfer of funds from one bank to another electronically. A branch of the bank should be NEFT enabled for these type of transactions.

Four features of NEFT are

(i) NEFT is an electronic payment system that uses a secure mode of transferring funds from one bank branch to another bank branch.

(ii) It uses the Public Key Infrastructure (PKI) technology to ensure end-to-end security and rides on the Indian Financial Network (INFINET).

(iii) It facilitate the transaction in a particular period of time.

(iv) There is no limit (either minimum or maximum) on the amount of funds that could be transferred using NEFT.

Concept Enhancer There is a fee applicable on all NEFT transactions, the amount varies from ₹ 2.5 to ₹ 25, depending on the amount being transferred.

7. Write a short note on core banking solutions. *ISC 2018 (4M)*

Ans Core Banking Solutions, (CBS) is a system that facilitates speedy and instant banking from anywhere and at all times. Under this method, a customer of a bank can operate his account through all CBS branches of the bank, in the country as well as in abroad. Using this system a customer can withdraw cash from any of the CBS branches, he can transfer funds or even get his passbook updated.

Value Points

For getting maximum marks, following points can be included in the answer

- Add meaning of core banking solutions.
- Add features of core banking solutions.

8. Explain the meaning of e-banking. State any three features of e-banking. *ISC 2016 (4M)*

Ans Electronic banking is a service provided by banks, in which a customer is allowed to conduct banking transactions over the internet, using a personal computer, mobile telephone or handheld computer (PDA).

Features of e-banking are as follows

(i) E-banking checks balance and transfers of funds across accounts.

(ii) Review and access the online record of day-to-day banking transactions.

(iii) Pay bills day and night.

Common Mistake Many candidates are not able to define e-banking properly due to lack of essential keywords in their answer. Some candidates give advantages of e-banking instead of features. So understanding of question and concept is required.

Additional Questions

2 Marks Questions

1. State any two payments which can be made online.

Ans (i) Payments can be made for online shopping through net banking transfer or payment through debit card or credit card option.

(ii) Insurance premium can be paid online.

2. List the various types of e-banking facilities.

Ans Various types of e-banking facilities are

(i) Debit cards (ii) Credit cards

(iii) Tele-banking (iv) ATM

(v) SMS alerts

(vi) EFT (Electronic Fund Transfer)

4/5 Marks Questions

1. Discuss some technological development taking place in banking sector.

Ans Now-a-days banks have entered into a revolutionary system of banking through the development of information technology.

Banking has reached the doorsteps of customer increasing the convenience, speed and security of banking transaction.

Some of the ways in which technology has helped banks are (any four)

(i) **Internet banking** People with computer network and internet connection can conduct their banking business online. Many facilities like, fund transfer, account status, online bill payments, shopping can be done through internet banking.

(ii) **Mobile banking** Now-a-days customers are being benefitted by mobile banking. Through the use of mobiles, funds can be transferred and received, SMS alerts are received for any debits or credits in the account and railway reservations have been possible.

Technological Developments in Banking Sector
- Internet banking
- Mobile banking
- Debit card and credit card
- ATM
- Electronic Fund Transfers

(iii) **Debit card and credit card** Debit cards and credit cards allow withdrawal money any time. The difference is that a debit card is attached to one's saving/current account and money is withdrawn from his own balance.

Whereas in case of credit cards the amount withdrawn is a credit availed from bank and interest and processing fee are charged thereon.

(iv) **ATM** (Automated Teller Machine) Customers can withdraw money, get account updates, etc. Consequently cheques and drafts can also be deposited at multipurpose ATMs.

(v) **Electronic Fund Transfers** (EFT) This system allows direct transfer of funds from one account to another electronically.

This system allows the benefit of saving time and avoiding inconvenience of handling large amounts of cash.

2. Discuss the benefits of e-banking.

Ans Electronic banking or e-banking means banking transactions being carried on with the help of computer networks. Anyone having an account in the bank with PC and an internet connection can avail services of internet banking. E-banking offers benefits to both the customers and the banks.

Benefits to the Customers

(i) **Anytime banking** Benefit of banking services can be availed 24 hours a day and 365 days a year through e-banking.

(ii) **Anywhere banking** A customer at home or at some other city or country, can avail the benefit of banking services.

(iii) **Increase in customer satisfaction** The convenience, speed and security offered increases customer satisfaction.

(iv) **Avoid inconvenience** Huge amounts of cash have not to be physically transferred.

Benefits to Banks

(i) **Less burden on branches** As most of the transactions are done electronically, there is less burden on the staff.

(ii) **Reduction in number of branches** This helps in reducing fixed/capital expenditure on buying the offices and also the expense of paying office rent.

(iii) **Offers bank a competitive advantage** To combat increasing competition, increasing customer satisfaction is the key to success.

CHAPTER TEST

01 Mark Questions

1. What are NEFT and RTGS about?
(a) Cheque truncation process
(b) Electronic fund transfer from bank to bank
(c) Electronic payment products within a bank
(d) Various deposit products

2. PIN stands for which of the following?
(a) Permanent Identity Number
(b) Portable Identification Number
(c) Permanent Identification Number
(d) Personal Identification Number

3. Credit card is an essential component of which of the following?
(a) Electronic commerce (b) Internal commerce
(c) Both (a) and (b) (d) None of these

4. E-banking allows 24 hour access to bank accounts. State true or false.

5. A PIN number is not needed for a debit card. State true or false.

6. ……… is a financial instrument to remit money from one place to another.

7. Credit card is a payment card which enables a purchase by money borrowed from the ……… .

8. What is real time gross settlement?

9. What is NEFT?

10. **Assertion** (A) Maximum limit of NEFT per transaction is ₹ 1,00,000.
Reason (R) NEFT works on the principle of gross batch settlement.
Alternatives
(a) Both Assertion (A) and Reason (R) are true and Reason (R) is the correct explanation of Assertion (A)
(b) Both Assertion (A) and Reason (R) are true, but Reason (R) is not the correct explanation of Assertion (A)
(c) Both Assertion (A) and Reason (R) are true
(d) Both Assertion (A) and Reason (R) are false

02 Marks Questions

11. What are the main forms of e-banking?

12. State any two types of SMS alerts.

13. What is EFTS?

14. Give two examples of e-banking.

03/04/05 Marks Questions

15. Apart from withdrawal of funds, mention any three more services provided by ATMs.

16. Write a short note on online payment.

17. Write a short notes on debit cards and credit cards.

18. What are the merits of e-banking to banks?

19. Explain how funds can be transferred through mobile banking.

20. What do you understand by e-banking? Describe features and advantages of e-banking.

Answers

1. (b) Electronic fund transfer from bank to bank
2. (d) Personal Identification Number
3. (a) Electronic commerce
4. True
5. False
6. Demand draft
7. card issuer
10. (d) Both Assertion (A) and Reason (R) are false

06

Management : An Introduction

TREND ANALYSIS 5 YEARS

		Average No. of Questions Across all Sets					
		Types of Questions	2024	2023	2020	2019	2018
TOPIC 01	Management : Meaning, Objectives and Characteristics	1 Mark	1	—	—	—	—
		2 Marks	—	—	1	1	1
		3/4/5 Marks	—	1	1	1	—
TOPIC 02	Importance and Nature of Management	1 Mark	—	—	—	—	—
		2 Marks	—	—	—	—	—
		3/4/5 Marks	—	—	—	1	1

TOPIC 1

Meaning, Objectives and Characteristics of Management

Meaning and Definition of Management

Management is an activity which is necessary wherever there is a group of people working in an organisation towards a common goal. It is a process of planning, organising, actuating and controlling the organisation's operations and activities, effectively and efficiently.

According to **Harold Koontz** and **Heinz Weihrich**, "Management is the process of designing and maintaining an environment in which individuals, working together in groups, efficiently accomplish selected aims."

Concept of Management

The two concepts of management are

(i) **Traditional approach** The traditional view point of management is concerned with accomplishing organisational objectives by directing the efforts of others or it is an art of getting things done through others.

(ii) **Modern approach** Management is a process of getting things done with the aim of achieving goals effectively and efficiently.

Management Used in Different Senses

The term management is used with different connotations, which are discussed below

(i) **Management as an activity** Management is a human activity which directs and controls the organisation for achieving common goals. As an activity, management integrates the inputs of men, money, material, machinery and methods and makes a productive enterprise out of them.

(ii) **Management as a group** An organisation is a collection of diverse individuals with different needs. All managers, from chief executive to first line supervisors, are part of it. This requires team work and coordination of individual efforts in a common direction.

(iii) **Management as a discipline** Management is a specialised branch of knowledge which involves study of principles and practices of management.

(iv) **Management as a process** Management is a series of continuous, composite, but separate functions of planning, organising, staffing, directing and controlling. These functions are simultaneously performed by all managers all the time.

Approaches of Management Thought

The different approaches of management thought, which were advocated by eminent experts are

(i) **Classical concept** This approach consisted of scientific management, administrative management and bureaucratic management. This concept emphasised management as a process.

"Management is a distinct process consisting of planning, organising, actuating and controlling, performed to determine and accomplish stated objectives by use of human beings and other resources." ***—George R Terry***

(ii) **Productivity concept** Maximising productivity was emphasised by this concept or school of thought.

"Management is the art of knowing exactly, what you want people to do and seeing that they do it in the best and cheapest way." ***—FW Taylor***

(iii) **Human relations** (Neo-classical concept) This school of thought developed during 1920-1950, gave special attention to human factor.

"Management is an art of getting things done through and with people in formally organised groups." ***—Harold Koontz***

(iv) **Decision-making and leadership concept** This concept emphasised on management as a function of decision-making and leadership.

"Management is an art and science of decision-making and leadership." ***—Donald J Clough***

(v) **Integration concept** (Modern management) It views modern organisations as complex system and management as the force that integrates human and non-human resources into an effective operating unit.

"Management is defined as the process of planning, organising, actuating and controlling an organisation's operations in order to achieve coordination of human and material resources essential in the effective and efficient attainment of objectives." ***—Robert L Trewelly and M Gene Newport***

Objectives of Management

The main objectives of management are

(i) **Profitability** The basic objective of any organisation is to earn enough profits to meet the various needs of an organisation. This can be achieved by efficiently using the resources.

(ii) **Growth and prosperity** A business needs to add to its prospects in the long-run and should fully exploit its growth potential. Management must maximise prosperity by the best utilisation of resources. This will ensure prosperity for both employee and employer.

(iii) **Development of people** Management should seek to develop human talent by providing training and participation in management.

(iv) **Change and innovation** Management helps in the development of the organisation and thoughts that helps in the development of the society. It comes up with newer products and methods, adopts new technology and serve as an agent of change and progress.

(v) **Decision-making** Right decisions at the right time are important for the success of an organisation. The quality and timing of decisions determines the growth and progress of the organisation.

(vi) **Improving image** A good image of the organisation depends upon the effective and efficient functioning of the management.

(vii) **Quality goods at fair prices/social objectives** It involves creation of benefit for the society. This includes providing good quality products at reasonable prices, using environmental friendly methods of production and by giving employment opportunities to the disadvantaged sections of the society.

(viii) **Discipline and morale** Management helps in improving discipline by effective deployment of tasks, ensuring establishment of clearcut authority and responsibility. Effective supervision, motivation and other controlling techniques help in the attainment of this objective.

Characteristics of Management

Following are the main characteristics of management

(i) **Management is goal-oriented** Every organisation has a set of basic goals, which are a reason for its existence.

(ii) **Management is a group activity** It unites the efforts of diverse individuals towards fulfilling the common organisational goal.

(iii) **Management is universal** It is present in all organisations whether big or small, business or non-business.

(iv) **Management is a dynamic function** An organisation interacts with external environment which changes continuously. Management strives to adapt to the changing environment.

(v) **Management is an intangible** Its presence can only be felt by orderliness and accomplishment of targets, as it is an invisible force.

(vi) **Management is both an art and a science** Management is a science, as it contains certain principles and an art, as it is a skilful application of acquired knowledge of management principles.

(vii) **Management is an integrating force** It integrates diverse individual efforts towards attainment of organisational objectives.

(viii) **Multi-disciplinary** Its theoretical knowledge is drawn from various disciplines like anthropology, sociology, psychology, economics, etc.

(ix) **Continuous activity** The functions of management are simultaneously performed by all the managers all the time.

(x) **Distinct process** Management consists of a distinct and continuous process of planning, organising, staffing, directing and controlling.

(xi) **Social process** Management aims at getting work done by a group of people, by establishing harmony among them, thereby, considered as a social process.

(xii) **System of authority** Management refers to the authority that regulates all operations in the enterprise, at all levels in the organisation.

PYQs Previous Years' Questions

1 Mark Questions

1. Management as a ………… refers to a systematised branch of knowledge and a separate field of study. *ISC 2024*

Ans discipline

2. Management as an activity brings together five M's of management. Which of the following options is not one of the M's? *ISC Sem I 2021*

(a) Mobility (b) Methods
(c) Materials (d) Money

Ans (a) Mobility

3. Which concept of management considers it a series of interrelated functions, to be performed sequentially? *ISC Sem I 2021*

(a) Management as a discipline
(b) Management as a process
(c) Management as an activity
(d) Management as a group

Ans (b) Management as a process

4. With reference to the concept of management as a group, choose the odd one out. *ISC Sem I 2021*

(a) Board of directors (b) Chief executive
(c) Head of department (d) Workers

Ans (d) Workers

5. With reference to management as a process, choose the odd one out. *ISC Sem I 2021*

(a) Staffing (b) Group activity
(c) Organisation (d) Planning

Ans (b) Group activity

6. The phrase 'management is all pervading' implies *ISC Sem I 2021*

(a) management is required in all organisations
(b) management is required at all levels of organisation
(c) management is required at the top level of the organisation
(d) management is required at all levels of authority and in all organisations

Ans (d) management is required at all levels of authority and in all organisations

7. One of the objectives of management is **ISC Sem I 2021**
(a) profitability (b) contingency
(c) dynamism (d) universality

Ans (a) profitability

8. The meaning of the term management is used in various senses like **ISC Sem I Specimen 2021**
(a) activity (b) group
(c) discipline (d) integration

Ans (d) integration

9. Which of the statements given below aptly describes management as a discipline? **ISC Sem I Specimen 2021**
(a) Management as a discipline is a systematised body
(b) Management as a discipline means obedience to rules in the organisation
(c) Management as a discipline means order in the organisation
(d) Management is a discipline refers to equity in the organisation

Ans (a) Management as a discipline is a systematised body

10. Management of an organisation strives to achieve different social objectives. One of the social objectives is **ISC Sem I Specimen 2021**
(a) profit
(b) modernisation
(c) expansion
(d) pollution free environment

Ans (d) pollution free environment

2 Marks Questions

1. Define management as an activity. **ISC 2020**

Ans Management is a human activity which directs and controls the organisation for achieving common goals. As an activity, management integrates the inputs of men, money, material, machinery and methods and makes a productive enterprise out of them.

2. "Management is universal." Comment. **ISC 2019**

Or What is meant by universality of management? **ISC 2011**

Ans The activities involved in managing an enterprise is common to all organisations whether, economic, social or political. The organisation may be big or small, or in any part of the world.

The basic functions performed by the management remain the same. Therefore, we can also say, management is unviersal or all pervasive, i.e. present everywhere.

3. Why is management considered to be a discipline? **ISC 2018, 09, 04**

Or Write briefly on management as a discipline.

Ans Management has a specialised body of knowledge. The theories and principles, techniques and methods provide the basic groundwork for the development of management as a discipline.

Professional courses such as Master of Business Administration (MBA), Bachelor of Business Administration (BBA) and other such courses are pursued for the study of management. Various institutes and colleges are providing management education and training, as a separate discipline.

4. Define management as a process. **ISC Specimen 2018, 17, 06**

Ans Management as a process means the primary functions or activities that management performs to get things done. Management as a process consists of planning, organising, staffing, directing and controlling functions.

They are a series of interrelated and continuous functions aimed to integrate human elements with physical and financial resources to achieve a predetermined objective. Management is a process of releasing and directing human energy towards attaining a definite goal.

5. Explain management as a group. **ISC 2013, 05**

Or What is management as a group activity? **ISC 2005**

Ans Management is a collective noun, as it refers to a group of people working together for meeting common organisational goals. All the managers, from chief executive to first line managers, are collectively a part of 'management'.

As a group, management is rule framing and enforcing body. It consists of hierarchy of managers responsible for decision-making and enforcing them by supervising, directing and controlling the activities of the organisation.

6. Explain the integration concept of management. **ISC 2012**

Or What is the integration concept of management? **ISC 2007**

Ans The integration concept emphasises on integration and coordination of human, physical and financial resources to enable a business enterprise to effectively and efficiently achieve the desired goals.

"Management is the force that integrates human and non-human resources into an effective operating unit."

7. Define the term 'management'. ***ISC 2001***

Ans According to **Robert L Trewelly** and **M Gene Newport**, "Management is defined as the process of planning, organising, actuating and controlling an organisation's operations in order to achieve coordination of human and material resources essential in the effective and efficient attainment of objectives."

8. Explain the classical concept of management. ***ISC 2001***

Ans This approach consisted of scientific management, administrative management and bureaucratic management. This concept emphasised management as a process.

"Management is a distinct process consisting of planning, organising, actuating and controlling, performed to determine and accomplish stated objectives by use of human beings and other resources."

9. Why is management considered to be multi-disciplinary? ***ISC 2000***

Ans The theoretical knowledge of management is derived from various disciplines such as Anthropology, Sociology, Psychology, Economics, etc. Because of this it is considered to be multi-disciplinary.

3/4/5 Marks Questions

1. Discuss any four objectives of management. ***ISC 2023 (4M)***

Or Define management. Briefly explain any three objectives of management. ***ISC 2020 (4M)***

Or Explain any three objectives of management. ***ISC 2016 (3M)***

Ans Management is defined as the process of planning, organising, actuating and controlling an organisation's operations and activities effectively and efficiently.

The main objectives of management are as follows

(i) **Profitability** The basic objective of management is to earn enough profits to meet the various needs of an organisation.

Firstly, it is necessary for the survival of business and then for growth and expansion of the business. This can be achieved by efficiently using the resources.

(ii) **Growth and prosperity** A business needs to add to its prospects in the long-run and should fully exploit its growth potential. Management must maximise prosperity by the best utilisation of resources.

(iii) **Development of people** Management should seek to develop human talent by providing training and participation in decision-making.

(iv) **Decision-making** Right decisions at the right time are important for the success of an organisation. The quality and timing of decisions determines the growth and progress of the organisation.

Concept Enhancer Management involves creation of benefits for the society through providing good quality products at reasonable price and using environment friendly methods of production.

2. Explain three important characteristics of management. ***ISC 2019 (3M)***

Or What are essential characteristics of management? ***ISC 2005 (5M)***

Or State two characteristics of management. ***ISC 2004***

Ans The main features which highlight the characteristics of management are as follows (any five)

(i) **Management is a goal-oriented process**

Management always aims at achieving certain specified objectives.

It seeks to achieve pre-determined objectives through efficient use of human and non-human resources.

(ii) **Management is a continuous process**

Management is an ongoing process. The management functions are simultaneously performed by all managers, all the time.

It involves continuous handling of problems and issues.

Managers identify problems and try to solve them by taking appropriate actions on a regular basis.

Characteristics of Management
- A goal-oriented process
- A continuous process
- A group activity
- A dynamic function
- A social process
- Intangible

(iii) **Management is a group activity** An organisation is a collection of diverse individuals with different needs.

Every member of the group has a different purpose for joining the organisation, but as members of the organisation, they work towards fulfilling the common organisational goal. This requires team work and coordination of individual efforts in a common direction.

(iv) **Management is a dynamic function** Every organisation interacts with environment. In order to survive, it is necessary that an organisation must change itself according to the needs of environment.
This maintains the competitive edge of the organisation by adapting to the changes in the environment and even modify the environment for its success.

(v) **Management is a social process** Human factor is an important and inseparable part of the organisation. Management strives to achieve its objectives by coordinating the efforts of people working in an organisation.

(vi) **Management is an intangible** It is an invisible force. It can only be felt and not seen.
Good management can be felt and noticed by meeting of targets, happy employees, orderliness, etc. within the organisation.

3. "Management is getting things done through people". Discuss. *ISC 2003 (5M)*

Ans This is the most simple and popular definition of management, according to the traditional concept of management. The definition only emphasises on accomplishing the objectives of the organisation by guiding human efforts. It just focusses on management as an art.

It lays stress only on achievement of business objectives and does not mention social obligations of management.

This definition therefore, suffers from certain limitations like

(i) It does not specify the functions performed by the manager.
(ii) It does not talk about coordination.
(iii) It does not mention the scientific aspect of management.
(iv) It does not state as to how management strives for efficiency and effectiveness.

According to **Koontz** and **O' Donnell**, "Management is the creation and maintenance of an internal environment in an enterprise, where individuals, working in groups, can perform efficiently and effectively towards attainment of group goals."

The definition emphasises on

(i) Conducive internal environment
(ii) Working of groups
(iii) Efficiency and effectiveness

However, it also suffer from the limitations of ignoring the nature of management and goals of individuals.

According to **Robert L Trewelly** and **M Gene Newport**, "Management is defined as the process of planning, organising, actuating and controlling an organisation's operations in order to achieve coordination of human and material resources essential in the effective and efficient attainment of objectives." This definition gives a balanced view of management.

Thus, we can say management is

(i) A purposive activity
(ii) Group activity
(iii) Integrating activity
(iv) Social process
(v) Continuous process
(vi) Distinct process
(vii) Goal-oriented
(viii) Aims at achieving efficiency and effectiveness

TOPIC 2

Importance and Nature of Management

Importance of Management

The following points highlight the importance of management

(i) **Achievement of goals** Management unites the efforts of diverse individuals towards the achievement of common organisational goals.

(ii) **Optimum utilisation of resources** It allows correlation and coordination among human, physical and financial resources and thus, enables an organisation to optimally use the resources and achieve the desired goals.

(iii) **Increases efficiency** By minimising the cost through better planning, directing, staffing and controlling the activities of an organisation, management achieves efficient utilisation of physical, human and financial resources.

(iv) **Raises the standards of living** By providing quality goods at reasonable prices, it helps to improve the living standard of the society.

(v) **Generates employment** Employment is generated by establishment of new enterprises and expansion of the existing ones.

(vi) **Development of the society** By performing functions to achieve multiple objectives, management helps in development of an organisation and thereby developing the society by providing good quality products, generating employment, adopting new techniques, innovation, etc.

(vii) **Profits for survival and growth** In an uncertain environment, management continuously helps in adapting to the changes and earn enough profits for survival, growth and expansion of the organisation.

Nature of Management

Management is regarded as an art by some and science by others. The truth seems to be somewhere in between, as it has characteristics of both science as well as art. Management is also considered as a profession.

Management as a Science

Management may be regarded as a science because of following reasons

(i) **Systematised body of knowledge** Management has a systematised body of knowledge. It has its own theories and principles that have developed over a period of time.

It also draws some principles from other disciplines such as Economics, Sociology, Psychology and Mathematics.

(ii) **Principles based on scientific observation and experiments** Like Science, management principles are based on scientific enquiry and observations.

(iii) **Universal validity and application** Like Science, principles of management are universally applicable.

(iv) **Cause and effect relationship** Principles of management establish cause and effect relationship. e.g. If unity of command is not there, there may be confusion and chaos.

Although, the principles of management are not as exact as the principles of Physics or Chemistry; management principles are flexible and can be modified to suit different situations. Thus, management can be called as 'an inexact science' or 'soft science' also.

Management as an Art

Management may be regarded as an art because of the following reasons

(i) **Existence of theoretical knowledge** A successful manager practices the art of management in the day-to-day job of managing an enterprise based on study, observation and experience.

(ii) **Personalised application** The use of basic knowledge varies from individual to individual, therefore, it is a personalised concept, e.g. Two dancers, two speakers will always differ in demonstrating their art.

(iii) **Based on practice and creativity** A good manager works through a combination of practice, creativity, imagination, initiative and innovation. He uses tactics and creativity to develop his own style.

Thus, management is an art because it satisfies all the characteristics of an art.

Management as a Profession

Profession means a vocation requiring special knowledge, practical training, code of conduct and service motive. Let us see, whether management is a profession, on the following bases

(i) **Systematised body of knowledge** All professions are based on a systematised body of knowledge, consisting of laws, theories and principles. Management also has a set of principles which help managers in practicing management.

(ii) **Restricted entry** The entry to all professions is restricted through a prescribed qualification. But, there is no restriction on anyone being appointed as a manager in any business enterprise.

(iii) **Professional association** It is not obligatory for managers to get registered with any professional body like the Medical Council or Bar Council of India, which regulates the professional conduct of doctors and lawyers, respectively.

(iv) **Ethical code of conduct** Legal and medical professions are bound by a code of conduct which guides the behaviour of its members. AIMA has devised a code of conduct for Indian managers, but there is no statutory backing for this code.

(v) **Service motive** Like other professionals, managers are expected to serve the society rather than simply earning profits.

Thus, although management does not possess all the essential attributes of a profession, management is definitely on a path of becoming a full fledged profession.

PYQs Previous Years' Questions

1 Mark Questions

1. Which of the following is not correct with regard to the importance of management? *ISC Sem I 2021*
   (a) Management generates employment opportunities
   (b) Management improves standard of living of people
   (c) Management is a system of authority
   (d) Management lends of development of nation

Ans (c) Management is a system of authority

2. Management is an art because it has the feature of *ISC Sem I 2021*
   (a) creativity (b) observation and experiments
   (c) service motive (d) cause and effect relationship

Ans (a) creativity

3. Management is considered as *ISC Sem I 2021*
   (a) an art (b) a science
   (c) an art and a science (d) Neither art nor science

Ans (c) an art and a science

4. One of the features of management as a profession, is *ISC Sem I 2021*
   (a) restricted entry (b) creativity
   (c) cause and effect relationship (d) personal skill

Ans (a) restricted entry

5. Since management deals with humans, it is considered as a .... *ISC Sem I 2021*
   (a) physical science (b) social science
   (c) home science (d) life science

Ans (b) social science

6. Management as a science is *ISC Sem I Specimen 2021*
   (a) a systematised body of knowledge
   (b) perfection through practice
   (c) multi disciplinary
   (d) integrating force

Ans (a) a systematised body of knowledge

2 Marks Question

1. Mention two points of importance of management. *ISC 2005*

Ans Two main points of importance of mangement are

(i) **Achievement of goals** Management plays an important role in the achievement of objectives of an organisation. Management is a goal-oriented process. With a view to realise the pre-determined goals, manager plans carefully, organises the resources properly, hires competent people, provides necessary guidance and unites the efforts of different individuals towards achieving the pre-determined goals.

(ii) **Optimum utilisation of resources** It allows correlation and coordination among human, physical and financial resources and thus, enables an organisation to optimally use the resources and achieve the desired goals.

3/4/5 Marks Questions

1. Why is management considered an art? *ISC Specimen 2023 (4M)*

Or Write a short note on features of management as an art. *ISC 2019 (4M)*

Or Explain, why management is considered to be an art? *ISC 2014 (4M)*

Ans Art is the skillful and personalised application of existing knowledge to achieve desired goals.

Management is said to be an art since, it satisfies the following features of an art are as

(i) **Existence of theoretical knowledge** Manager practices the art of management in day-to-day job of managing an enterprise on the basis of study, observation and experience.

(ii) **Personalised application** Because of the availability of the theoretical knowledge of management, a manager is able to apply it in personalised application and this application varies from individual to individual.

(iii) **Based on practice and creativity** Art requires creativity. Similarly, manager also requires creativity to apply the acquired knowledge in a personalised and skillful manner.

Common Mistake Students usually get confused while framing answer to this question. They are advised to focus on words like, theoretical knowledge, personalised, application, needs practice, etc.

2. Explain why management is considered to be a science. **ISC 2018 (4M)**

Or Why is management considered as a science? **ISC 2016 (3M)**

Ans Management may be regarded as a science because of following reasons

(i) **Systematised body of knowledge** Management has a systematised body of knowledge. It has its own theories and principles that have developed over a period of time.

It also draws some principles from other disciplines such as Economics, Sociology, Psychology and Mathematics.

(ii) **Principles based on scientific observation and experiments** Like science, management principles are based on scientific enquiry and observations.

(iii) **Universal validity and application** Like science, principles of management are universally applicable.

(iv) **Cause and effect relationship** Principles of management establish cause and effect relationship e.g. If unity of command is not there, there may be confusion and chaos.

Although, the principles of management are not as exact as the principles of Physics or Chemistry; management principles are flexible and can be modified to suit different situations. Thus, management can be called as 'an inexact science' or 'soft science' also.

Common Mistake Some students are generally confused in management as it is science or art. Features of management as a science must be explained clearly with the help of point in favour and against.

3. "Management is the dynamic, life giving element in every business." In the context of this statement, explain the importance of management in modern times. **ISC Specimen 2018, 17 (5M)**

Or Explain the importance of management in modern time. **ISC 2012 (5M)**

Or Discuss the importance of management for a successful functioning of an organisation. **ISC 2010 (5M)**

Ans Management is certainly a dynamic and life giving element in every business. The importance of management in modern time can be highlighted by the following points

Refer to text on page 69 and 70.

4. Write a short note on 'Management as science and art'. **ISC 2011 (4M)**

Or Management is both a science and an art. Explain. **ISC 2006, ISC 2001**

Ans Refer to Q.No. 1 and 2 (3/4/5 Marks) on page 71 and 72.

5. Why is management considered to be a profession? **ISC 2004**

Ans Refer to text on page 70.

6. "Government without good management is like a house built on sand." In the light of the above statement, explain the importance of management in modern time. **ISC 2000 (5M)**

Ans As we are all aware that good management is a pervasive activity required in all types of organisations big or small, put as public, households or firms and even for the government of a country. So, we can easily say that a government without good management is like a house build on sand, sure to collapse even on the context of a small disturbance. In the light of the above statement, the importance of management in modern times can be highlighted by the following points

(i) **Optimum utilisation of resources** A government is often faced with scarcity of resources. On the basis of sound management activities, government can strive for optimum utilisation of resources leading to a country's economic growth.

(ii) **Achievement of group objectives** A government operates in groups. Good management practices help the government to achieve group objectives thereby paving the way towards prosperity.

(iii) **Generation of employment opportunities** Good management policies of the government help in increasing employment opportunities, thereby fulfilling the social and economical needs.

(iv) **Sound organisational structure** Management establishes a sound government and establishes clearcut authority and responsibility relationships, thereby encouraging the spirit of cooperation, fellow feeling and mutual understanding among various levels of governance.

Value Points

For getting maximum marks, following points can be included in the answer

- Add about optimum utilisation of resources.
- Add about fulfilling social and economical needs.

CHAPTER TEST

01 Mark Questions

1. Management is not ....
(a) a pure science (b) an art
(c) Both art and science (d) an applied science

2. Management is the process of
(a) managing the activities of the organisation
(b) controlling affairs of the organisation
(c) administering the departments of the organisation
(d) All of the above

3. Which of the following are some of the characteristics of management?
(a) Management is a goal oriented process
(b) Management is multi-dimensional
(c) Management is all pervasive (d) All of the above

4. Management is related to people in defined roles and working within a structured organisation. State true or false.

5. Management is the ability to direct staff towards achieving goals. State true or false.

6. Management is a .... directed process as it aims at achieving specific goals.

7. ... is a systematised body of knowledge that explains certain general truths or operation of general laws.

8. Define management as an activity.

9. Write short note on features of management as an art.

10. **Assertion** (A) Management principles can be applied to all types of activities.

Reason (R) Management involves the decisions by a manager and it is not a group activity.

Alternatives
(a) Both Assertion (A) and Reason (R) are true and Reason (R) is the correct explanation of Assertion (A)
(b) Both Assertion (A) and Reason (R) are true, but Reason (R) is not the correct explanation of Assertion (A)
(c) Both Assertion (A) and Reason (R) are true
(d) Both Assertion (A) and Reason (R) are false

02 Marks Questions

11. What is meant by traditional approach of management?

12. Explain productivity concept of management.

13. How is traditional concept of management different from modern concept?

14. Write two importance of management.

03/04/05 Marks Questions

15. 'Management is all pervasive'. Explain.

16. Why is management considered to be 'goal-oriented', 'intangible' and 'continuous process'?

17. Explain the different approaches of management thought.

18. Management is not a full fledged profession. Discuss.

19. Management is something between both science and art. Do you agree? Discuss.

20. What are the objectives of management? Discuss.

Answers

1. (a) a pure science
2. (d) All of the above
3. (d) All of the above
4. True
5. True
6. goal
7. Science
10. (b) Both Assertion (A) and Reason (R) are true, but Reason (R) is not the correct explanation of Assertion (A)

07

Principles of Management

TREND ANALYSIS 5 YEARS		Average No. of Questions Across all Sets					
		Types of Questions	2024	2023	2020	2019	2018
TOPIC 01	Introduction to Principles of Management	1 Mark	1	—	—	—	—
		2 Marks	—	—	—	—	—
		3/4/5 Marks	—	—	—	—	1
TOPIC 02	Taylor's Principles of Scientific Management	1 Mark	—	—	—	—	—
		2 Marks	—	—	—	—	—
		3/4/5 Marks	—	—	—	1	—
TOPIC 03	Fayol's Principles of Management and Comparison	1 Mark	—	1	—	—	—
		2 Marks	—	—	—	—	—
		3/4/5 Marks	1	—	1	—	1

Introduction to Principles of Management

Management principles are broad and general guidelines for decision-making and behaviour. They provide cause and effect relationship between variables and predict the result, if applied in a given situation. But, they are not rigid as the principles of pure science. This is because these principles deal with human behaviour and human behaviour is not static.

The principles have been formed by

(i) **Observation and practice** Formed by experience and collective wisdom of managers which they gained through observation and practice.

(ii) **Experimentation** By conducting experiments to test their validity.

Nature/Characteristics of Principles of Management

Following are the nature/characteristics of principles of management

(i) **Universal applicability** These principles are universal and can be applied in all types of organisations, whether it is profit making or non-profit making, private or government and manufacturing or service sector enterprise.

(ii) **Dynamic/Relativity** Management principles are general guidelines. They cannot be applied blindly in all the situations, as they do not provide readymade strait jacket solutions to all managerial problems. They have to be modified according to different situations and continuously changing business environment.

(iii) **Flexible** The management principles are dynamic, but not static or rigid prescriptions, which are to be followed absolutely. They are flexible in nature and can be modified by the manager, as per the given situation.

(iv) **Cause and effect relationship** These principles establish cause and effect relationship. It indicates the consequence of implementing a particular principle over a given situation.

(v) **Equal importance** All principles are of equal importance, as they may be used with equal efficiency in different situations.

(vi) **Influencing human behaviour** Management is a social science and deals with human behaviour. It aims at influencing human behaviour.

Need/Importance of Principles of Management

Need/Importance of principles of management are

(i) **Improving efficiency of managers** It increases the efficiency of management, as through these principles, a manager adopts a systematic and logical approach to overcome the problems and discards hit and trial approaches.

(ii) **Management training and education** These principles provide basic groundwork for the development of management as a discipline.

(iii) **Improving art of management** Managers can improve their knowledge and understanding of managerial situations.
These principles enable managers to learn from past mistakes and conserve time by solving recurring problems quickly. Hence, we can say that these principles provide managers an insight of real world situations.

(iv) **Fulfilling the social responsibilities** Management principles are evolved or developed to serve the demands of society. These principles establish certain ethics in response to social responsibility towards the society.

(v) **Useful for conducting research** The principles laid down, have increased the horizon of knowledge and have provided ideas and vision for further research.

(vi) **Emergence of clearer and systematic thinking** The principles work as a guideline for better understanding of nature of management.

(vii) **Evaluate managerial behaviour** These principles develop scientific approach, as they give realistic, subjective and an objective measurement for evaluation.

(viii) **Spread knowledge** It is an organised body of knowledge which has helped in the progress of management education.

Taylor's Principles of Scientific Management

It was FW Taylor, an American, who first used scientific methods of study to solve managerial problems. Therefore, he is known as 'The Father of Scientific Management'.

According to **FW Taylor**, "Scientific management means knowing exactly what you want men to do and seeing that they do it in the best and the cheapest way."

The basic principles of scientific management are as follows

(i) **Science, not rule of thumb** Scientific attitude and methods should be used for solving problems, instead of following rule of thumb, i.e. old methods of doing work.

(ii) **Harmony, not discord** Close cooperation between employees and employers is necessary for mutually beneficial relationship.

(iii) **Maximum, not restricted output** Higher profits are desired for mutual gains of management and workers. Optimum utilisation of resources and maximum output will help to achieve this.

(iv) **Division of work and responsibility** Taylor suggested separation of planning from operational work. Management should fix responsibility for planning and supervision on different individuals.

(v) **Scientific selection, training and development of workers** Employees should be scientifically selected and trained according to the requirement of the job. Each and every worker should be encouraged to develop his full potential through continuous appraisal.

Fayol's Principles of Management

Henry Fayol was born in 1841 in France. He was a mining engineer and a great classical management theorist. He was known as 'The Father of General Management'.

Fayol developed his own concept of administration. He had given 14 principles of management, which are described below

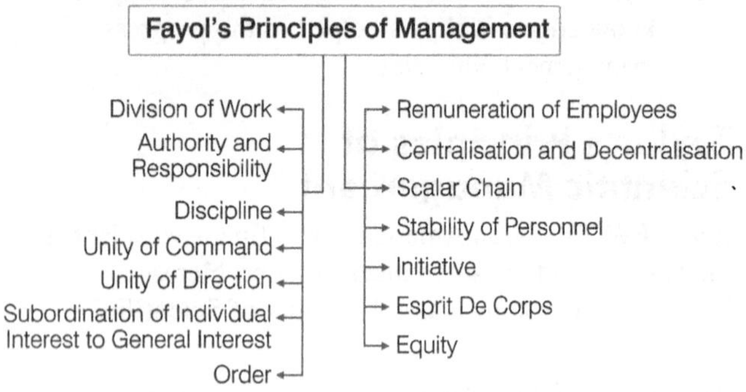

(i) **Division of work** Fayol has advocated division of work. According to him, if work is divided into small tasks, then this will help in taking the advantage of specialisation.

The intent of division of work is to produce more and better work with the same effort. It is the most efficient way to use human effort.

(ii) **Authority and responsibility** Authority means the right to give orders and obtain obedience. On the other hand, responsibility means obligation to complete the assigned task on time.

According to Fayol, there must be a balance between authority and responsibility. Excess of authority without matching responsibility, may bring negative results. Thus, there should be parity between them.

(iii) **Discipline** It is the sincerity and obedience towards organisational rules and regulations, as these are necessary for the smooth functioning of an organisation.

According to Fayol, good superiors at all levels, fair agreements and judicious application of penalties are helpful in maintaining discipline.

(iv) **Unity of command** The principle of unity of command states that each participant in a formal organisation should receive orders and is responsible to only one superior. If in any case, employee gets orders from two superiors at the same time, the principle of unity of command is violated.

(v) **Unity of direction** It implies that there should be one head and one plan for a group of activities having the same objective. In other words, the related activities should be put under one group, there should be one plan of action for them and they should be in the control of one manager.

(vi) **Subordination of individual interest to general interest** The interest of an organisation is to achieve its goals.

These goals are achieved after integrating the efforts of different individuals, who are working in the organisation to satisfy their own personal needs. Sometimes, an individual starts giving priority to his own interest, but according to Fayol in all situations, company's interest should supersede the interest of individual.

(vii) **Order** As per this principle, there should be an orderly arrangement of men and material, which implies that there is a fixed place for everything and everyone in the organisation.

(viii) **Remuneration of employees** According to Fayol, the quantum and methods of remuneration payable to employees should be fair and reasonable. It should be satisfactory to both employers and employees.

(ix) **Centralisation and decentralisation** The concentration of decision-making authority is called 'centralisation' whereas, its dispersal among more than one person is known as 'decentralisation'. According to Fayol, an organisation should strive to achieve a proper balance between centralisation and decentralisation.

(x) **Scalar chain** According to Fayol, scalar chain refers to the chain of authority and communication that runs from top to bottom and should be followed by managers and their subordinates.

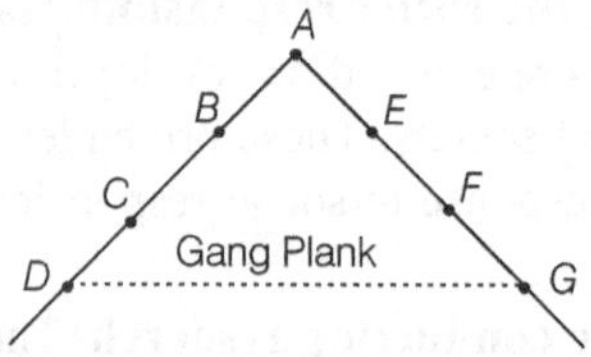

The given figure illustrates the scalar chain. If D and G wants to communicate, the message should usually move up through C, B, A, E, F and then G. Communication through this process takes time, that's why, Fayol suggested the concept of **gang plank**, which permits the direct communication between D and G in case of emergency.

(xi) **Stability of personnel** According to Fayol, suppose an individual gets selected for a post, then he should be given appropriate time to prove his abilities.
We can say, he should be kept at the post for a fixed tenure. This ensures stability and thus, the employee can get reasonable time to explore his skills.

(xii) **Initiative** Fayol suggested that employees at all levels should take initiative or action without any force or boundations. This will help to motivate them and they will work hard for the betterment of the organisation.

(xiii) **Esprit de corps** It means union is strength. Fayol emphasised on teamwork. He suggested that every employee must consider him as a part of team. This spirit brings harmony in the groups and they strive to work hard to achieve the targets of an organisation.

(xiv) **Equity** This principle emphasises kindliness and justice in the behaviour of managers towards workers. It will bring loyalty and devotion in the behaviour of employees and they will put in their best to achieve the targets.

Taylor Vs Fayol : A Comparison

Comparison between Taylor and Fayol

Basis	Henry Fayol	FW Taylor
Perspective	Top level of management	Shop or floor level of a factory
Applicability	Universally applicable	Applicable to specialised situations
Basis of formation	Personal experience	Observations and experimentation
Focus	Improving overall administration	Increasing productivity
Personality	Practioner	Scientist

Relevance of Principles in Today's Scenario

The principles of management have been a foundation of decision-making and guiding human behaviour. However, they need to be little modified, according to the changing times, as discussed in the chart below

Principle	Relevance	Changes required
Division of work	The work cannot be done by single person.	Degree of division of work differs from one organisation to another.
Authority and responsibility	Managers are empowered.	Employees should be empowered.
Discipline	Essential for smooth functioning.	Self-discipline and informal controls through peer pressure.
Unity of command	Usually followed.	Some cases may require orders from multiple bosses.
Unity of direction	Departments of a firm usually follow this.	Some organisations may be of matrix structure.
Subordination of individual interest to general interest	Employees are committed to the organisation.	It should be both ways, employees and organisations should be committed to each other.
Remuneration	Reasonable reward system.	Performance based reward system.
Centralisation and decentralisation	Some decentralisation is evident in each organisation.	Projects and tasks require decentralisation.
Scalar chain	Formalised communication channels usually followed.	Needs less formalised and flatter communication channels for speeding up decision-making.
Stability of tenure	In the interest of employers too.	Have to retrench inefficient employees.
Initiative	Initiatives are taken from employees in many cases, like feedback, suggestions, etc.	More encouragement by reward system should be done.
Esprit de corps	Unity is relevant.	High morale should be maintained for congenial environment.
Equity	Employers have to adhere to equity concept for better relations with employees.	Commitment can be obtained through a sense of ownership.

PYQs Previous Years' Questions

1 Mark Questions

1. Principles of management are not as accurate as principles of science because *ISC 2024*

(a) they are absolute

(b) they deal with human behaviour which is unpredictable

(c) they are rigid

(d) they are not universally accepted

Ans (b) they deal with human behaviour which is unpredictable

2. Deepti and Sudha are managers in ABC Ltd. and are working together on a project. They report to Mrs. Verma a senior manager. Sudha asks Deepti to submit a report on the project to her without informing Mrs. Verma. Which principle of management in not followed in this case? *ISC 2023*

Ans Unity of command

3. Esprit de corps means *ISC Specimen 2023, Sem I Specimen 2021*

(a) buyer beware (b) product is our strength

(c) service is our motto (d) union is strength

Ans (d) union is strength

4. The principles of management have developed through *ISC Sem I 2021*

(a) rule of thumb

(b) observation and experiments

(c) customers' experience

(d) sellers' experience

Ans (b) observation and experiments

5. With reference to the need for principles of management, choose the odd one out. *ISC Sem I 2021*

(a) To train manager (b) To spread knowledge

(c) To increase efficiency (d) To increase flexibility

Ans (d) To increase flexibility

6. Every activity should be scientifically planned rather than doing it on trial and error basis or traditional methods. Which principle of scientific management states so? *ISC Sem I 2021*

(a) Harmony, not discord

(b) Division of work and responsibility

(c) Science, not rule of thumb

(d) Maximum, not restricted output

Ans (c) Science, not rule of thumb

7. The principle of esprit de corps was stated by *ISC Sem I 2021*

(a) Peter F Drucker (b) Henry Fayol

(c) FW Taylor (d) Earnest Dale

Ans (b) Henry Fayol

8. A manager encourages his subordinates to suggest new ways of doing the assigned tasks. Which principle of management is being followed in this case? *ISC Sem I 2021*

(a) Stability of tenure (b) Scalar chain

(c) Initiative (d) Equity

Ans (c) Initiative

9. Which principle of management will be violated if the tools of production are not in a proper place in the factory? *ISC Sem I 2021*

(a) Equity (b) Initiative

(c) Stability of tenure (d) Order

Ans (d) Order

10. According to Henry Fayol, the principle of authority and responsibility means *ISC Sem I 2021*

(a) authority and responsibility go hand in hand

(b) authority and responsibility do not coexist

(c) no parity between authority and responsibility

(d) authority does not require taking responsibility

Ans (a) authority and responsibility go hand in hand

11. Gang plank is considered as direct .... communication. *ISC Sem I 2021*

(a) horizontal (b) vertical

(c) diagonal (d) downward

Ans (a) horizontal

12. With reference to the effects of violation of principle of order, choose the odd one out. *ISC Sem I 2021*

(a) Insecurity among employees

(b) Wastage of resources

(c) Increase in the cost of operation

(d) Confusion and chaos

Ans (a) Insecurity among employees

13. Which principle of management states that every subordinate should receive orders from and be accountable for only one superior? *ISC Sem I Specimen 2021*

(a) Unity of direction (b) Unity of command

(c) Centralisation (d) Scalar chain

Ans (b) Unity of command

14. Which principle of management states that there should be a place for everything and everything be in its place? *ISC Sem I Specimen 2021*

(a) Equity (b) Discipline
(c) Order (d) Esprit de corps

Ans (c) Order

15. The principle through which Henry Fayol points out the danger and cost of unnecessary labour turnover is *ISC Sem I Specimen 2021*

(a) Order (b) Stability of tenure
(c) Equity (d) Remuneration

Ans (b) Stability of tenure

16. The supervisor of the production department needs to communicate with the supervisor of the sales department urgently. To facilitate quick communication he establishes a *ISC Sem I Specimen 2021*

(a) Scalar chain (b) Unity of command
(c) Gang plank (d) Direct communication

Ans (c) Gang plank

17. Ram and Rajan have similar qualifications and perform the same type of jobs in the organisation, but they are paid different salaries. Name the principle of Henry Fayol violated in this case. *ISC Sem I Specimen 2021*

(a) Equity (b) Order
(c) Remuneration (d) Centralisation

Ans (a) Equity

18. The principles of management, as advocated by Henry Fayol are *ISC Sem I Specimen 2021 (M)*

(a) Scalar chain
(b) Equity
(c) Order
(d) All of the above

Ans (d) All of the above

19. The characteristics of principles of management are *ISC Sem I Specimen 2021*

(a) Universality (b) Dynamic
(c) Contingent
(d) Train managers

Ans (b) Dynamic

20. One of the principles of scientific management is *ISC Sem I Specimen 2021*

(a) Science not rule of thumb.
(b) Systematised body of knowledge.
(c) Specialised knowledge having a code of conduct.
(d) Perfection through practice.

Ans (b) Systematised body of knowledge.

2 Marks Questions

1. Explain the principle of authority and responsibility, as laid down by Henry Fayol. *ISC Specimen 2018, 17*

Or

Explain the principle of authority and responsibility. *ISC 2002, 2000*

Ans Henry Fayol had given fourteen principles of management, one of which is authority and responsibility. Authority means the right to give orders and obtain obedience. On the other hand, responsibility means obligation to complete the assigned task on time.

According to Fayol, there must be a balance between authority and responsibility. Excess of authority without matching responsibility, may bring negative results. Thus, there should be parity between them.

Value Points

For getting maximum marks, following points can be included in the answer

- Meaning of authority as well as responsibility.
- Balance between authority and responsibility.

2. Explain the principle of 'Esprit de corps' as advocated by Henry Fayol. *ISC 2016*

Ans 'Esprit de corps' literally means 'union is strength'. By formulating this principle, Fayol emphasised on teamwork. He suggested that every employee must consider himself as a part of team.

This consideration on the part of the employee brings harmony in groups and they strive to work hard to achieve the targets of an organisation.

3. Distinguish between unity of command and unity of direction. *ISC 2015, 07*

Ans Difference between unity of command and unity of direction

Basis	Unity of command	Unity of direction
Meaning	As per this principle, an employee should receive orders from one boss only.	This principle insists on one plan and one head.
Purpose	Main purpose of this principle is to avoid the state of confusion from the mind of an employee.	Main purpose of this principle is to direct the efforts of employees of one department in achieving the target.

4. What is principle of equity as laid down by Henry Fayol? *ISC 2011*

Ans This principle emphasises kindliness and justice in the behaviour of managers towards workers. It will bring loyalty and devotion in the behaviour of employees and they put their best to achieve the targets.

5. What is meant by gang plank? *ISC 2010*

Or What is scalar chain in management? *ISC 2002*

Ans Principle of scalar chain states that there should be formal lines of authority from the highest to lowest ranks in the organisation structure. It suggests that communication from top to bottom should follow official lines of command.

However, 'gang plank' is a shorter route that can help the employees at the same level in different departments to communicate in order to avoid delay in communication.

For example, If in XYZ Ltd, E wants to communicate with R. He will have to follow the path in chain like first, he delivers informations to D, then D to C, B, A, M, N, O and at last O transfer the message to R. But, in case of emergency, E can directly contact with R, according to the concept of gang plank.

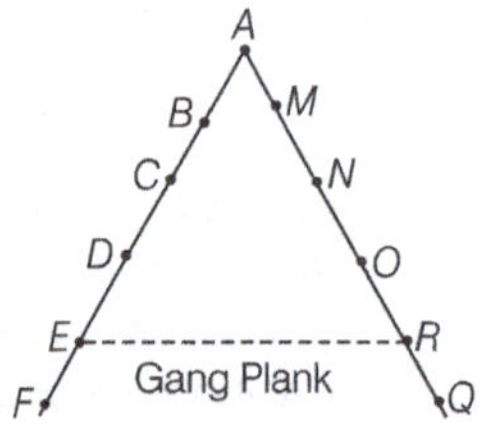

6. What is the need for principles of management? *ISC 2009*

Ans Principles of management are needed, as they help in

(i) Improving efficiency of management.
(ii) Management training and education.
(iii) Fulfilling the social responsibilities.
(iv) Spreading knowledge.

7. What is meant by 'order' as a principle in Fayol's management? *ISC 2008*

Ans As per this principle, there should be an orderly arrangement of men and material which implies that there is a fixed place for everything and everyone in the organisation. Arrangement of things is known as 'material order' whereas arrangement of men is known as 'social order'.

8. What is meant by a principle of management? *ISC 2004*

Ans Management principles are broad and general guidelines for decision-making and behaviour.

They provide cause and effect relationship between variables and predict the result if applied in a given situation.

But, they are not rigid as of pure science. This is because these principles deal with human behaviour and human behaviour is not static.

9. What is meant by 'unity of direction'? *ISC 2004*

Ans It implies that there should be one head and one plan for a group of activities having the same objective. In other words, the related activities should be put under one group, there should be one plan of action for them and they should be in the control of one manager.

10. What is meant by 'unity of command'? *ISC 2003*

Ans The principle of unity of command states that each participant in a formal organisation should receive orders and is responsible to only one superior. If in any case, employee gets orders from two superiors at the same time, the principle of unity of command is violated.

11. Who is known as 'The Father of Scientific Management'? *ISC 2002*

Ans FW Taylor is known as 'The Father of Scientific Management'.

3/4/5 Marks Questions

1. From the statements given below, identify and briefly explain each principle of management by Henri Fayol. *ISC 2024 (4M)*

(i) A place for everything and everything in its place.
(ii) Absence of nepotism and favouritism.

Ans (i) "A place for everything and everything in its place."

Here, the principle of management is 'order'. As per this principle, there should be an orderly arrangement of men and material, which implies that there is a fixed place for everything and everyone in the organisation.

(ii) "Absence of nepotism and favouritism."

Here the principle of management is 'equity'. As per Fayol, management should deal with employees with equity based on kindliness and justice to encourage workers to fulfil their duties with devotion and loyalty. There should neither be nepotism nor favouritism and all should be given just and fair treatment.

2. State any three differences between the principles of Taylor and Fayol. *ISC Specimen 2023 (5M)*

Or Give four differences between Taylor's and Fayol's principles of management. *ISC 2020 (4M)*

Or Give three points of difference between Taylor's and Fayol's principles of management.
ISC Specimen 2018, 17 (3M)

Or Bring out the distinction between principles of Fayol and Taylor. **ISC 2008 (5M)**

Ans Difference between Taylor's and Fayol's principles of management

Basis	FW Taylor	Henry Fayol
Perspective	Taylor's principles are for shop floor/lower level.	Fayol's principles were formed from top level management perspective.
Applicability	Taylor's techniques are applied in specialised situations and are less flexible.	Fayol's principles are universally applicable and flexible.
Basis of formation	Based on observations and experiments.	Based on personal experiences.
Focus	Taylor focussed on increasing productivity of workers.	Fayol focussed on overall improvement of administration of the organisation.
Personality	Taylor was a scientist and is known as 'The Father of Scientific Management'.	He was a practioner, known as 'Father of Management.'
Expression	Taylor's contribution is expressed as scientific management.	Fayol's contribution is expressed as general theory of administration.

3. Discuss the need for the principles of management. **ISC Specimen 2023, 18, 04, 01 (4M)**

Ans Need/Importance of principles of management are

(i) **Improving efficiency of managers** It increases the efficiency of management, as through these principles, a manager adopts a systematic and logical approach to overcome the problems and discards hit and trial approaches.

(ii) **Management training and education** These principles provide basic groundwork for the development of management as a discipline.

(iii) **Improving art of management** Managers can improve their knowledge and understanding of managerial situations.

These principles enable managers to learn from past mistakes and conserve time by solving recurring problems quickly. Hence, we can say that these principles provide managers an insight of real world situations.

(iv) **Fulfilling the social responsibilities** Management principles are evolved or developed to serve the demands of society.

These principles establish certain ethics in response to social responsibility towards the society.

Concept Enhancer Principles of management work as a guideline for better understanding of nature of management and develop scientific approach for evaluation.

4. State and explain the principles of management as laid down by FW Taylor. **ISC 2019, 16 (5M)**

Or State and explain any four principles of FW Taylor. **ISC 2014 (4M)**

Or State and explain five principles of scientific management as laid down by FW Taylor. **ISC 2010, 06 (5M)**

Or Discuss any four principles of management as formulated by FW Taylor. **ISC 2006**

Ans The basic principles of scientific management are as follows

(i) **Science, not rule of thumb** The first principle of scientific management requires scientific study and analysis of each element of a job, in order to replace the old approach.

Development of a science for each element of a man's job requires that decisions should be made on the basis of facts rather than on opinions and beliefs.

The work assigned to an employee should be observed and analysed with respect to each element or part and the time involved in it.

The purpose of such observation and analysis is to decide the best way of performing the work and to determine the standard output. Taylor stressed that each job should be based on scientific study and not on intuition or experience.

Principles of Scientific Management
- Science, not rule of thumb
- Harmony, not discord
- Scientific selection, training and development
- Division of work and responsibility
- Maximum, not restricted output

(ii) **Harmony, not discord** There should be harmony not conflict between the management and the workers. This requires change of mental attitudes of the workers and the management towards each other. Taylor called it 'Mental revolution'.

Mental revolution, on the part of management requires that they should provide standardised materials, machines and equipments.

They should create suitable working conditions and resolve all problems scientifically.

Mental revolution on the part of workers, requires that they should be disciplined, loyal and sincere in fulfilling the tasks assigned to them.

Instead of fighting for dividing surplus or profit, the management and workers should cooperate to increase them.

(iii) **Scientific selection, training and development** Industrial efficiency depends upon the efficiency of workers, and workers efficiency depend upon proper training and their proper selection.

Taylor suggested that due care should be taken while selecting the employees and after selecting, they must be given job according to their physical, mental and intellectual capabilities.

Employees must be sent for training from time to time to update their knowledge. This will ensure greatest efficiency and prosperity for both workers and management.

(iv) **Division of work and responsibility** According to Taylor, there must be an equal division of work and responsibility between workers and management.

Taylor emphasised on division of work and specialisation. He advocated separate planning and execution functions. According to him, planning should be given to those who have technical mastery, intelligence and grit. While execution should be given to those with energy and good health.

(v) **Maximum, not restricted output** Management should share gains of the company with the workers. Scientific management emphasised that true interests of the two are one and the same, that prosperity for employer cannot exist for a long time, unless, it is accompanied by prosperity of employees. Thus, both should work for maximum output by increasing the efficiency and profits of the business.

5. Explain the following principles of management, as advocated by Henry Fayol

(i) Stability of tenure (ii) Discipline
(iii) Unity of command (iv) Unity of direction
(v) Order **ISC 2018 (5M)**

Or Briefly discuss any five principles of management as formulated by Fayol. **ISC 2013**

Ans Refer to text on page 76 and 77.

6. Briefly discuss any five features of principles of management. **ISC Specimen 2018, 17 (5M)**

Or Write any two features of principles of management. **ISC 2014, 12**

Ans Refer to text 'nature of principles of management' on page 74 and 75.

Value Point

For getting maximum marks, following point can be included in the answer

- Stress upon the important keywords like, universality, dynamism, flexibility, contingent and relative principle.

7. Explain the meaning of 'Fayol's principle of centralisation'. **ISC 2014 (4M)**

Ans The concentration of decision-making authority is called centralisation, whereas, its dispersal among more than one person is known as decentralisation.

It can also be said that everything that increases the importance of subordinate's role is decentralisation and everything that reduces it, is centralisation.

According to Fayol, 'There is a need to balance subordinate involvement, through decentralisation, with managers retention of final authority through centralisation'.

The degree of centralisation depends upon the circumstances in which the organisation is working. Generally, large organisation are more decentralised and small firm are centralised in their functioning.

8. Describe the following principles of management. **ISC 2011**

(i) Authority and responsibility
(ii) Stability of personnel
(iii) Division of work

Ans Refer to text on page 76 and 77.

9. Discuss the universality of Henry Fayol's principles of management. **ISC 2007**

Ans Universality of management principles means that they are applicable everywhere, in all types of organisations, whether big or small.

They may be economic, social or political organisation, the activities performed for attaining the objectives of the organisation are same.

The basic principles may remain the same, however application of management principles differ from organisation to organisation, depending upon the culture and needs of that organisation.

Fayol's Principles in Respect to their Universality

(i) **Division of work** This principle is applicable everywhere, as no person can solely perform all the functions. Division of work also creates specialisation, which increases efficiency, but degree of division of work may depend on organisation to organisation e.g. Project based organisation or divisional structure may require performance of more than one function by a manager.

(ii) **Discipline** Discipline is necessary in every organisation. Here discipline when applied, would mean that workers and management both honour their commitments.

(iii) **Authority and responsibility** This principle is also valid in all organisation. However, previously managers were empowered but now employees are empowered.

(iv) **Order** According to this principle, people and materials must be in suitable places at appropriate time for maximum efficiency. This principle is also universally applicable and still has a relevance.

(v) **Equity** Unless and until, the employees are treated with equity, without any bias and prejudices, the organisation's environment cannot remain healthy. Thus, this principle is also universally applicable.

Case Based Questions

Case 1

Super Enterprises has been a successful business enterprise in India. Recently, it found that there was dissatisfaction among the employees due to low pay and benefits. The company took timely action of assuring the employees an increase in their salary and productivity bonus.

This was done to the satisfaction of the employees. The management of the company realised that the performance of the employees improved and the company was able to maximise output at a competitive cost.

However, there was a group workers who did not want to cooperate with the organisation and the other employees. The manager Mr. R was worried that this would bring down the spirit of the whole team.

So, he resolved this issue by having discussions with the group of workers and explaining to them the importance of cooperation among the employees. ***ISC Sem I 2021***

(i) The principle of management applied by Super Enterprises by taking 'Timely action' is
- (a) stability of tenure
- (b) subordination of individual interest to general interest
- (c) remuneration
- (d) order

Ans (c) remuneration

(ii) Which characteristics of management is highlighted in the timely action taken by Super Enterprises?
- (a) Management is both art and science
- (b) Management is universal
- (c) Management is an intangible
- (d) Management is dynamic

Ans (d) Management is dynamic

(iii) The manager Mr. R was worried about the violation of one of Fayol's principles of management. Identify the principle.
- (a) Esprit de corps
- (b) Initiative
- (c) Order
- (d) Equity

Ans (a) Esprit de corps

(iv) Which principle of management states that all employees should be treated with justice and kindness without discrimination?
- (a) Unity of direction
- (b) Subordination of individual interest to group interest
- (c) Equity
- (d) Scalar chain

Ans (c) Equity

(v) The knowledge on management is drawn from several subject like Economics, Psychology, etc. When characteristic of management is highlighted in this statement?
- (a) Management is multi-disciplinary
- (b) Management is a distinct entity
- (c) Management is both art and science
- (d) Management is an intangible

Ans (a) Management is multi-disciplinary

Common Mistake Students usually do not focus on the concept given in case. They need to focus on complete understanding of concept given in the paragraph. Before starting the reading of paragraph, first read questions and then try to solve as per demand and requirement of question.

Case 2

Aapka Vidyalaya' believes in the holistic development of students and encourages team building through a mix of curricular, co-curricular and sports activities. On its Founder's Day, a stage performance had to be put up. A committee of ten prefects was constituted to plan different aspects of the function. They all decided to use recycled paper for decoration.

There was a spirit of unity and harmony and all the members supported each other. With mutual trust and a sense of belonging, the programme was systematically planned and executed. Kartik, one of the prefects, realised that the group had unknowingly applied one of the principles of management while planning and executing the programme. He was so inspired by the success of this function that he asked his father to apply the same principle in his business. His father replied that he was already using this principle. ***ISC Sem I Specimen 2021***

(i) Identify the principle of management applied for the success of the programme.
(a) Espirit de corps (b) Unity of direction
(c) Authority and responsibility
(d) Division of work

Ans (a) Espirit de corps

(ii) Who had advocated this principle?
(a) Henry Fayol (b) FW Taylor
(c) George Terry (d) James Lundy

Ans (a) Henry Fayol

(iii) Who is considered as the father of scientific management?
(a) Henry Fayol (b) FW Taylor
(c) George Terry (d) James Lundy

Ans (b) FW Taylor

(iv) Who is considered as the father of modern management?
(a) Lawrence Appley (b) Peter Drucker
(c) George Terry (d) Henry Fayol

Ans (b) Peter Drucker

(v) Principles of management
(a) are considered as the fundamental statements of truth.
(b) explain the relationship between two constants.
(c) increase efficiency. (d) clarify the thinking.

Ans (b) explain the relationship between two constants.

Case 3

Nutan Tiffin Box service was started in Mumbai by the Mumbai Dabbawalas. The Dabbawalas who are the soul of entire Mumbai aim to provide prompt and efficient services by providing tasty homemade tiffin to all office goers at the right time and place. The service is uninterrupted even on the days of bad weather, political unrest and social disturbances. Recently, they have started online booking system through their website 'mydabbawala.com'. Owing to their tremendous popularity amongst the happy and satisfied customers and members, the Dabbawalas were invited as guest lecturer by top business schools. The Dabbawalas operate in a group of 25-30 people along with a group leader. Each group teams up with other groups in order to deliver the tiffins on time. They are not transferred on frequent basis as they have to remember the addresses of their customers. They follow certain rules while doing trade-no alcohol during working hours; no leaves without permission; wearing white caps and carrying ID cards during business hours.

Recently, on the suggestion of a few self-motivated fellow men, the Dabbawalas thought out and executed a plan of providing food left in tiffins by customers to slum children. They have instructed their customers to place red sticker if food is left in the tiffin, to be fed to poor children later. ***ISC Sem I Specimen 2021***

(i) Which principle of management given by Fayol is mentioned in the above case?
(a) Order (b) Equity
(c) Centralisation (d) Espirit de corps

Ans (a) Order

(ii) Which characteristics of management are highlighted in the above case?
(a) Management is multi-disciplinary
(b) Management is goal-oriented
(c) Management helps in minimisation of cost
(d) Management ensures profitability

Ans (b) Management is goal oriented

(iii) Management is important because it helps in
(a) achievement of group goals
(b) change and innovation
(c) discipline and morale (d) creativity

Ans (a) achievement of group goals

(iv) Management can be termed as
(a) a science and an art. (b) an art and a profession.
(c) a profession and a science.
(d) a science, an art and a profession.

Ans (d) a science, an art and a profession.

(v) One of the objectives of management is
(a) development of people. (b) development of nation.
(c) higher standard of living.
(d) generation of employment.

Ans (a) development of people.

CHAPTER TEST

01 Mark Questions

1. Which of the following best describes the principles of management?
(a) They help managers take decisions while performing managerial functions
(b) They denote a cause and effect relationship
(c) They are guidelines for further action in management functions
(d) All of the above

2. Which of the following describes the principle of harmony, not discord?
(a) The management should properly investigate any task
(b) The management should engage in scientific enquiry
(c) The management should focus on observation and analysis
(d) The management should share the gains or profits of a company with their workers

3. Which of the following is the main objective of the principle of order?
(a) It focuses on providing orderly arrangements for the resources within an organisation
(b) It concentrates on building a framework for giving orders to the employees within an organisation
(c) It focuses on creating a framework for receiving orders from the top management within an organisation
(d) None of the above

4. The principles of management are universal in nature. State true or false.

5. Management principles are formed by experience and collective wisdom of managers. State true or false.

6. The principles of management emphasis logical decision-making and avoiding bias or prejudice at all costs. The above statement points out that knowledge of these principles help in ....

7. Henri Fayol is known as ....

8. Which principle of scientific management says that employees must be rewarded when they make suggestions that lead to cost savings within the company?

9. What is gang plank?

10. **Assertion** (A) Each member of the organisation should receive orders only from one superior.

Reason (R) Management principles are applied differently under different situations.

Alternatives
(a) Both Assertion (A) and Reason (R) are true and Reason (R) is the correct explanation of Assertion (A)
(b) Both Assertion (A) and Reason (R) are true, but Reason (R) is not the correct explanation of Assertion (A)
(c) Both Assertion (A) and Reason (R) are true
(d) Both Assertion (A) and Reason (R) are false

02 Marks Questions

11. Define scientific management.

12. Explain the principle 'Science, not rule of thumb'.

13. Give one reason, why Fayol's principles of management are universal?

14. How do management principles help in 'fulfilling social responsibility'?

03/04/05 Marks Questions

15. Explain the following principles
(i) Equity (ii) Initiative
(iii) Esprit de corps

16. Write short notes on the following
(i) Scalar chain
(ii) Division of work

17. Explain the nature of principles of management by giving any five points.

Answers

1. (d) All of the above
2. (d) The management should share the gains or profits of a company with their workers
3. (a) It focuses on providing orderly arrangements for the resources within an organisation
4. True
5. True
6. scientific decision-making
7. the father of general management
10. (b) Both Assertion (A) and Reason (R) are true, but Reason (R) is not the correct explanation of Assertion (A)

08

Functions of Management

TREND ANALYSIS 5 YEARS

Topic		Types of Questions	2024	2023	2020	2019	2018
		Average No. of Questions Across all Sets					
TOPIC 01	Introduction to Functions, Planning	1 Mark	—	2	—	—	—
		2 Marks	—	—	—	—	—
		3/4/5 Marks	2	1	1	2	1
TOPIC 02	Organising	1 Mark	1	—	—	—	—
		2 Marks	—	—	—	—	—
		3/4/5 Marks	1	1	1	1	1
TOPIC 03	Staffing	1 Mark	1	—	—	—	—
		2 Marks	—	—	1	1	1
		3/4/5 Marks	1	1	2	—	1
TOPIC 04	Directing	1 Mark	2	—	—	—	—
		2 Marks	—	1	1	1	1
		3/4/5 Marks	1	1	2	2	2
TOPIC 05	Controlling	1 Mark	—	—	—	—	—
		2 Marks	—	1	—	—	—
		3/4/5 Marks	1	1	—	1	—
TOPIC 06	Coordination	1 Mark	—	1	—	—	—
		2 Marks	—	—	—	—	—
		3/4/5 Marks	—	—	—	—	1

TOPIC 1

Functions of Management and Planning

Functions of Management

Management has been defined as a process of getting things done with the aim of achieving goals effectively and efficiently. Process, in this definition means a series of functions performed by the management.

Functions of management can be categorised as

(i) **Managerial functions** They are common to all enterprises. The managerial functions are planning, organising, staffing, directing and controlling.

(ii) **Operative functions** They differ from organisation to organisation. Production, purchase, marketing, finance and personnel are the different operative functions.

Functions of Management According to Different Management Thinkers

Different management thinkers have stipulated the following functions of management

(i) According to **Henry Fayol** Planning and forecasting, organising, commanding, coordinating and controlling.

(ii) According to **George R Terry** Planning, organising, actuating and controlling.

(iii) According to **Luther Gullick** Planning, organising, directing, staffing, coordinating, reporting, budgeting, coined as acronym- 'PODSCORB'.

(iv) According to **Harold Koontz and Cyril O' Donnell** Planning, organising, staffing, directing and controlling. Koontz and O'Donnell considered coordination as the 'essence of management'.

(v) **According to Ernest Dale** Planning, organising, staffing, direction, control, innovation, representation.

Meaning of Planning

Planning is deciding in advance the objectives to be achieved during a given period, formulating alternative courses of action to achieve them and selecting the best course of action. It involves selection of objectives to be achieved and policies and procedures to be followed, etc.

According to **Theo Haimann**, "Planning is deciding in advance what is to be done. In future when a manager plans, he projects a course of action for the future, attempting to achieve a consistent and coordinated structure of operations aimed at the desired results."

Features of Planning

Following are the features of planning which throw light on its nature and scope

(i) **Planning is a primary function** Planning lays down the base for other functions of management. All other managerial functions are performed within the framework of the plans drawn.

(ii) **Planning is goal oriented** Planning starts with the determination of objectives. It identifies the actions that would lead to the desired results quickly and economically. It contributes to the achievement of predetermined goals.

(iii) **Planning is pervasive** It is required at all levels of management as well as in all the departments of the organisation.

(iv) **Planning is continuous** Planning is an ongoing process as it follows a cycle. Once a plan is drawn, it is implemented, followed by another plan and so on.

(v) **Planning is futuristic** Planning is essentially looking ahead. It is prepared for the future. The purpose of planning is to meet future events effectively.

(vi) **Planning involves decision-making and choice** Planning is essentially, the process of choosing among various alternatives. So, in order to make a choice, examination and evaluation of each alternative is necessary.

(vii) **Planning is an intellectual process** Planning is a mental exercise as it requires creativity, imagination and higher thinking with sound judgement.

(viii) **Planning aims at efficiency** Planning is done to achieve desired objectives at minimum cost by optimising the utilisation of resources.

Importance of Planning

Following points highlight the importance of planning

(i) **Focuses on objectives** Objectives or goals to be achieved are decided before plans are drawn. The objectives decided serve as guidelines for future course of actions.

(ii) **Planning provides direction and make activities meaningful** It clearly defines what employees have to do, when to do, how to do and for whom to do.

(iii) **Planning reduces the risk of uncertainties** Planning is an activity, which enables a manager to look ahead and anticipate changes and deal with changes and uncertain events.

(iv) **Planning reduces overlapping and wasteful activities** Planning serves as a base for coordination. Various activities of different departments and divisions are carried on in an effective manner, which reduces overlapping and wasteful activities.

(v) **Planning promotes innovative ideas** Planning requires high thinking and it is an intellectual process, so there is a great scope of finding better ideas and better methods to perform a particular job.

(vi) **Planning facilitates decision-making** Planning helps the manager to look into the future and choose from amongst the various alternative courses of action.

(vii) **Planning establishes standards for controlling** Planning provides the standards against which actual performance is measured. It helps in finding deviations and thus, we can say planning provides the basis for controlling.

Limitations of Planning

Following are the limitations of planning

(i) **Planning leads to rigidity** When in an organisation, a well defined plan is drawn, then a manager may not be in a position to change it. This leads to rigidity.

(ii) **Planning reduces creativity** Planning is done by the top management and due to this, much of the initiative or creativity inherent in middle and lower level managers or other members gets lost or reduced.

(iii) **Planning involves huge cost** Planning is an expensive process. Money, time and lots of efforts have to be spent in planning and forecasting.

(iv) **Planning is a time consuming process** Sometimes, plans to be drawn up take so much of time that there is not much time left for their effective implementation.

(v) **Lack of accuracy** Plans may be misleading and inaccurate due to lack of reliable data, errors in judgement, lack of experience, etc.

(vi) **External limitations** These can be due to
- (a) Unforeseen events and changes.
- (b) Change in social, technological, economic environment.
- (c) Political interference.
- (d) Competitors' strategies.

(vii) **False sense of security** Following a predetermined path in a dynamic environment may lead to a placid attitude and leads to failure of plans.

Process/Steps of Planning

As we all know, planning is to decide in advance what to do and how to do in future. It is an activity, which follows certain logical steps

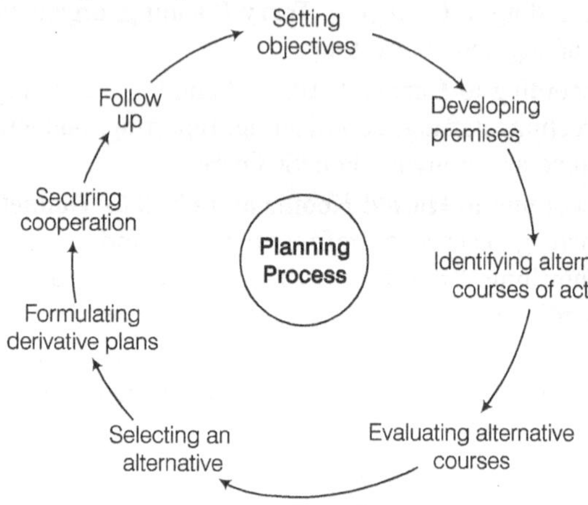

Process of Planning

(i) **Setting objectives** The first step in planning is to define and describe clearly the objectives of the organisation as a whole.

(ii) **Developing premises** Planning is concerned with future, which is uncertain. Therefore, the manager is required to make certain assumptions about the future and these assumptions are known as premises.

(iii) **Identifying alternative courses of action** After objectives and planning premises are established, it is necessary to collect and analyse all relevant information. It is desirable to identify those alternatives, which are strategic, promising or directly related to the situation.

(iv) **Evaluating alternative courses** The next step is to weigh the pros and cons of each alternative and evaluate each alternative in the light of the objectives to be achieved.

(v) **Selecting an alternative** The best plan has to be adopted and implemented and the selection of such an alternative is made by the manager.

(vi) **Formulating derivative plans** After the basic plan is decided, a detailed/derivative plan is formulated which defines the policies, procedures, rules, programmes, budgets, etc.

(vii) **Securing cooperation** Plans can only be successful if they are whole heartedly accepted by all the members.

(viii) **Follow up action** Plans should be reviewed periodically to ensure its relevance and effectiveness.

Types of Plans

Following are the various types of plans

(i) **Objective** Every organisation is established to achieve some purpose, which is stated as it's objective. These are the ends results to be achieved. Therefore, in simple words, objectives are stated as 'for what an organisation strives for'.

Following are the **features** of objectives

(a) They are clearly and specifically defined.
(b) They are expressed in quantitative terms.
(c) They are time-bound.
(d) They must be acceptable and achievable.
(e) They specify the Key Result Areas (KRAs), where deviations should not occur.
(f) They should be flexible and adaptable to change.

(ii) **Policy** It is a general statement that defines the boundaries, within which decisions are made and they direct decisions towards the accomplishment of objectives. Policy comes under the standing plan, as it answers to recurring problems of a similar nature e.g. Policy of organisation regarding expulsion of employee, promotion of employee, etc.

Following are the **features** of policies

(a) It is a type of standing plan.
(b) It is a broad guideline specifying the way to achieve objectives.
(c) It helps in decision-making and judgement.
(d) Major and minor policies are framed for outsiders and insiders respectively.
(e) It provides the route to reach the goals.

(iii) **Procedure** It describes the exact manner, in which a certain activity is to be performed. It is a chronological sequence of steps to be taken. These are designed to execute policies and achieve objectives.

These also come under the standing plan, as they prescribe ways to handle routine problems.

Following are the **features** of procedures

(a) They are decided on the basis of objectives and policies.
(b) They are standardised in all respects, *viz* material, machines, techniques, etc.
(c) They are evaluated periodically to adapt to changes.
(d) They are not based an guess work, but on logical reasoning.

(iv) **Method** It provides the prescribed ways or manner, in which a task has to be performed considering the objectives. Methods are formalised and standardised ways of accomplishing repetitive and routine jobs and thus, are considered as standing plans.

Following are the **features** of methods

(a) It is a type of standing plan.
(b) It is formed on the basis of planned operations and procedures.
(c) It helps in day-to-day working and smooth operations of business.
(d) It helps to save time, money and effort of resources.
(e) It is one of the steps of 'procedure'.

(v) **Rules** These are specific statements that inform what is to be done. There is no discretion allowed in rules, as they must be followed strictly and one cannot make any changes in them.

Following are the **features** of rules

(a) These deal with specific situation.
(b) These help to control behaviour of the employees.
(c) These are not flexible.
(d) These facilitate discipline in the organisation.
(e) These may be a part of a procedure.

(vi) **Programme** It is a detailed statement about a project which outlines the objectives, policies, procedures, budgets which are to be implemented in the project.

It is a concrete action plan indicating how, when and by whom work is to be done.

It also comes under the single-use plans, as it is developed for a particular project.

Following are the **features** of programme

(a) It is a type of single-use plan.
(b) It is formed on the basis of objectives and policies.
(c) It includes the minutest details of work to be done.
(d) It facilitates smooth functioning in the organisation.

(vii) **Budget** A budget is a statement of expected results expressed in numerical or financial terms. It is a projection designed to define the anticipated costs and results in numerical terms of a single project. Thus, it comes under the category of single-use plan.

Following are the **features** of budget

(a) It is prepared for a specific future time period.

(b) It is directed towards a specific goal.

(c) It helps to reflect cost and cash flows involved in an activity.

(d) It is expressed in quantitative/numeric terms.

Comparison Among Types of Plans

Basis	Objectives	Policy	Procedure	Method	Programme	Rules	Budget
Meaning	These are the end results to be achieved.	It defines the boundaries within which decisions are made.	It states the exact manner for performing a particular activity.	It states the way in which a task is to be performed.	It is a detailed statement including objectives, strategies, policies, rules, budgets, etc.	It informs what is to be done and what not.	It is a statement of expected results in numerical terms.
Type of plan	Single-use plan	Standing plan	Standing plan	Standing plan	Single-use plan	Standing plan	Single-use plan
Purpose	It is the base of planning process.	It links the enterprise to its environment.	It helps in easy conduct of activities.	It helps in speedy completion of tasks.	It arranges activities and resources to complete a project.	It facilitates in regulated working in the enterprise.	It helps in efficient use of resources.
Focus	It focuses on achievement of goals.	It focuses on thinking and decision-making.	It focuses on routinising recurring jobs.	It focuses on achieving efficiency and economy.	It focuses on successful launch of a project.	It focuses on maintaining discipline.	It focuses on time bound achievement of goals.

PYQs Previous Years' Questions

1 Mark Questions

1. The type of plan considered as a guide to decision making in repetitive situation is called *ISC 2023*

(a) policy (b) rule (c) programme (d) strategy

Ans (a) policy

2. A .... is a comprehensive plan designed to implement the policies and accomplish the objectives of an organisation. *ISC 2023*

Ans programme

3. Which function of management emphasises on thinking before taking an action? *ISC Sem I 2021*

(a) Planning (b) Organising (c) Staffing (d) Directing

Ans (a) Planning

4. Despite changes in the environment, the management of a company continues with the existing plans. Which limitation of planning is highlighted in this case? *ISC Sem I 2021*

(a) Human elements (b) Psychological barrier

(c) Rigidity (d) Time consuming

Ans (c) Rigidity

5. Programme as a type of plan is *ISC Sem I 2021*

(a) a single use, comprehensive plan

(b) an action plan to face environmental uncertainties

(c) manner in which activities are to be performed

(d) a penalty for violation laid down

Ans (a) a single-use, comprehensive plan

6. A budget is considered as *ISC Sem I 2021*

(a) a single-use plan

(b) a standing plan

(c) a single-use as well as a standing plan

(d) neither a single use nor a standing plan

Ans (a) a single-use plan

7. Which of the following types of plan does not allow for any flexibility or discretion? *ISC Sem I Specimen 2021*

(a) Rule

(b) Policy

(c) Strategy

(d) Procedure

Ans (a) Rule

8. Planning requires logical and systematic thinking rather than guesswork or wishful thinking. Which feature of planning is highlighted in the above case? ***ISC Sem I Specimen 2021***

(a) Planning focuses on achieving objectives
(b) Planning is a mental exercise
(c) Planning is the primary function of management
(d) Planning is pervasive

Ans (b) Planning is a mental exercise

9. Which of the following statements is not true with reference to planning? ***ISC Sem I Specimen 2021***

(a) Planning is a pre-requisite for controlling
(b) Planning does not lead to rigidity
(c) Planning enables a manager to look ahead and anticipate changes
(d) Planning facilitates co-ordination among departments and individuals in the organisation

Ans (b) Planning does not lead to rigidity

10. The following is not a type of plan ***ISC Sem I Specimen 2021***

(a) Policy (b) Procedure
(c) Budget (d) Values of an organisation

Ans (d) Values of an organisation

11. Which type of a plan is 'offering 30% jobs to women in an organisation'? ***ISC Sem I Specimen 2021***

(a) Policy (b) Rule
(c) Procedure (d) Programme

Ans (a) Policy

12. Which type of a plan is a chronological sequence of steps to be taken in a pre-determined order? ***ISC Sem I Specimen 2021***

(a) Rule (b) Programme
(c) Procedure (d) Objective

Ans (c) Procedure

13. 'Office phone should not be used for personal calls'. This type of a plan is a ***ISC Sem I Specimen 2021***

(a) rule (b) policy
(c) procedure (d) objective

Ans (a) rule

14. One of the limitations of the planning function of management is ***ISC Sem I Specimen 2021***

(a) once plans are formulated people tend to strictly adhere to them
(b) planning bridges the gap between the present and the future
(c) planning reduces the risk of uncertainty
(d) planning is an economical process

Ans (a) once plans are formulated people tend to strictly adhere to them

15. Which statement given below cannot be used to describe budget as a type of plan? ***ISC Sem I Specimen 2021***

(a) Budgets are quantitative statements indicating expected results and expenditure required to achieve the results
(b) A budget reflects capital outlay
(c) A budget is a plan of action designed to achieve a specific goal
(d) A budget is designed to achieve discipline and order

Ans (d) A budget is designed to achieve discipline and order

2 Marks Questions

1. What is referred to as 'PODSCORB'? ***ISC 2001***

Ans Luther Gullick specified the functions of management as an acronym 'PODSCORB'

Where; P $\rightarrow$ Planning, O $\rightarrow$ Organising
D $\rightarrow$ Directing, S $\rightarrow$ Staffing
CO $\rightarrow$ Coordinating, R $\rightarrow$ Reporting
B $\rightarrow$ Budgeting

2. Give the broad categories of functions of management. ***ISC 2000***

Ans Functions of management can be categorised as

(i) **Managerial functions** They are common to all enterprises. The managerial functions are planning, organising, staffing, directing and controlling.

(ii) **Operative functions** They differ from organisation to organisation. Production, purchase, marketing, finance and personnel are the different operative functions.

Concept Enhancer Management is defined as a process of getting things done with the aim of achieving goals effectively and efficiently. Here, process means a series of functions performed by the management.

3/4/5 Marks Questions

1. Though planning is an important function of management, it may not always give desired results.

Justify this statement by explaining any four limitations of planning. ***ISC 2024 (4M)***

Or Sometimes effective plans fail to achieve the desired result. In the light of this statement, explain any four limitations of planning. ***ISC Specimen 2023 (4M)***

Or Planning is not a guarantee of success. In this context, explain the limitations of planning. ***ISC 2018, 2000 (4M)***

Or Define planning. Write any three limitations of planning. **ISC 2012 (4M)**

Or Explain any two limitations of planning. **ISC 2000**

Ans Planning is deciding in advance the objectives to be achieved during a given period, formulating alternative courses of action to achieve them and selecting the best course of action.

According to **Theo Haimann**, "Planning is deciding in advance what is to be done. When a manager plans, he projects a course of action for the future, attempting to achieve a consistent and coordinated structure of operations aimed at the desired results."

Following are the limitations of planning

(i) **Planning leads to rigidity** When in an organisation, a well defined plan is drawn, then a manager may not be in a position to change it. This leads to rigidity.

(ii) **Planning reduces creativity** Planning is done by the top management and due to this, much of the initiative or creativity inherent in middle and lower level managers or other members gets lost or reduced.

(iii) **Planning involves huge cost** Planning is an expensive process. Money, time and lots of efforts have to be spent in planning and forecasting.

(iv) **Planning is a time consuming process** Sometimes, plans to be drawn up take so much of time that there is not much time left for their effective implementation.

Concept Enhancer Planning does not guarantee success, i.e. following a predetermined path in a dynamic environment may lead to a placid attitude and leads to failure of plans.

2. Explain method as a type of plan. **ISC 2024 (3M)**

Ans Method provides the prescribed ways or manner, in which a task has to be performed considering the objectives. Methods are formalised and standardised ways of accomplishing repetitive and routine jobs and thus, are considered as standing plans.

Following are the **features** of methods

(i) It is a type of standing plan.

(ii) It is formed on the basis of planned operations and procedures.

(iii) It helps in day-to-day working and smooth operations of business.

(iv) It helps to save time, money and effort of resources.

(v) It is one of the steps of 'procedure'.

3. Planning is of vital importance in the managerial process. Give any four reasons to support this statement. **ISC 2023 (4M)**

Or

Explain any three points of importance of planning. **ISC 2019 (3M)**

Or

'Planning is beneficial to all'. In the light of this statement, discuss the importance of planning. **ISC 2015 (5M)**

Ans Following are the points that highlight the importance of planning

(i) **Focuses on objectives** Objectives or goals to be achieved are decided before plans are drawn. The objectives decided serve as guidelines for future course of actions.

(ii) **Planning provides direction and make activities meaningful** It clearly defines what employees have to do, when to do, how to do and for whom to do.

(iii) **Planning reduces the risk of uncertainties** Planning is an activity, which enables a manager to look ahead and anticipate changes and deal with changes and uncertain events.

(iv) **Planning reduces overlapping and wasteful activities** Planning serves as a base for coordination. Various activities of different departments and divisions are carried on in an effective manner, which reduces the overlapping and wasteful activities.

(v) **Planning promotes innovative ideas** Planning requires high thinking and it is an intellectual process, so there is a great scope of finding better ideas and better methods to perform a particular job.

Value Points

For getting maximum marks, following points can be included in the answer

- Guidelines for future course of action.
- Base for coordination.

4. Explain the first five steps involved in the process of planning, as a function of management. **ISC 2020 (5M)**

Ans First five steps in the process of planning are

(i) Setting objectives

(ii) Developing premises

(iii) Identifying alternative courses of action

(iv) Evaluating alternative courses of action

(v) Selecting an alternative

For explanation, refer to text on page 88.

5. Discuss any four features of objectives, as a type of a plan. *ISC 2019 (4M)*

Ans Features of objectives are

(i) They are clearly and specifically defined in quantitative terms.
(ii) They are acceptable and achievable.
(iii) They should be flexible and adaptable to change.
(iv) They specify key result areas, where deviations should not occur.

6. Explain any four features of a budget. *ISC Specimen 2018, 17 (4M)*

Ans Four features of a budget are explained below

(i) **Budget is prepared for a specific future time period** Budget is a statement of expected results which are expressed in numerical terms and which relate to a specific future time period . It always has a reference of time. e.g. Budget for the month of February, budget for 2016-17 etc.

(ii) **Budget is a single-use plan** Budget is a projection designed to define the anticipated costs and results in numerical terms of a single project. Thus, it is a single-use plan.

Features of Budget
- Budget is prepared for a specific future time period
- Budget is a single-use plan
- Budget aims toward a specific goal
- It is quantitative in nature

(iii) **Budget aims toward a specific goal** Budget is prepared for the achievement of a specific goal. It has no relevance without pre-defined goals and objectives.

(iv) **It is quantitative in nature** A budget reflects the outcomes of a project in quantitative or numerical terms.

7. Write a short note on programme, as a type of plan. *ISC Specimen 2018, 17 (4M)*

Ans Programmes are the detailed statements about a project which outline the objectives, policies, procedures, budgets etc. which are to be implemented in the project. These are concrete action plans indicating how, when and by whom work is to bc done. These also come under the single-use plans, as they are developed for a particular project.

Following are the features of programme

(i) It is a type of single use plan.
(ii) It is formed on the basis of objectives and policies.
(iii) It includes the minutest details of work to be done.
(iv) It facilitates smooth functioning in the organisation.

8. Distinguish between method and procedure. *ISC 2016 (3M)*

Ans Difference between method and procedure

Basis	Procedure	Method
Meaning	It states the exact manner for performing a particular activity.	It states the way in which a task is to be performed.
Purpose	It helps in easy conduct of activities.	It helps in speedy completion of tasks.
Focus	It focusses on routinising recurring jobs.	It focusses on achieving efficiency and economy.

9. Write the meaning of following types of plans *ISC 2014 (3M)*

(i) Policy (ii) Procedure (iii) Method

Ans (i) **Policy** It is a general statement that defines the boundaries, within which decisions are made and they direct decisions towards the accomplishment of objectives.

Policy comes under the standing plan, as it answers to recurring problems of a similar nature. e.g. Policy of organisation regarding expulsion of employee, promotion of employee, etc.

(ii) **Procedure** It describes the exact manner, in which a certain activity is to be performed. It is a chronological sequence of steps to be taken. These are designed to execute policies and achieve objectives. These also come under the standing plan, as they prescribe ways to handle routine problems. e.g. Procedure may be for purchase of raw material, selection of employees, redressal of grievances, etc.

(iii) **Method** Refer to Q.No. 2 (3/4/5 Marks) on page 92.

10. Explain the features of planning as a function of management. *ISC 2014 (4M)*

Or List any two features of planning as a function of management. *ISC 2010*

Ans Features of planning as a function of management are

(i) **Planning is a primary function** Planning precedes all other functions of management. It provides basis and direction to managerial efforts. Planning serves as a guide for organising, staffing, directing and controlling. The management process starts with planning and all other functions follows it.

Features of Planning
- Planning is a primary function
- Planning is pervasive
- Planning is continuous
- Planning is futuristic

(ii) **Planning is pervasive** It means, it is required in all types of organisation, whether big or small, business or non-business, social, political or religious in all departments of an organisation and at all levels of management, i.e. top, middle and lower.

(iii) **Planning is continuous** Plans are made for a specific period of time. At the end of that period, new plans are laid down. Thus, planning is a continuous activity. As a matter of fact, the planning process continues till the existence of enterprise.

(iv) **Planning is futuristic** Planning essentially involves looking ahead and preparing for the future.

The purpose of planning is to meet future events effectively to the best advantage of an organisation.

11. Explain any five functions of the management of an organisation. ***ISC 2006, 02***

Or

'To manage is to forecast and plan, to organise, to command, to coordinate and to control.' Discuss. ***ISC 2004***

Ans The functions of management refer to those activities which are required to be undertaken for the achievement of organisational goals.
Following are the functions of management (any five)

(i) **Planning** It is the primary function of management. It involves determinations of objectives and selecting a course of action.
As ME Hurley has said, "Planning is deciding in advance what is to be done. It involves the selection of objective, policies, procedures and programmes from among various alternatives."
Planning is an intellectual process and is closely connected with creativity and innovation. Planning provides a rational approach for achieving predetermined objectives.

(ii) **Organising** Once the plans are established for the accomplishment of an organisational goal, the organising function examines the activities and resources required to implement the plan. Organising function involves grouping of the required tasks into manageable departments and establishing the authority responsibility relationship.

According to Henry Fayol, "To organise a business means to provide it with everything useful for its functioning-raw materials, tools, capital and personnel."

(iii) **Staffing** Staffing simply stated, is finding the right people for the right job. It is concerned with human resources of an organisation.

It refers to the managerial function of recruiting, selecting, developing and motivating human resource for achievement of organisational goals.

As Koontz and O' Donnell has put it, "The managerial function of staffing involves manning the organisational structure through proper and effective selection, appraisal and development of personnel to fill the roles designed in the structure".

(iv) **Directing** It is also known as the 'commanding' or 'actuating' function, since it is concerned with the execution of plans.

Directing is the process of instructing, guiding, supervising, motivating and leading the subordinates. It is concerned with the execution of plans through organised action. Therefore, it is also called 'management in action'.

According to Koontz and O' Donnell, "Direction is a complex function that includes all those activities which are designed to encourage subordinates to work efficiently and effectively."

(v) **Controlling** It refers to measurement of performance, comparing it with standards and taking corrective actions.

Controlling function of a manager is a pervasive function. Managers at all levels of management need to perform controlling function to keep a control over activities in their areas.

As defined by Koontz and O' Donnell, "Managerial control implies the measurement of accomplishment against the standard and the correction of deviations to assure attainment of objectives according to plans."

(vi) **Coordination** It is not regarded as a separate function, but it is considered as the essence of management. It involves synchronisation of different actions, so that planned objectives can be achieved with minimum conflict.

Coordination is a deliberate action on the part of management to achieve unity of action.

As defined by Mooney and Railey,
"Coordination is the orderly arrangement of group efforts to provide unity of action in the pursuit of a common purpose."

Common Mistake Sometimes, students are not able to recall all functions of management. So, they should use the acromym 'PODSCORB' to recall all functions.

12. Comment briefly on 'planning provides the basis of control'. *ISC 2005*

KEY IDEA
In order to understand these type of questions, we should focus on the key words of the statement and then correlation of the basic concepts.

Ans Planning involves setting of goals. The entire managerial process is concerned with accomplishing predetermined goals through planning, organising, staffing, directing and controlling.

Planning provides the goals or standards against which actual performance is measured.

Then, by measuring actual performance, managers are able to see whether they have been able to achieve the goals.

This enables them to find out the deviations and take corrective actions. Only when the standards are set, then only we can find out the deviations and take corrective actions.

Thus, we can say that planning is the basis of control.

TOPIC 2

Organising

Meaning of Organising

Organising is a process of identifying and grouping the work to be performed, defining and delegating responsibility and authority and establishing relationships for the purpose of enabling people to work most effectively together in accomplishing objectives.

According to **Henry Fayol**, "To organise a business means to provide it everything useful for its functioning *viz* raw material, tools, capital and personnels."

Features of Organising

Features of organising are

(i) **Division of work** The total work is divided into many parts, which is to be performed by one or a group of persons.

(ii) **Authority responsibility structure** The position of each employee is defined with regard to authority and responsibility.

(iii) **Grouping of activities** Activities are grouped on some common basis like functions, products, process, regions, etc.

(iv) **Installing sound communication system** It is necessary to establish a good communication system for providing information about position, authority, responsibility, duties, etc.

(v) **Flexibility** The organising process should be flexible. Thus, any changes can be dealt with effectively.

(vi) **Coordination** Different departments, units and personnel should work towards a common goal. Thus, coordination is required.

(vii) **Achieving organisational objectives** Every effort in organising process is done to ensure achievement of organisational goals.

Importance of Organising

Following points highlight the importance of organising

(i) **Benefits of specialisation** Organising facilitates the systematic allocation of work. This reduces the work load as well as enhances productivity, because the work is allocated as per specialisation.

(ii) **Clarity in working relationships** The establishment of working relationships clarifies lines of communication and specifies who is accountable to whom.

(iii) **Optimum utilisation of human resources** Organising leads to proper usage of all material, financial and human resources by proper assignment of jobs. There is avoidance of duplication of work and overlapping responsibilities among various employees.

(iv) **Training and development of personnel** Organising stimulates creativity amongst the managers. Effective delegation allows the manager to reduce their workload by assigning routine jobs to their subordinates.

(v) **Expansion and growth** Organising helps in the growth and diversification of an enterprise by enabling it to deviate from existing norms and taking up new challenges.

(vi) **Security and support** People working at assigned positions in organisations feel safe and secure.

(vii) **Adaptation to change** A properly designed organisation structure gives flexibility and adapts to the changes easily. In case of increase in workload or, addition of a product line, the structure is modified accordingly.

Process/Steps of Organising

The process/steps of organising are as follows

(i) **Identification and division of work** The first step in the process of organising involves identifying and dividing the work that has to be done in accordance with previously determined plans.

(ii) **Departmentalisation/Grouping of activities** Once, work has been divided into small and manageable activities then those activities, which are similar in nature are grouped together. This process is called 'Departmentalisation'.

(iii) **Assignment of duties** In this step, work is allocated to different individuals as per the knowledge and skills acquired by them, as it is essential for effective performance that a proper match is made between the nature of a job and the ability of an individual.

(iv) **Delegation of adequate authority** It is difficult for managers to fulfil their duties until and unless adequate authority is given to him.

(v) **Establishing reporting relationships** Each individual should know well in advance to whom he is accountable. In this step, such establishment is created, so that hierarchical structure should be followed with proper coordination.

Types of Organisation Structure

The various types of organisation structure are

1. Line (or Scalar) Organisation

Line organisation refers to direct chain of command through which authority flows from top to bottom. It is also known as 'hierarchical', or 'scalar' organisation. There is unity of command. The quantum of authority is highest at the top and reduces at the successive levels.

Features of Line Organisation

Features of line organisation are

(i) It is the simplest form of organisation.

(ii) All the orders and instructions flow from the top.

(iii) The principle of unity of command is generally observed.

Merits of Line Organisation

Merits of line organisation are

(i) It is easy to form, and the simplest form of organisation.

(ii) Decision-making takes place at a fast pace.

(iii) It has a unified supervision/control system.

(iv) Discipline is maintained due to unity of command.

(v) Responsibility and authority are clearly defined.

Demerits of Line Organisation

Demerits of line organisation are

(i) Managers are overburdened with a number of tasks and responsibility.

(ii) There is lack of specialisation in activities/departments.

(iii) It suffers from the drawbacks of autocratic leadership.

(iv) It is inflexible and has little scope of expansion.

Types of Line Organisation

Line organisation is of the following types

(i) **Pure line organisation** In this organisation, the activities at a particular level are similar. The divisions are created solely for the purpose of supervision and control.

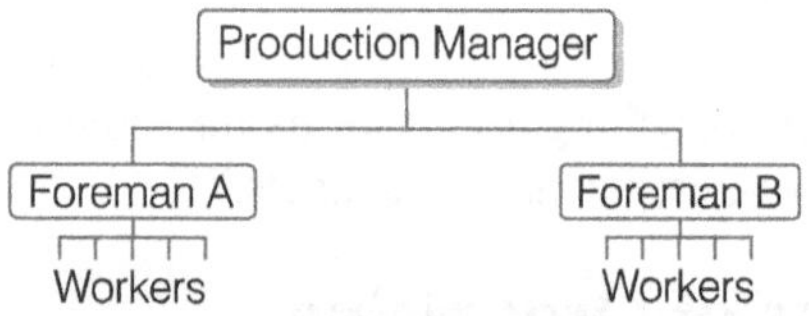

(ii) **Departmental line organisation** The organisation is divided into departments. The work here differs in various departments, but within one department similar activities are performed.

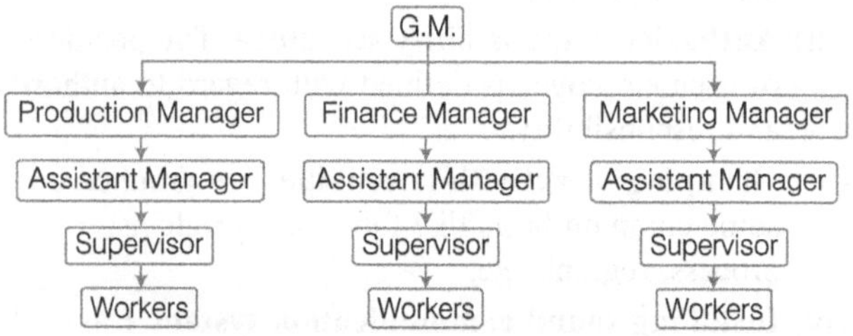

2. Line and Staff Organisation

In line and staff organisation, the structure is that of the line organisation, but staff officers i.e. the functional experts are provided to advise the line authorities. Thus, line and staff organisation is a combination of line structure and the functional structure.

In line structure too much control is there and in functional structure control is divided. Thus, it attempts to reap the benefits of both the structures.

Features of Line and Staff Organisation

Features of line and staff organisation are

(i) In this type of organisation there are two types of relationships, *viz.* line and staff.
(ii) This structures distinguishes two aspects of administration, *viz.* planning and execution.
(iii) Staff officers and line officers work independently.

Merits of Line and Staff Organisation

Merits of line and staff organisation are

(i) It enjoys the benefits of specialisation in different activities.
(ii) Specialists and experts in each area help in better decision-making.
(iii) Unity of command ensures discipline in the organisation.
(iv) There is flexibility and more chances of growth.
(v) Responsibility is adequately divided amongst different executives.

Demerits of Line and Staff Organisation

Demerits of line and staff organisation are

(i) There is a problem of coordination among different individuals/departments.
(ii) There is a lack of coordination among the executives.
(iii) Lack of accountability among staff members make them complacent.
(iv) It is more expensive than line organisation.

Difference between line organisation and line & staff organisation

Basis	Line organisation	Line & Staff organisation
Suitability	Small enterprises	Large enterprises
Departments	For basic activities	For basic and specialised activities
Degree of specialisation	Low degree of specialisation	High degree of specialisation
Economy	More economical	Less economical
Work load of managers	More	Less

3. Functional Structure

Under functional structure, each major or basic function is organised as a separate department, e.g. Production, finance, sales, etc. Functional structure is the most widely used basis for grouping activities. It exists almost in every organisation at some level.

It is most suitable when the size of the organisation is large, has a diversified activities and operations require a high degree of specialisation.

Features of Functional Organisation

Features of functional organisation are

(i) In this organisation activities of an enterprise are grouped into different departments on the basic of their functions.
(ii) It is suitable only for large organisations.
(iii) It is a complex organisation which is based on the principle of specialisation.

Merits of Functional Structure

Merits of functional structure are

(i) A functional structure provides occupational specialisation, since emphasis is placed on specific functions.
(ii) It promotes control and coordination within a department because of similarity in the tasks being carried on.
(iii) It increases managerial and operational efficiency and this results in higher profit.
(iv) It makes training of employees easier as it focuses on a limited range of skills.
(v) It ensures the performance of all activities necessary for achieving organisational objectives. Due attention can also be given to different functions.

Demerits of Functional Structure

Following are the demerits of functional structure

(i) A functional structure places less emphasis on the overall objectives of the enterprise than the objectives pursued by a functional head. Such practices may lead to functional empires wherein the importance of a particular function may be over emphasised and organisational interests may be overlooked.
(ii) As a number of sub-units gets created within a functional unit, personal contact is lost, communication becomes slow and problems of coordination and control develop.

4. Divisional Structure

In divisional organisation structure, the activities of the organisation are grouped into a number of divisions. Divisions are created when product expansion, diversification, manufacturing and marketing are being done.

It is most suitable, when the size of the organisation is large and variety of products are manufactured using different productive resources.

Features of Divisional Structure

Features of divisional structure are

(i) It promotes specialisation.
(ii) It causes decentralisation of authority.
(iii) It provides opportunity for managerial appraisal.

Merits of Divisional Structure

Merits of divisional structure are

(i) All the activities related to one type of product are grouped under one division, which brings integration and coordination in the activities.
(ii) Decisions are taken much faster in divisional structure.
(iii) It facilitates expansion and growth, as new divisions can be added without interrupting the existing operations.
(iv) It provides for accurate measurement of performance. Fixation of responsibility and accountability is easy.

Demerits of Divisional Structure

Demerits of divisional structure are

(i) There is a duplication of physical facilities and functions.
(ii) It suffers from the problem of underutilisation of plant capacity.
(iii) Managers in each department focus on their own product, without thinking of the whole organisation.
(iv) Conflict may arise between different divisions on allocation of funds and other resources.

Difference between Functional Structure and Divisional Structure

Basis	Functional structure	Divisional structure
Formation	It is formed on the basis of functions.	Its formation is based on the product lines and is supported by functions.
Specialisation	Functional specialisation, hence economical.	Product specialisation, hence costly.
Coordination	Difficult for a multi-product company.	Easy, because all functions related to a particular product are integrated in one department.

Formal Organisation

An organisation structure, which is designed and established by the management to achieve organisational goals, is termed as formal organisation. It is an official system of clearly defined activities and relationships, which are intended to divide and integrate the activities of the organisation.

Features of Formal Organisation

Some important features of formal organisation are

(i) It is a means to achieve objectives specified in the plans.
(ii) It facilitates interlinking of various departments, levels and people in the organisation.
(iii) It is deliberately designed by the top management.
(iv) It places more emphasis on work rather than interpersonal relations.
(v) It clarifies relationships and helps to known who has to report to whom.

Merits of Formal Organisation

Merits of formal organisation are

(i) **Fixation of responsibility** In formal organisation, it is easier to fix responsibility, since mutual relationships among the members are clearly defined.
(ii) **Clarity of roles** Under this, there is a clarity of jobs to be performed by members of the organisation. This helps in avoiding duplication of work.
(iii) **Unity of command** It is maintained through an established chain of command.
(iv) **Effective accomplishment of goals** It leads to effective accomplishment of goals by providing rules and procedures and by placing more emphasis on work.
(v) **Stability in the organisation** There is stability in the organisation because behaviour of employees can be accurately predicted, since there are specific rules to guide them.

Demerits of Formal Organisation

Demerits of formal organisation are

(i) **Delay in decision-making** Established chain of command and communication may lead to procedural delays.
(ii) **Lack of creative efforts** Rigid laid down policies may not provide adequate recognition to creative talent.

Informal Organisation

An organisational structure, which is the result of social relationships and interaction among people, is termed as informal organisation. This type of structure is unplanned and arises spontaneously from within the formal organisational structure.

Features of Informal Organisation

Some important features of informal organisation are

(i) It originates from within the formal organisation, due to interaction among employees.
(ii) The standard of behaviour evolves from group norms.

(iii) Communication is free and independent.
(iv) It emerges spontaneously and is not created deliberately.
(v) It has no definite structure or form.

Merits of Informal Organisation

Various merits of informal organisation are

(i) **Faster spread of information** Under informal organisation, fixed lines of communication are not followed. Thus, informal organisation leads to faster spread of information as well as quick feedback.

(ii) **Fulfilment of social needs** It helps to fulfil the social needs of the members of the organisation. This enhances their job satisfaction, since it gives them a sense of belongingness in the organisation.

(iii) **Fills inadequacies of formal structure** It contributes towards fulfilment of organisational objectives by compensating for inadequacies in the formal organisation, e.g. Employees reactions towards plans and policies can be tested through informal network.

Demerits of Informal Organisation

Demerits of informal organisation are

(i) **Rumours** Informal organisation may create rumours, which go against the interest of formal organisation.

(ii) **Resistance to change** Informal groups unite together and oppose changes due to which growth of an organisation suffers.

Difference between Formal Organisation and Informal Organisation

Basis	Formal organisation	Informal organisation
Meaning	Structure of authority relationships.	Network of social relationships among employees.
Formation	Deliberately planned and created by the management.	Emerges spontaneously as a result of social interactions among employees.
Purpose	To achieve planned goals of the organisation.	To satisfy social and cultural needs of members and fulfil common interests.
Structure	Has a well-defined structure of tasks and relationships.	No clear-cut structure. A complex network of relations .
Nature	Rigid, stable and predictable.	Flexible, unstable and unpredictable.
Interdependence	It exists independently.	It exists within the framework of formal organisation.

Meaning of Delegation of Authority

It is a process of entrusting responsibility and authority to the subordinates and creating accountability on those employees, who are entrusted with responsibility and authority. Delegation refers to the downward transfer of authority from a superior to a subordinate. It is a prerequisite for the efficient functioning of an organisation because it enables a manager to use his time on high priority activities.

According to **Theo Haimann**, "Delegation of authority merely means the granting of authority to subordinates to operate within prescribed limits."

Elements of Delegation of Authority

Following are the essential elements of delegation

(i) **Authority** The term authority implies the right of an individual to take decisions and to command his subordinates.

The concept of authority arises from the established scalar chain, which links the various job positions and levels of an organisation. Authority helps to maintain order in the organisation, and determines the superior subordinate relationship.

(ii) **Responsibility** It is the obligation of a subordinate to properly perform the assigned duty. It arises from a superior subordinate relationship because the subordinate is bound to perform the duty assigned to him. Thus, it flows upwards.

(iii) **Accountability** It implies being answerable for the final outcome. Once authority has been delegated and responsibility accepted, one cannot deny accountability. It is the obligation to carry out responsibility and exercise authority. It flows upward as subordinate will be accountable to his superior.

Importance of Delegation of Authority

Importance of delegation of authority are

(i) **Effective management** By empowering the employees, and delegating routine matters to them, the top management gets more time to concentrate on important matters.

(ii) **Motivation of employees** Delegation provides a feeling of status and recognition to subordinates. It provides a psychological benefit and employees are motivated to perform well and try to improve their performance.

(iii) **Facilitation of growth** Delegation helps in the expansion of an organisation by providing a ready workforce to take up leading positions in new ventures.

(iv) **Better coordination** The elements of delegation namely authority, responsibility and accountability helps to define the powers, duties and responsibility related to various positions in an organisation. This helps to avoid overlapping and duplication of work and facilitates coordination.
(v) **Basis of management hierarchy/scalar chain** Delegation of authority establishes superior-subordinate relationships, which is the basis of hierarchy of management.
(vi) **Quick decisions** When authority is delegated, lower level employees can take decisions quickly without consulting the senior executives.

Limitations of Delegation of Authority

Delegation of authority has the following limitations
(i) If the subordinates are not efficient, then it can affect the quality of work.
(ii) It may make the top level management complacent.
(iii) It may lead to unrest and competition among employees.

Meaning of Decentralisation

Decentralisation of authority means systematic dispersal of authority in all departments and at all levels of management for taking decisions and actions appropriate at the respective levels. An organisation is said to be decentralised when managers at middle and lower levels have been given the authority to take decisions for their respective areas.

According to **Louis Allen,** "Decentralisation refers to systematic effort to delegate to the lowest level all authority except that which can be exercised at central points."

Merits of Decentralisation

Following are the merits of decentralisation
(i) Develops initiative among employees.
(ii) Develops managerial talent for the future.
(iii) Facilitates quick decision-making.
(iv) Provides relief to top management.
(v) Facilitates growth and better control.

Demerits of Decentralisation

Following are the demerits of decentralisation
(i) The quality of decisions may fall.
(ii) Lower level employees may misuse their power.

Difference between Centralisation and Decentralisation

Basis	Centralisation	Decentralisation
Decision-making authority	Top level management.	Spread over different levels of organisation
Quality of decision	Quality decisions.	Not so high quality decisions.
Time involved in decision-making	Delay in decision-making.	Quick decisions.
Applicability	Suitable for small organisations.	Suitable for large organisations.
Flow of orders, instructions, etc.	Higher level to lower levels.	At all levels.
Development of juniors	Less scope	High scope
Burden of top executives	Highly burdened	Routine decisions taken by lower management and burden is relatively less.
Motivation and morale of employees	Low	High
Ability to tackle emergency situations	Effective	Not so effective

Difference between Delegation and Decentralisation

Basis	Delegation	Decentralisation
Nature	Compulsory act	Optional policy
Purpose	Reduce manager's work load	Increase subordinate's role in management
Scope	Narrow scope	Wide scope
Autonomy	Less freedom to act independently	More freedom to act independently

PYQs Previous Years' Questions

1 Mark Questions

1. ……… organisations are formed spontaneously as a result of social interaction among employees in an organisation. *ISC 2024*

Ans Informal

2. Which one of the following is not a feature of an informal organisation? *ISC Sem II 2022*
   (a) There are no written rules and regulations.
   (b) They are often created spontaneously by people with common interests.
   (c) Membership is voluntary.
   (d) They are based on division of labour.

Ans (d) They are based on division of labour.

3. Grouping of activities based on product line is a part of *ISC Sem II Specimen 2022*
   (a) Functional organisation
   (b) Divisional organisation
   (c) Delegated organisation
   (d) Autonomous organisation

Ans (b) Divisional organisation

4. Which of the following is not true about formal organisation? *ISC Sem II Specimen 2022*
   (a) They are deliberately planned and created by management
   (b) They are stable and predictable
   (c) Violation of rules in a formal organisation may lead to penalties
   (d) Leaders are chosen

Ans (d) Leaders are chosen

2 Marks Questions

1. Briefly explain the meaning of the term functional organisation structure. *ISC Sem II 2022 (M)*

Ans **Functional organisation** An organisational structure in which departments are created on the basis of different functions performed in the organisation is called a functional structure.

2. What is meant by divisional organisation? *ISC Sem II 2022*

Ans An organisation in which various departments are created on the basis of products is called a divisional organisation. Each unit has a divisional manager, who is responsible for performance and has authority over their division.

3. The employees of ABC Co. have formed a Dramatics Club for their recreation. Name the type of organisation formed by them and state one of the features of such an organisation. *ISC Sem II Specimen 2022*

Ans Informal organisation

Some important features of informal organisation are (any one)

(i) It originates from within the formal organisation, due to interaction among employees.
(ii) The standard of behaviour evolves from group norms.

4. Mention the steps involved in the organising function of management. *ISC 2013*

Ans The steps of organising function are

(i) Defining activities and division of work.
(ii) Grouping of activities.
(iii) Assigning duties.
(iv) Delegating authority.
(v) Establishing reporting relationship.
(vi) Coordinating activities.

3/4/5 Marks Questions

1. Decentralisation of authority implies a systematic dispersal of authority at all levels of management for decision-making.
   In the light of the above statement, explain any four merits of decentralisation in an organisation. *ISC 2024 (4M)*

Ans The merits of decentralisation in an organisation are as follows

(i) **Develops initiative among subordinates** Decentralisation helps to promote self-reliance and confidence amongst the subordinates. Its policy helps to identify those executives who have the necessary potential to become dynamic leaders.

(ii) **Quick decision-making** Under decentralisation, decisions are taken at levels which are nearest to the points of action and there is no requirement for approval from many levels. This makes process much faster and facilitates quick decision-making.

(iii) **Develops managerial talent for the future** Decentralisation gives subordinates a chance to prove their abilities. It also helps to identify those who may not be successful in assuming greater responsibility.

(iv) **Better control** Decentralisation makes it possible to evaluate performance at each level and held the departments accountable for their results.

2. Give any three differences between centralisation and decentralisation. *ISC 2023 (3M)*

Or Differentiate between centralisation of authority and decentralisation of authority. *ISC 2016 (4M)*

Or Distinguish between centralisation and decentralisation. *ISC 2014 (3M)*

Ans Difference between centralisation and decentralisation are

Basis	Centralisation	Decentralisation
Meaning	It is concentration of decision-making power in a few hands.	It is dispersal of decision-making authority to the lowest level.
Quickness of decision-making	Fast decision-making.	Delayed decision-making.
Development of juniors	Less scope.	Wide scope.
Applicability	Small organisations.	Large organisations.

3. Organisation is an important tool to achieve objectives of the enterprise. In the light of this statement, explain any four points on the importance of organisation. *ISC Specimen 2023 (4M)*

Or Explain any four points on the importance of organising, as a function of management. *ISC Sem II 2022 (4M)*

Or Give three points in support of the statement, "Organising is an important function of management." *ISC Specimen 2018, 17 (3M)*

Ans "Organising is an important function of management". Points in support of this statement are

(i) **Benefits of specialisation** Organising facilitates the systematic allocation of work. This reduces the work load as well as enhances productivity, as the work is allocated as per specialisation.

(ii) **Clarity in working relationships** The establishment of working relationships clarifies lines of communication and specifies who is accountable to whom.

(iii) **Optimum utilisation of human resources** Organising leads to proper usage of all material, financial and human resources by proper assignment of jobs. There is avoidance of duplication of work and overlapping of responsibilities among various employees.

(iv) **Training and development of personnel** Organising stimulates creativity amongst the managers. Effective delegation allows the manager to reduce their workload by assigning routine jobs to their subordinates.

Concept Enhancer A properly designed organisation structure gives flexibility and adapts to the changes easily. It also helps in growth and diversification of an enterprise.

4. Organising involves a series of steps that need to be taken to achieve the desired goals. Explain these steps. *ISC Specimen 2023 (3M)*

Or Explain the various steps involved in the process of organising. *ISC 2018,14 (5M)*

Or Explain the steps involved in organising as a function of management. *ISC 2010*

Ans Refer to text on page 96.

5. Why is delegation an important management tool? *ISC Sem II Specimen 2022*

Or Explain the importance of delegation of authority. *ISC 2019 (5M)*

Ans Refer to text on page 99 and 100.

6. Distinguish between a formal organisation and an informal organisation. *ISC 2020 (3M)*

Ans Difference between formal and informal organisation

Basis	Formal organisation	Informal organisation
Origin	It is created by conscious managerial decisions.	It arises spontaneously with in the formal organisation.
Authority	Members are bound by hierarchical structure.	All members have equal authority.
Flow of communic -ation	It moves according to the scalar chain of authority.	It moves in any direction.

7. Write five features of an informal business organisation. *ISC 2017 (5M)*

Ans Some important features of informal organisation are as follows

(i) It originates from within the formal organisation, due to interaction among employees.

(ii) The standard of behaviour evolves from group norms.

(iii) Communication is free and independent.

(iv) It emerges spontaneously and is not created deliberately.

(v) It has no definite structure or form.

8. Differentiate between functional organisation and divisional organisation. *ISC 2015 (3M)*

Ans Difference between functional organisation and divisional organisation

Basis	Functional organisation	Divisional organisation
Formation	It is formed on the basis of functions.	Its formation is based on the product lines and is supported by functions.
Specialisation	Functional specialisation, hence economical.	Product specialisation, hence costly.
Coordination	Difficult for a multi-product company.	Easy, because all functions related to a particular product are integrated in one department/division.

9. Explain any five features of organising as a function of management. *ISC 2007 (5M)*

Ans Five features of organising function of management are

(i) **Division of work** It essentially means that after identifying the activities to be performed. The work should be divided into parts. This enables specialisation, because jobs are assigned to different individuals, according to their qualification and capabilities.

(ii) **Authority responsibility structure** The hierarchy of organisational structure clearly defines the authority-responsibility relationship, as it clearly defines who has to take orders from whom.

(iii) **Flexibility** The organisational structure should be flexible, so that any challenge can be dealt by adopting new changes like developing further division of work and grouping of activities in case of growth and expansion of business.

Features of Organising
- Division of work
- Authority responsibility structure
- Flexibility
- Achieving organisational goals
- Coordination

(iv) **Achieving organisational goals** The division of work is done keeping in view the overall organisational objectives.

(v) **Coordination** For the proper functioning of organisation, it creates an environment of coordination between departments and people.

10. What is 'organisational structure'? Why is it needed? *ISC 2003 (3M)*

Ans Organisational structure is the outcome of the organising process. It can be defined as the framework within which managerial and operating tasks are performed.

It specifies relationships between people, work and resources. It allows correlation and coordination among human, physical and financial resources to accomplish organisational goals.

TOPIC 3

Staffing

Meaning of Staffing

Staffing may be defined as the process of hiring and developing the required personnel to fill in various positions in the organisation. It implies placing the right man at the right job. This function of management is concerned with determining the manpower requirement of an enterprise.

According to **Koontz** and **O' Donnell**, "The managerial function of staffing involves manning the organisational structure through proper and effective selection, appraisal and development of personnel to fill the roles designed in the structure".

Features of Staffing

The features of staffing are

(i) **Deals with human resource** This function is people-oriented and aims at efficient utilisation of human resource.

(ii) **Pervasive function** It is required in all types of organisations, big or small, profit making and non-profit making. It is also performed at all levels of organisation.

(iii) **Continuous function** It is a continuous and never ending process. The process of hiring, training and compensating people is a never ending process.

(iv) **Multi-disciplinary** It has been developed with a combination of many disciplines like psychology, sociology, anthropology, etc.

(v) **Extends beyond personnel department** It is both a line and staff function. When every manager performs this function it is a line function, but when personnel department is performing it by giving specialised services, it is a staff function.

Importance/Need of Staffing

Following points highlight the need of staffing

(i) **Filling jobs with competent personnel** Staffing involves manning the organisation structure through proper recruitment and selection process, thereby, employing competent personnel to attain organisational objectives.

(ii) **Effectiveness of operations** Performance of the organisation depends on the quality of the persons employed. Better performance can be achieved by proper selection, training and development of the employees.

(iii) **Improves job satisfaction and morale** It helps employees to utilise their potential for maximum individual satisfaction from work. It improves job satisfaction by providing fair remuneration and regular assessment.

(iv) **Survival and growth** Competent personnel not only bring the organisation into existence, but also act as a key factor for the survival and growth of the enterprise.

(v) **Optimum utilisation of human resource** It helps in avoiding over manning, underutilisation of manpower and high labour cost. It also helps in preventing the disruption of work by indicating in advance about the likely shortage of employees.

Steps in Staffing Process

The staffing process begins with estimating the requirement of human resource and exploring different sources from where they can be obtained.

Following are the steps in the staffing process

(i) **Estimating the manpower requirements** It involves forecasting and determining the number and kind of manpower required by the organisation in future. It involves workload analysis and workforce analysis. Workload analysis helps a manager to assess the number and type of human resources necessary to perform various jobs in the organisation, whereas, workforce analysis helps him to know the number and type already available.

(ii) **Recruitment** It may be defined as the process of searching for prospective employees and stimulating them to apply for jobs in the organisation. The objective of recruitment is to create a pool of prospective candidates, from which the best candidate can be selected.

(iii) **Selection** In this step, right candidate is chosen for the right job from the pool of candidates obtained through recruitment.
This process ensures that the organisation gets best among available and it enhances the self-esteem and prestige of those who are selected. It involves a series of tests, interviews and negotiations.

(iv) **Placement and orientation** Placement means occupying the post or position for which the person has been selected. Orientation/Induction implies introducing the selected employee to other employees and familiarising him with rules and policies of the organisation, by giving him a brief presentation about the company, his superiors, subordinates and colleagues.

(v) **Training and development** These involve improving job knowledge, skills and attitudes of employees on a regular basis so that they may perform their jobs efficiently. Apart from this, training helps in career building and increases motivation of employees.

Meaning of Recruitment

Recruitment may be defined as the process of publishing the information about the vacancies in the organisation. In other words, it is concerned with searching prospective employees and stimulating them to apply for jobs in the organisation. The objective of recruitment is to procure sufficiently large number of qualified candidates, so that the most eligible employee can be selected.

Sources of Recruitment

There are two sources of recruitment, *viz* internal and external.

1. Internal Sources

These refer to employing persons from within the organisation. The important internal sources of recruitment are as follows

(i) **Promotion** It means shifting an employee to a higher post carrying higher salary, status and responsibility.

(ii) **Transfer** It refers to shifting an employee to a similar job with no change in salary, status and responsibility, to another department or shift.

2. External Sources

These refer to the recruitment of candidates from outside the organisation.

The important external sources of recruitment are

(i) **Direct recruitment** Under this, a notice is placed on the notice board of the enterprise, specifying the details of the jobs available.

(ii) **Advertisement** Advertising in newspapers, journals and on television is a common method of encouraging people to apply for jobs. This will provide a wide range of candidates to select from.

(iii) **Employment exchange** These help to match personnel demand and supply by serving as a link between job seekers and employers.

(iv) **Labour contractors or jobbers** Labour contractors maintain close contacts with labourers and they can provide a number of workers at short notice.

(v) **Web publishing** Internet is becoming a common source of recruitment these days. There are many websites like naukri.com, monster.com, designed to provide information to both job seekers and employers.

(vi) **Casual callers** Many business organisations keep a database of unsolicited applicants in their files. Such files can be recalled to fill the current vacant positions in the organisation.

(vii) **Recommendations of employees** It is a very common and economical method to fill the vacant positions in the organisation. In this, existing employees refer a candidate who is their relative or friend.

(viii) **Educational institution/Campus recruitment** Industries have technical requirements. Thus, they approach technical institutes and conduct test and interviews on the campus for selecting their personnel.

(ix) **Placement agencies** These agencies provide manpower provision to organisations. Generally, senior executives are hired by them. They lessen the burden of the companies by taking up their recruitment task.

Meaning of Selection

Selection is the process of carefully screening the candidates, so as to identify and choose the most suitable person for the job. In other words, it is the process of identifying and choosing the best person out of a number of prospective candidates for a job.

'Selection is the process by which an organisation chooses from a list of screened applicants, the person or persons who best meet the selection criteria for the position available.'

Selection Process

The process of selection is as follows

(i) **Preliminary screening** The initial screening is done through a preliminary interview in order to eliminate the unsuitable candidates, by going through the information provided in their application forms.

(ii) **Blank application** A blank application form is given to the candidate to fill all personnel and professional details. The application blank provides a detailed written record of the candidate.

(iii) **Selection tests** Candidates are required to take tests which measures the individual's job related proficiency and skills. Various types of tests are aptitude test, personality test, interest test, intelligence tests, etc.

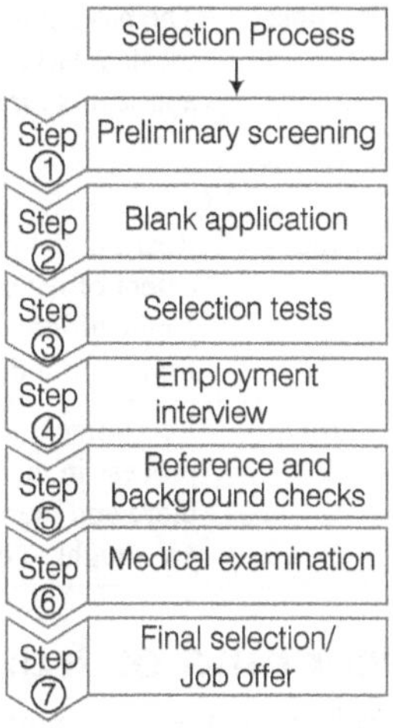

(iv) **Employment interview** It involves an oral face-to-face interaction with the candidate.

It helps to check the details of application blank provided and also judge certain qualities like

(a) Quickness of response.

(b) Personality.

(c) Suitability for the job.

(v) **Reference and background checks** Many employers request names, addresses and telephone numbers of references for the purpose of verifying information and gaining additional information about an applicant.

(vi) **Medical examination** After reference check and before the job offer, the candidate is required to undergo a medical fitness test.

The job offer is given to the candidate, only when the examiner has declared him fit after the medical examination.

(vii) **Final selection/Job offer** The final decision has to be made from among the candidates, who have passed the tests, interviews and reference checks. The next step in the selection process is job offer to those applicants, who have passed all the previous hurdles with great patience and dignity.

When the candidate accepts the job offer, the contract of employment is made which is in a written form and includes job title, duties, responsibilities, date when continuous employment starts and the basis for calculating service, rates of pay, allowances, hours of work, leave rules, sickness, grievance procedure, etc.

Difference between Recruitment and Selection

Basis	Recruitment	Selection
Meaning	Recruitment is the process of searching and motivating candidates to apply for a job.	Selection is that process of staffing, which rejects the unsuitable candidates and chooses the suitable candidates.
Sequence	Recruitment is the process which ends with staffing and precedes selection in the process of staffing.	Selection is the last step of recruitment in the process of staffing.
Purpose	The basic purpose is to create a large pool of applicants for the jobs.	The basic purpose is to eliminate as many candidates as possible until the most suitable person gets finalised.
Scope	Recruitment relates to the extent of receipt of applications and selection from within them.	Selection involves sorting of the candidates.
Nature	Recruitment is a positive process in the sense that more and more applicants are sought to be attracted.	Selection is a negative process in the sense that more applications are rejected than selected.

Meaning of Training

Training is the systematic development of knowledge, skills and aptitutes required by an individual to perform adequately a given task or job.

The purpose of training is to achieve a change in the behaviour of those trained and to enable them to do their jobs in a better way. Training is not a 'one step' process, but is a continuous or a never ending process.

According of **Terry Heap**, "Training is the creation of an environment where employees acquire job related knowledge, skills, abilities and attitudes."

Advantages of Training

Advantages of training are

(i) **Reduced learning time** A trained employee takes less time in learning the job as compared to untrained employee. As a result, there is less wastage of resources and higher productivity in the organisation.

(ii) **Better performance** The performance of trained employees is always better than the performance of untrained employees. In the training programmes, their qualities and capabilities are improved and employees get some experience of working on the job before they are actually assigned the job. This improves their performance and efficiency level.

(iii) **Higher morale** Training increases the satisfaction and morale of employees and thus, builds confidence in them.

(iv) **Helps in solving operational problems** While performing various activities, the organisation faces various problems such as problem of absenteeism, wastage of resources, dissatisfaction of employees, lack of team work, etc.
Through training, these operational problems can be avoided or removed in the organisation because supervisors are trained for improvement of superior subordinate relationship and for encouraging and motivating their subordinates.

(v) **Managing manpower need** Some organisations have specialised technique of production, but the ready staff is not available. In that case, organisations hire untrained people and train them with the required skills according to their organisation's need. By training, they solve long-term problem of manpower requirement.

(vi) **Helps to adopt changes** Training helps the employees to adapt to environmental changes.

(vii) **More safety** Trained employees can handle the machines and equipments safely, impart good productive results in return and there are less chances of accidents.

(viii) **Promotion and career growth** Training make employees capable of taking challenging jobs. Training provides new knowledge and skills to the workers and this will enhance their earning opportunities also.

Types/Methods of Training

The methods of training are broadly categorised as follows

1. On-the-job Methods

It refers to those methods that are applied to the work place, while the employee is actually working. Some important on-the-job methods are

(i) Apprenticeship programmes
(ii) Coaching
(iii) Internship training
(iv) Job rotation
(v) Induction

2. Off-the-job Methods

Off-the-job methods are used away from the work place. Some important off-the-job methods are

(i) Classroom lectures
(ii) Films
(iii) Case studies
(iv) Computer modelling
(v) Vestibule training
(vi) Programmed instruction.

Meaning of Development

It refers to the learning opportunities designed to the help employees enhance their personality. It helps individuals to progress towards maturity, not only to become good employees but also good human beings.

Difference between Training and Development

Basis	Training	Development
Meaning	Training is a process of imparting knowledge for doing specific jobs.	Development is a process of learning, so that employee can grow.
Nature	Training is a job oriented process.	Development is a career oriented process.
Purpose/ Objective	The basic purpose of training is to enable the employees to do current job or some intended purpose.	The basic purpose of development is to enable the overall growth of the employees.
Focus	Training focuses on technical skills.	Development focuses on conceptual and human ideas.
Level of trainees involved	Training is required by supervisors and labourers.	Development is usually required at managerial levels.
Scope of learning	Training has a narrow scope because it is a part of development.	Development has a wide scope as training itself is a part of development.
Depth of knowledge imparted	Training means making employees skillful in a particular job.	Development means making employees skillful in many fields.
Duration	Training is a short-term process.	Development is an on going and long-term process.

PYQs Previous Years' Questions

1 Mark Questions

1. Best Pest Control Services has seventy five technicians who are experts in pest control. The management decides to train these technicians again in order to keep pace with the growing technological changes and improve pest control techniques.

   What type of training should the management impart to these technicians? *ISC 2024*

   (a) Orientation training (b) Job training
   (c) Refresher training (d) Safety training

Ans (c) Refresher training

2. ……… function of management is related to placing the right person in the right job. *ISC Specimen 2023*

Ans Staffing

3. The process of filling job vacancies within the organisation from the existing work force is termed as *ISC Sem II 2022*

   (a) Internal recruitment
   (b) External recruitment
   (c) Selection
   (d) Staffing

Ans (a) Internal recruitment

4. The process of meaning various jobs in the organisation with the right person is known as ……… . *ISC Sem II Specimen 2022*

Ans Staffing

2 Marks Questions

1. Briefly explain the meaning of training. *ISC Sem II 2022*

Ans Training is the systematic development of knowledge, skills and aptitutes required by an individual to perform adequately a given task or job. The purpose of training is to achieve a change in the behaviour of those trained and to enable them to do their jobs in a better way.

2. State any two points of difference between recruitment and selection. ***ISC Sem II 2022, 19, 14***

Ans Difference between recruitment and selection are

Basis	Recruitment	Selection
Meaning	Recruitment is the process of searching and motivating candidates to apply for a job.	Selection is the process of staffing, which rejects the unsuitable candidates and chooses the suitable candidates.
Purpose	The basic purpose is to create a large pool of applicants for the jobs.	The basic purpose is to eliminate as many candidates as possible until the most suitable candidate gets finalised.

Concept Enhancer Recruitment is a positive aspect while selection is a negative aspect.

3. What is pre-requisite of selection? Which function of management ensures the right person at the right job? ***ISC Sem II Specimen 2022***

Ans Recruitment is pre-requisite of selection. Staffing function of management ensures the right person at the right job.

4. Moon Ltd. imported new machinery from Germany. However, the productivity of the business did not improve with the use of this machinery. On investigation, it was found that the workers were not able to operate the high-tech machinery effectively, causing poor performance and wastages.

What can be done by Moon Ltd. to overcome the above problem? ***ISC 2020***

Ans Moon Ltd. should provide vestibule training to its workers. This training is conducted away from the workplace. In this method of training, employees are trained on special machines in separate room. An artificial work environment is created which closely resembles the real working conditions.

5. Explain any two sources of external recruitment used in today's world. ***ISC 2018***

Ans The important external sources of recruitment are as follows

(i) **Direct recruitment** Under this, a notice is placed on the notice board of the enterprise, specifying the details of the jobs available.

(ii) **Advertisement** Advertising in newspapers, journals and on television is a common method of encouraging people to apply for jobs. This will provide a wide range of candidates to select from.

6. Give two points of difference between training and development. ***ISC Specimen 2018, 17***

Ans Differences between training and development are

Basis	Training	Development
Meaning	Training is a process of imparting knowledge for doing specific jobs.	Development is a process of learning, so that employee can grow.
Nature	Training is a job oriented process.	Development is a career oriented process.

Concept Enhancer Development is on going process while training is time restricted process.

7. What are the steps involved in the process of recruitment? ***ISC 2015***

Ans Recruitment involves the following steps

(i) Identifying the sources of supply of adequate number and right type of personnel required.

(ii) Publicising information about job vacancies in the organisation, e.g. Advertisement for vacancies in a newspaper so as to stimulate the prospective candidates to offer themselves for employment.

(iii) Assessing alternative sources of manpower and choosing the best source.

(iv) Contacting the chosen source of recruitment to secure applications.

8. Write short note on staffing as a function of management. ***ISC 2012***

Or What is staffing? ***ISC 2010***

Ans Staffing may be defined as the process of hiring and developing the required personnel to fill in various positions in the organisation. It implies placing right man at the right job.

This function of management is concerned with determining the manpower requirement of an enterprise.

The main features are

(i) It is concerned with human resource.

(ii) It is a pervasive function.

(iii) It is a continuous process.

3/4/5 Marks Questions

1. Differentiate between recruitment and selection by giving any four points. ***ISC 2024 (4M)***

Ans Refer to text on page 106.

2. Explain any four differences between training and development. ***ISC 2023***

Ans Refer to text on page 107.

3. Explain any four external sources of recruitment. ***ISC Sem II Specimen 2022 (4M)***

Or Explain any three sources of external recruitment. ***ISC 2020 (3M)***

Or Explain any five sources of external recruitment. ***ISC 2014 (5M)***

Ans Refer to text on page 105.

4. Enumerate any five points of importance of staffing as a function of management. ***ISC 2020 (5M)***

Or Discuss the importance of staffing as a function of management. ***ISC 2007 (5M)***

Or Highlight the significance of 'staffing' as a management function. ***ISC 2001***

Ans Staffing is that function of management, which helps in obtaining right people and putting them on the right job. The importance of staffing as a function of management are

(i) **Filling jobs with competent personnel** Staffing involves manning the organisation structure through proper recruitment and selection process, thereby, employing competent personnel to attain organisational objectives.

(ii) **Effectiveness of operations** Performance of the organisation depends on the quality of the persons employed. Better performance can be achieved by proper selection, training and development of the employees.

(iii) **Improves job satisfaction and morale** It helps employees to utilise their potential for maximum individual satisfaction from work. It improves job satisfaction by providing fair remuneration and regular assessment.

(iv) **Survival and growth** Competent personnel not only bring the organisation into existence, but also act as a key factor for the survival and growth of the enterprise.

(v) **Optimum utilisation of human resource** It helps in avoiding over manning, underutilisation of manpower and high labour cost. It also helps in preventing the disruption of work by indicating in advance about the likely shortage of employees.

Importance of Staffing
- Filling jobs with competent personnel
- Effectiveness of operations
- Improves job satisfaction and morale
- Survival and growth
- Optimum utilisation of human resource

5. Explain any three types of training that can be given to an employee. ***ISC 2018***

Ans Three types of training are as follows

(i) **Coaching** In this method, the employee is trained on-the-job by his immediate superior. This ensures that the employee is able to acquire knowledge and skills, while doing the job. This method is used at top management levels.

Types of Training
- Coaching
- Job-rotation
- Vestibule training

(ii) **Job-rotation** In this method, the employee is moved from one job the the another at planned intervals. This method gives adequate exposure to the employee.

(iii) **Vestibule training** This training is conducted away from the work place. In this method of training, employees are trained on special machines in separate classrooms.

An artificial work environment is created which closely resembles the real working conditions. This method is used for space programmes or where the machinery is expensive.

6. Explain the first five steps involved in the selection of suitable workforce in an organisation. ***ISC Specimen 2018, 17 (4M)***

Ans The first five steps in the process of selection are

Step 1 **Preliminary screening** The initial screening is done through a preliminary interview in order to eliminate the unsuitable candidates, by going through the information provided in their application forms.

Step 2 **Application blank** A blank application form is given to the candidate to fill all personnel and professional details.

The application blank provides a detailed written record of the candidate.

Step 3 **Selection tests** Candidates are required to take tests which measures the individual's job related proficiency and skills. Various types of tests such as aptitude test, personality test, interest test, intelligence tests, etc can be conducted.

Step 4 **Employment interview** It involves an oral face to face interaction with the candidate. It helps to check the details of application blank provided and also judge certain qualities like

(a) Quickness of response.
(b) Personality.
(c) Suitability for the job.

Step 5 **Medical examination** After the selection decision and before the job offer, the candidate is required to undergo a medical fitness test. The job offer is given to the candidate, only when the examiner has declared him fit after the medical examination.

Common Mistake Majority of the candidates write steps of staffing or steps of recuritment instead of steps of selection. Several candidates give a wrong sequence of steps. So, stress upon the right steps of selection process as well as correct sequence of them as required.

7. Discuss the first five steps involved in the process of staffing. **ISC 2016 (5M)**

Ans Refer to text on page 104.

TOPIC 4

Directing

Meaning of Directing

Directing means giving instructions and guiding people in doing work. It is that part of the management process which ensures that the members of an organisation work efficiently and effectively for the attainment of desired objectives.

According to **Theo Haimann**, "Directing consists of the processes and techniques utilised in issuing instructions and making decisions that operations are carried on as originally planned."

Features of Directing

Features of directing are

(i) **Management function** It is an important function of management and the managers gets the work done through directing, that involves guiding, supervising and motivating the employees.

(ii) **Translates plans into action** All activities of an organisation are initiated through direction. It is a key managerial function. All other functions of management prepare a setting for action, but directing initiates action in the organisation.

(iii) **A continuous process** It is an ongoing process. It does not mean issuing an order or instruction, but a manager must continuously guide, inspire and supervise his subordinates, so that organisational goals could be achieved on time. This function continues throughout the lifetime of an organisation.

(iv) **Pervasive function** Every manager from top to bottom performs the function of directing or in other words, we can say, directing takes place wherever superior subordinate relations exist.

(v) **Downward flow of order** Directing is initiated at top level and flows to the bottom, which means it flows downward in the hierarchy. Every manager can direct his immediate subordinate and take instructions from his immediate boss.

(vi) **Linking function** It serves as a link between planning and controlling.

(vii) **Human factor** It is an interpersonal aspect of management, as it deals with human behaviour.

Importance of Directing

Efficient directing provides the following benefits

(i) **Initiate action** All activities are initiated through direction. It is this function, which starts actual work by converting plans into action.

(ii) **Improves efficiency** Directing guides employees to fully realise their potentials and capabilities. Through this function, managers utilise the potential of employees and persuade them to work to the best of their ability and contribute their maximum efforts towards the achievement of organisational objectives.

(iii) **Ensures coordination** Directing integrates employees efforts in the organisation in such a way that every individual's effort contributes to the welfare of the organisation. Thus, it ensures that employees work efficiently for the attainment of goals.

(iv) **Provides stability and growth** The work in the organisation starts with directing the employees towards the predetermined goals of the organisation. If this function of management is executed successfully, then it results in unity of direction and achievement of organisational goals. Organisation can expand and grow only when right direction is provided.

(v) **Facilitates change** Business environment is changing very frequently, but the people generally have a tendency to resist change. In this context, directing helps a manager to persuade his subordinates to carry out changes from time-to-time and to cope with change in the environment, since it is necessary to adapt to changes in modern business.

Elements of Directing

Directing functions of management includes the following elements

(i) Supervision (ii) Motivation
(iii) Leadership (iv) Communication

Meaning of Supervision

Supervision means instructing, guiding and monitoring the subordinates to ensure that they perform their jobs in accordance with the plans and instructions.

According to **George R. Terry**, "Supervision is the achieving of results by means of intelligent utilisation of human talents and facilitating resources in a manner that provides the greatest challenge and interest to the human talent."

Functions of a Supervisor

Functions of a supervisor are

(i) **Scheduling the work** A supervisor plans and schedules the activities for smooth flow of work. Scheduling means laying down the time for completion of activities.

(ii) **Issues orders and instruction** Instructions are given on how the work is to be performed and orders to start, stop or modify the actions to be performed by the subordinates.

(iii) **Motivation** The supervisor motivates his subordinates by providing financial and non-financial incentives. He inspires them for higher quality of work and productivity.

(iv) **Preserving records** The supervisor keeps a record of output and other related aspects of each employee. He sends the necessary information to the top management.

(v) **Liaison between management and workers** The supervisor is an important link between the management and the workers. He explains management policies to the workers and also passes on the management's instructions.

He has a close contact with the workers and tries to understand their problems. He brings worker's problems to the notice of the top management.

(vi) **Grievance handling** A supervisor is in direct touch with the workers, so that he can handle their grievances effectively. He should maintain good relations with the workers, so that the workers come to him if they have any grievance.

When a grievance is reported, he should try to remove it. But, if he can not redress the grievance, he should report it to the upper level management.

(vii) **Arranging training** The supervisor leads the workers of his department. He fixes production targets for them and provides them the necessary guidance for doing the work assigned to them. He provides on the job training to the workers working under him.

(viii) **Monitoring performance** The supervisor checks whether the actual work is done according to the targets or not.

(ix) **Ensuring safety** Supervisor regularly monitors the working condition of machines and equipments. He tries to minimise the accidents. Proper training for machine handling is provided by him.

(x) **Reporting feedback** He prepares the progress report of work, fullfils targets, etc.

Span of Control/Span of Supervision

Span of control/supervision means the number of subordinates that a supervisor can manage effectively and efficiently.

If the number of subordinates reporting directly to a manager are too many, control may become ineffective and if the number is too small, full use of manager/supervisor's capacity is not made.

Factors Affecting Span of Control

Following are the factors affecting span of control

(i) **Nature of work** If the nature of work is of routine, repetitive and simple; then wider span of supervision control can be there, but in case of complex and complicated work, narrow span of control should be followed i.e. few persons under the supervisor/manager should be there.

(ii) **Ability of supervisor** Competent, experienced and trained supervisor is relatively capable of supervising large number of employees.

(iii) **Ability of the subordinates** Strict and narrow supervision is required for unskilled and semi-skilled employees whereas wider span of control can be there in case employees are trained and experienced.

(iv) **Degree of decentralisation** Large number of employees can be easily managed under decentralised organisation, thus there is a wider span of control.
Whereas, in a centralised organisation, many decisions are to be taken up by the supervisor alone. Therefore, narrow span of control is applicable.

(v) **Clarity of plans and policies** When clear cut plans and policies are there, it is easy to supervise a large number of people.

(vi) **Communication and information effectiveness** Strong information system can help in wider span of control. Sophisticated control system techniques and standards reduce the need of close supervision.

(vii) **Location of operations** When operations are geographically dispersed, narrow span of control is possible.

Meaning of Motivation

Motivation means incitement or inducement to act or move. In the context of an organisation, it means the process of making the subordinates to act in a desired manner to achieve certain organisational goals.

It is the act of inspiring employees to work hard to achieve the desired goals of the organisation. The main motto of this process is to influence the behaviour of subordinates for better performance.

In the words of **William Scott**, "Motivation means a process of stimulating people to action to accomplish desired goals."

Features of Motivation

The important features of motivation are

(i) Motivation is a psychological phenomenon. It is a personal and internal feeling like an urge, drive, desires and aspirations of human beings.

(ii) Motivation inspires an employee to achieve goals. Thus, it encourages goal-directed behaviour.

(iii) Motivation may be positive or negative. Positive motivation means inspiring people to work better and negative motivation means forcing people to work by threatening or punishment.

(iv) Motivation is a complex process, as the individuals are heterogeneous in their expectations, perceptions and reactions.

Maslow's Need Hierarchy Theory

This theory was given by Abraham Maslow. It is based on human needs. Maslow has explained his theory as a hierarchy of five needs, which are depicted and explained below

Maslow's need hierarchy theory

(i) **Basic physiological needs** These are the basic needs, which a person is required to satisfy in order to survive. Hunger, thirst, shelter, sleep are some of the examples of these needs.

(ii) **Safety/Security needs** These needs are concerned with physical, economic and social security.

(iii) **Affiliation/Belonging/Social needs** These needs are concerned with affection, sense of belongingness, acceptance and friendship.

(iv) **Esteem needs** These include factors such as self-respect, status, recognition. When these needs are fulfilled, they enhance the self-confidence and prestige of employees.

(v) **Self-actualisation needs** It is the highest level of need in the hierarchy. It arises after the satisfaction of all previously discussed needs. These needs include growth, self-fulfilment and achievement of goals.

Assumptions of Maslow's Need Hierarchy Theory

Maslow's need hierarchy theory has the following assumptions

(i) People's behaviour is based on their needs. Satisfaction of such needs influences their behaviour.

(ii) People's needs are hierarchical in order. They start from basic needs and reach high level needs.

(iii) A satisfied need can no longer motivate a person, only next higher need can motivate a person.

(iv) A person moves to a higher level need, only when lower need is satisfied.

(v) A person is rational.

Meaning of Leadership

Leadership may be defined as the process of influencing the behaviour and performance of others in a group towards the achievement of goals. It is concerned with maintaining personal relations with followers and motivating them to contribute for achieving goals of the organisation.

In the words of **George Terry**, "Leadership is the activity of influencing people to strive willingly for group objectives."

Importance of Leadership

Following points highlight the importance of leadership

(i) **Effective direction** An organisation comes into existence with certain objectives. To attain these objectives, the activities of the organisation must be directed. Direction of the activities is effected through leadership. In short, effective leadership directs the activities of an organisation towards the attainment of the specified organisational goals.

(ii) **Source of motivation** Leadership is a source of motivation. Effective leadership motivates the subordinates to contribute their energies for the benefit of the organisation.

(iii) **Confidence** Leadership creates confidence in the subordinates by giving them proper guidance and advice.

(iv) **High morale** Good leadership increases the morale of the employees, which in turn, contributes to higher productivity.

(v) **Development of team spirit** Effective leadership promotes team spirit and team work which is quite essential for the success of an organisation.

Qualities of a Good Leader

Qualities of a good leader are

(i) **Knowledge** A good leader should have required knowledge and competence. Only such person can instruct subordinates correctly and influence them.

(ii) **Initiative** A leader should have the courage and ability to take initiative. He should not wait for opportunities to come to his way, rather he should grab the opportunities and use it to the advantage of a organisation.

(iii) **Integrity** A leader should possess high level of integrity and honesty. He should be a role model for others regarding ethics and values.

(iv) **Sound physique** A good leader must have good health and physical fitness. He requires tremendous stamina and urge for hard work.

(v) **Decisiveness** A leader should be quick in managing the work. Once he is convinced about a fact, he should be firm and should not change his opinions frequently.

(vi) **Self confidence and sense of responsibility** A leader must be confident, then only he will be able to tackle any situation successfully. Only a confident leader can create confidence in his subordinates. A leader must have the sense of responsibility for achievement of goals or targets of his group members.

(vii) **Social skills** A leader must be friendly with his subordinates. He must provide supportive environment to his subordinates, so that they do not hesitate to discuss their problems. He must understand people and try to maintain good relations with them.

(viii) **Motivation skills** A leader should be an effective motivator. He should understand the needs of people and motivate them by satisfying their needs.

(ix) **Communication skills** A good leader should be able to convey his ideas and thoughts in a precise and effective manner.

(x) **Vision and foresight** He needs foresight and judgement skills to take right decisions at the right time.

(xi) **Courage, tact and devotion** He is an example for others so he should be fair, honest, hardworking and devoted in his dealings. He should be courageous to face different situations and handle them tactfully.

(xii) **Empathy** The leader should be compassionate and be able to recognise and appreciate views of others.

(xiii) **Analytical capacity** Analysing the situations and different course of actions should be inherent in a leader.

Meaning of Communication

Communication is a process of exchange of ideas, facts, feelings, views, etc between two or more persons to create common understanding. It involves a systematic and continuous cycle of listening, understanding, etc.

In the words of **Rogers**, "Communication is a process by which people create and share information with one another in order to reach common understanding."

Features of Communication

Features of communication are

(i) **Two or more person** For sharing of ideas and messages, etc, atleast two or more persons are required, i.e. the sender and the receiver.

(ii) **Two way process** Communication is complete only when the receiver understands and responds to it.

(iii) **Continuous process** It is a continuous process as regular flow of communication is required for fulfilment of group activities.

(iv) **Pervasive function** It is required in all the organisations and at all levels of management.

(v) **Circular process** It is a circular process, as when the sender communicates the message, the receiver after decoding it, responds to the message, which is called 'feedback'.

(vi) **Flows in all directions** It flows horizontally across the departments, downwards from superior to subordinates and upwards from subordinates to superiors. Thus, it flows in all directions.

(vii) **Influencing human behaviour** It creates interpersonal relations and boosts morale by motivating and directing subordinates.

(viii) **Mutual understanding** Trust, loyalty, cooperation and team work can only be created through proper communication.

(ix) **Several media** Communication may be in written form, oral communication, body language, etc.

Objectives of Communication

Objectives of communication are

(i) **Acts as basis of coordination** Communication acts as basis of coordination. It helps in coordinating the activities of various departments and persons in an organisation.

(ii) **Helps in smooth working of an enterprise** Communication ensures smooth functioning of an enterprise. Existence of an organisation depends fully on communication, i.e. transmitting information.

(iii) **Acts as basis of decision-making** Communication provides needed information for decision-making. In its absence, it may not be possible for managers to take decision. Thus, it serves as a basis of decision-making.

(iv) **Increases managerial efficiency** Various functions of managers like providing informations, instructions, allocating jobs, resources would not be possible in the absence of communication. Thus, communication is essential for effective performance of managerial functions.

(v) **Establishes effective leadership** Communication is the basis of leadership. A good leader must possess efficient communication skills for influencing the behaviour of subordinates.

(vi) **Creates team work** Communication is designed to create cooperation and understanding.

(vii) **To secure feedback** Suggestions and complaints from employees, customers, suppliers, etc help the company to improve their methods and procedures.

Types of Communication

Following are the types of communication

(i) **Formal communication** It refers to the communication taking place through official channels in an organisation. Such type of communication takes place between managers or employees of same cadre.

It may be oral or written, but complete record of such type of communication is maintained in an organisation.

(ii) **Informal communication/Grapevine** It takes place in an organisation without following the formal lines of communication.

Such type of communication usually takes place among the workers to exchange their views and to satisfy their social needs.

The network of communication followed in the informal communication is referred to as 'grapevine network'.

Elements/Steps in the Communication Process

Main steps in the communication process are as follows

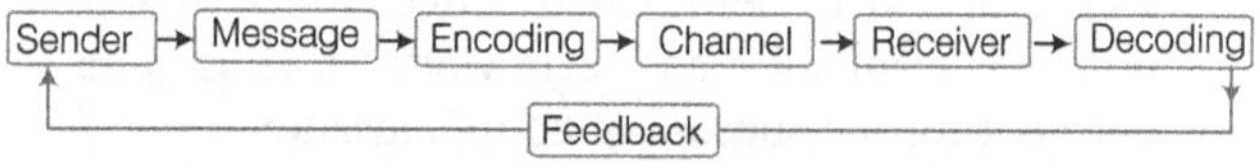

(i) **Sender** The person who sends the message, is known as 'the sender' or 'communicator'. He may be a speaker, a writer or an actor. He initiates the process of communication. He is the source of communication.

(ii) **Message** It is the subject matter of communication. It may consist of facts, information, ideas, opinions, etc. It exists in the mind of the sender.

(iii) **Encoding** The sender translates the message into words, symbols, gestures or other symbols, which he feels will make the receiver understand the message. This is known as 'encoding of message'.

(iv) **Channel or Media** The encoded message is transmitted through some medium, which is known as 'the communication channel'. e.g. Speaking, writing, movement of body parts, etc.

(v) **Receiver** The person, who receives the message, is called 'the receiver'. The receiver may be a listener, reader or viewer.

(vi) **Decoding** It means interpretation of the message by the receiver.

(vii) **Feedback** The receiver sends his response to the sender of the message. Such response is known as 'feedback'. When the feedback is received by the sender, the process of communication is complete.

Barriers to Communication

Barriers are any types of hurdles or bottlenecks in the way of communication. The following are the different barriers to communication

(i) **Language barriers/Semantic barriers** These barriers are due to meaning of words, language, symbols, etc. The same word or symbol has different meaning. Receiver may interpret it differently due to his own assumptions and there may be a case of faulty translation.

(ii) **Physical barriers** These are due to the distance between the sender and receiver e.g. a faulty telephone line may create noise in the communication process.

(iii) **Organisational barriers** Communication is hampered, if the policy of an organisation does not support free flow of communication. When there are several managerial levels, communication gets delayed and distorted.

(iv) **Status** The status of a conscious manager may not allow his subordinates to express their feelings freely. Subordinates at lower levels may hesitate to speak freely to high level managers.

(v) **Lack of attention** When the receiver's mind is preoccupied, he fails to listen to what is being said, e.g. a worker explains some problems to his supervisor. The supervisor is preoccupied with a telephone call and does not grasp the message.

(vi) **Premature evaluation** Communication is likely to fail if the receiver evaluates the meaning of message before the sender completes the message. Such premature evaluation may occur due to pre-conceived notions or prejudice against the communicator.

(vii) **Poor retention** The receiver, who cannot retain the information for a long time, may fail to understand it. Poor retention may be due to lack of interest.

(viii) **Distrust** When the sender and the receiver do not believe each other, the message may not be understood in its original sense.

(ix) **Wrong choice of medium** When a suitable medium is not used for communication, it may not be effective.

(x) **Other barriers** Other reasons like distance, shortage of time, fear of challenging the superiors, lack of confidence in subordinates etc, may also disrupt communication.

Measures to Overcome Barriers to Communication

Effective communication is essential for success of any organisation. Some measures for overcoming barriers and achieving effective communication are

(i) **Clarify the ideas before communicating** The message to be conveyed should be clear in all aspects. It should be analysed in depth and stated in precise and simple words.

(ii) **Well drafted message** The communicator should know the level of understanding and education level of the receiver. The message should be appropriate for the purpose for which it is being communicated.

(iii) **Proper language** Be aware of the language, tone and content of the message. The language used must be understandable to the receiver and should not offend the sentiments of the listener.

(iv) **Feedback** It should stimulate a response from the receiver. It should be two-way communication, i.e. telling and listening.

(v) **Be a good listener** Attentive and patient listening on the part of the management will encourage employees to communicate freely.

(vi) **Ensure proper feedback** The communicator may ensure the success of communication by asking questions regarding the message conveyed. Such feedback makes the process more responsive.

(vii) **Use of informal channel/grapevine** Informal channels should be intelligently used for faster and positive reactions and feedback.

(viii) **Consistency** The communication should be in line with the objectives and policies of an organisation.

(ix) **Gestures and tones** Facial expressions, gestures should be used to reinforce the message conveyed.

(x) **Physical layout of work place** The office space should be so designed, as to facilitate smooth communication.

PYQs Previous Years' Questions

1/2 Marks Questions

1. "Directing initiates action in an organisation." State whether this statement is true or false. *ISC 2024 (1M)*

Ans True

2. Which barrier to communication arises when the sender and receiver interpret a message differently? *ISC 2024 (1M)*

Ans Semantic or language barrier

3. What is meant by 'span of control'? *ISC 2023, Sem II Specimen 2022, 20, 15 (2M)*

Ans Span of control/supervision means the number of subordinates that a supervisor can manage effectively and efficiently. If the number of subordinates reporting directly to a manager are too many, control may become ineffective and if the number is too small, full use of manager/supervisor's capacity is not made.

4. At Support.com, there is no reward or appreciation for a good suggestion. Thus, the subordinates do not want to offer any useful suggestions to their superiors. Which type of barrier to communication has been created in the firm? *ISC Specimen 2023 (1M)*

(a) Semantic barrier (b) Personal barrier
(c) Organisational barrier (d) Psychological barrier

Ans (c) Organisational barrier

5. "Communication done through informal channels is also known as grapevine." State whether this statement is true or false. *ISC Sem II 2022 (1M)*

Ans True

6. With reference to Maslow's theory, state the meaning of safety or security needs. *ISC Sem II 2022 (2M)*

Ans These needs are concerned with physical, economic and social security in the form of job security, stability of income, etc. Physical protection from danger and economic security from old age, sickness and other factors form part of these needs.

7. Explain any two barriers to communication. *ISC Sem II 2022 (2M)*

Ans Two barriers to communication are

(i) **Physical barriers** These are due to the distance between the sender and receiver e.g. a faulty telephone line may create noise in the communication process.

(ii) **Organisational barriers** Communication is hampered, if the policy of an organisation does not support free flow of communication. When there are several managerial levels, communication gets delayed and distorted.

8. Briefly explain the meaning of motivation. *ISC Sem II 2022 (2M)*

Ans Motivation means incitement or inducement to act or move. In the context of an organisation, it means the process of making the subordinates to act in a desired manner to achieve certain organisational goals. It is the act of inspiring employees to work hard to achieve the desired goals of the organisation.

The main motto of this process is to influence the behaviour of subordinates for better performance. In the words of William Scott, "Motivation means a process of stimulating people to action to accomplish desired goals."

9. "Rational barrier is one of the types of barrier in the process of communication". State whether this statement is true or false. *ISC Sem II Specimen 2022 (1M)*

Ans False. Rational barrier is not a part of communication barrier. Communication barriers are psychological barriers, organisational barriers, semantic barriers, etc.

10. State any two qualities of a good leader. *ISC Sem II Specimen 2022 (2M)*

Ans Qualities of a good leader are

(i) **Knowledge** A good leader should have required knowledge and competence. Only such person can instruct subordinates correctly and influence them.

(ii) **Initiative** A leader should have the courage and ability to take initiative. He should not wait for opportunities to come to his way, rather he should grab the opportunities and use it to the advantage of a organisation.

11. Explain feedback as a part of the process of communication. *ISC 2019, 12, 05 (2M)*

Ans In the process of communication, when the sender sends the message and the receiver after decoding it responds to the message, then it is known as 'feedback'. It includes all those actions of receiver indicating that he has received and understood the message of sender.

12. Name the four elements of directing as a function of management. *ISC 2018 (2M)*

Or

Name the elements of directing functions of management. *ISC 2012*

Ans The elements of directing function are

(i) Supervision (ii) Motivation
(iii) Leadership (iv) Communicaiton

13. Why is feedback an important element in the communication process? *ISC 2016 (2M)*

Ans Feedback is an important element in the communication process because of the below mentioned reasons

(i) It helps the sender to assess whether the receiver has understood the message or not.

(ii) It completes the communication process.

14. Outline the steps involved in the process of communication. *ISC 2011 (2M)*

Ans Steps in the process of communication are

(i) **Sender** or communicator is the person, who sends a message or an idea.

(ii) **Message** It is what is conveyed by the sender. It consists of words, facts, ideas, opinions, etc. It is the subject matter of communication.

(iii) **Encoding** It is the use of appropriate verbal or non-verbal language for transmitting the message (words, symbols, gestures) known to both the parties.

Steps in Communication Process
- Sender
- Message
- Encoding
- Channel
- Receiver
- Decoding
- Feedback

(iv) **Channel** It is a medium or route, through which the message is passed from the sender to the receiver. It may be face-to-face, telephone, letter, radio, television, etc.

(v) **Receiver** Receiver or communicator is the person or group who is supposed to receive the message.

(vi) **Decoding** The receiver interprets the message to derive its meaning.

(vii) **Feedback** It is the response or reaction by the receiver. It represents the return flow of communication. With the help of feedback, the sender can judge the effectiveness of his message.

15. State any two features of communication. *ISC 2007 (2M)*

Ans Two features of communication are

(i) **Two or more persons** This process requires atleast two persons, a sender and a receiver.

(ii) **Two-way process** Mere sending the message is not communication. It is complete when the receiver understands and gives response and reaction to the sender.

16. What is 'grapevine' in communication strategy? *ISC 2004, 01 (2M)*

Ans The network of informal communication is called 'grapevine'. This is because it spreads throughout an organisation with its branches going out in all directions.

There is no clear line or direction in which communication flows. It disregards the officia lines/ channels developed through organisational chart.

17. State the importance of communication in two points. *ISC 2004 (2M)*

Ans Importance of communication are

(i) **Acts as a basis of coordination** Communication acts as a basis of coordination. It provides coordination among departments, activities and persons in the organisation.

Such coordination is provided for explaining about organisational goals, the mode of their achievement and inter relationships between different individuals, etc.

(ii) **Acts as a basis of decision-making** The decisions made in an organisation depend/largely on the amount and quality of information available. On the basis of communication of relevant information, one can take right decisions.

18. Why is directing called 'management in action'? *ISC 2002 (2M)*

Ans Directing may be regarded as the heart of management process as whatever activities are planned, are put into action through this function. Directing is the life spark of an enterprise and sets it into motion.

The purpose of directing is to activate employees through communication of plans and objectives to be achieved, supervise them and give them guidance from time to time, motivate them to accomplish their tasks and through effective leadership facilitate coordination and bring balance in the organisation. Thus, directing is called 'management in action'.

3/4/5 Marks Questions

1. Motivation is a psychological phenomenon which arises from human needs and wants.

In the light of above statement, explain Maslow's theory on motivation. **ISC 2024 (5M)**

Or Explain Maslow's theory. **ISC 2018 (5M)**

Or Write short note on 'Maslow's Theory of Needs'. **ISC 2014**

Ans **Maslow's need hierarchy** It is considered fundamental to understanding of motivation. Motivation has a direct link with needs. People have a wide range of needs.

Maslow classified human needs into five categories in order of priority.

Maslow's need hierarchy theory has the following assumptions

(i) People's behaviour is based on their needs. Satisfaction of such needs influences their behaviour.

(ii) People's needs are hierarchical in order. They start from basic needs and reach high level needs.

(iii) A satisfied need can no longer motivate a person, only next higher need can motivate a person.

(iv) A person moves to a higher level need, only when lower need is satisfied.

(v) A person is rational.

2. Directing is the heart of management process. Explain any four reasons to support this statement. **ISC 2023, Sem II 2022 (4M)**

Ans **Importance of directing** Refer to text on page 110 and 111.

3. Explain any four functions of a supervision. **ISC Specimen 2023, 14 (4M)**

Or What is meant by supervision? Explain three functions of a supervisor. **ISC 2019 (4M)**

Ans Supervision means instructing, guiding and monitoring the subordinates to ensure that they perform their jobs in accordance with plans and instructions.

The following are the functions of supervisor

(i) The supervisor maintains day-to-day contact and friendly relations with workers. A good supervisor acts as a guide, friend and philosopher to the workers.

(ii) He acts as a link between management and the operatives by conveying the management targets, policies, etc to the workers and the problems and ideas of the workers to the management. This helps in avoiding conflicts and misunderstandings between management and the workers.

(iii) He plays the key role in maintaining group unity and sorts out internal differences among the workers.

(iv) A good supervisor continuously analyses the work performed by the workers and gives them feedback and suggestions to improve their working skills.

Common Mistake Some candidates confuse functions of a supervisor with 'qualities of a good leader'. Students are advisable to learn both concepts under separate headings properly.

4. Mention two key objectives of communication. **ISC Sem II Specimen 2022, 01**

Or

Explain any four objectives of communication. **ISC 2020, 17, 11, 09 (4M)**

Or

Describe the importance of communication. **ISC 2015, 10 (4M)**

Ans Four objectives of communication are explained below

(i) **Acts as basis of coordination** Communication acts as basis of coordination. It helps in coordinating the activities of various departments and persons in an organisation.

(ii) **Helps in smooth working of an enterprise** Communication ensures smooth functioning of an enterprise. Existence of an organisation depends fully on communication, i.e. transmitting information.

(iii) **Acts as basis of decision-making** Communication provides needed information for decision-making. In its absence, it may not be possible for managers to take decision. Thus it serves as a basis of decision-making.

(iv) **Increases managerial efficiency** Various functions of managers like providing information, instructions, allocating jobs, resources would not be possible in the absence of communication.

Thus, communication is essential for effective performance of managerial functions.

Objectives of Communication

- Acts as basis of coordination
- Helps in smooth working of an enterprise
- Acts as basis of decision-making
- Increases managerial efficiency

5. Explain any five qualities that a good leader should possess. **ISC 2020, 14 (5M)**

Or Effectiveness of leadership depends on the qualities of the leader. Explain any four qualities that a good leader should possess. **ISC Specimen 2018, 17**

Ans Qualities of a good leader are as follows

(i) **Knowledge** A good leader should have required knowledge and competence. Only such person can instruct subordinates correctly and influence them.

(ii) **Initiative** A leader should have the courage and ability to take initiative. He should not wait for opportunities to come to his way, rather he should grab the opportunities and use it to the advantage of a organisation.

(iii) **Integrity** A leader should possess high level of integrity and honesty. He should be a role model for others regarding ethics and values.

(iv) **Sound physique** A good leader must have good health and physical fitness. He requires tremendous stamina and urge for hard work.

(v) **Decisiveness** A leader should be quick in managing the work. Once he is convinced about a fact, he should be firm and should not change his opinions frequently.

Value Points

For getting maximum marks, following points can be included in the answer

- Knowledge and competence
- High level of integrity and honesty
- Good health and physical fitness

6. What is meant by barriers to communication? Explain three suitable measures to overcome the barriers to effective communication. **ISC 2019 (5M)**

Or Explain any five ways of overcoming barriers to communication. **ISC 2015 (5M)**

Or State the measures to overcome the communication barriers. **ISC 2001 (5M)**

Ans Barriers to communication are any type of hurdles or bottlenecks in the way of communication. These can be language barriers, physical barriers, psychological barriers or organisational barriers.

For measures to overcome barriers to effective communication, refer to text page 115.

7. Explain any three barriers to communication. **ISC 2018, 14**

Or Explain the usual barriers to communication. **ISC 2004, 01 (5M)**

Or What is meant by barrier to communication? Explain any four types of barriers to communication. **ISC 2000**

Ans Refer to text on page 115.

8. Write briefly on 'direction as a function of management'. **ISC 2008 (3M)**

Ans It refers to the process of instructing, guiding, counselling, motivating and leading people in the organisation through effective communication, so that their efforts result in achievement of organisational objectives.

Characteristics of directing are

(i) **Initiating process** It involves giving orders and instructions to the employees and thereby, plans are converted into actions.

(ii) **Pervasive function** The directing function is performed by all managers at all levels to achieve the organisational goals.

(iii) **Continuous process** It is an activity that takes place throughout the life of an organisation, irrespective of people occupying managerial position.

9. What are the essentials of an ideal communication? **ISC 2003 (5M)**

Ans The following are the essentials of an ideal communication

(i) **Be aware of languages, tone and content of message** Language, tone and content of message should be so adjusted, according to the situation that it is easily understood by the receiver and stimulates them to respond.

(ii) **Be a good listener** Lot of problems can be solved due to attentive listening quality of the manager.

Essentials of Ideal Communication

- Be aware of languages, tone and content of message
- Be a good listener
- Follow-up communication
- Well drafted message
- Grapevine
- Mutual trust and faith

(iii) **Follow-up communication** Sometimes it is difficult to implement instructions in its totality by the subordinates. To overcome this, regular follow-up should be done by managers.

(iv) **Well drafted message** Message to be conveyed should be clear without the use of ambiguous words and should be understandable to the receiver.

(v) **Grapevine** Use of informal channels should be used tactfully for speed and positive response.

(vi) **Mutual trust and faith** Both the parties involved in communication will only be able to communicate freely, put suggestions and ideas and implement the required changes only when they have trust and faith on each other.

10. Communication is the number one problem of management. Explain. *ISC 2001 (5M)*

Ans Communication is the most important element for the success of an organisation. If communication is effective it can translate the organisational objectives into action, thus contributing towards organisation's success.

Plans will remain plans and not implemented untill properly communicated.

Whether it is conveying the plans and objectives to be achieved, supervising the employees, giving orders and asking for feedback, communicating regarding problems, grievances, etc the effectiveness of communication plays a major role.

As Louis A Alley has put it "Communication is a systematic and continuous process of telling, listening and understanding."

It is a systematic and continuous process and if not effective, can lead to hurdles in achieving objectives.

In the absence of effective communication following problems may be faced by an organisation

(i) Coordination between various activities, departments, level of management will not be upto the mark.
(ii) Smooth working of an enterprise will be disrupted.
(iii) Decision-making will be delayed.
(iv) Managerial efficiency will be reduced.
(v) Effective leadership cannot be established.

Value Points

For getting maximum marks, following points can be included in the answer

- Importance of communication.
- Problems faced by organisation in the absence of communication.

Additional Questions

2 Marks Questions

1. Give the meaning and definition of directing.

Ans Directing means giving instructions and guiding people in doing work. It is that part of the management process which ensures that the members of an organisation work efficiently and effectively for the attainment of desired objectives.

According to Theo Haimann, "Directing consists of the processes and techniques utilised in issuing instructions and making decisions that operations are carried on as originally planned."

2. Explain any two factors which affect span of control.

Ans Following are the factors affecting span of control

(i) **Nature of work** If the nature of work is of routine, repetitive and simple; then wider span of supervision control can be there, but in case of complex and complicated work, narrow span of control should be followed i.e. few persons under the supervisor/manager should be there.

(ii) **Ability of supervisor** Competent, experienced and trained supervisor is relatively capable of supervising large number of employees.

4 Marks Question

1. Explain briefly the features of directing.

Ans Refer to text on page 110.

TOPIC 5

Controlling

Meaning of Controlling

Controlling is one of the important functions performed by a manager. It ensures that activities in an organisation are performed as per the plans.

Controlling may be defined as the process, through which managers can ensure that actual activities and results are in conformity with the planned activities and results.

The main objective of this function is to check and ensure that performance of work is in accordance with plans.

According to **Koontz** and **O' Donnell**, "Managerial control implies the measurement of accomplishment against the standard and the correction of deviations to assure attainment of objectives according to plans."

Nature of Controlling

Following are the eminent features of controlling that describes its nature

(i) **Goal-oriented** Controlling ensures that an organisation's resources are being used effectively and efficiently for the achievement of predetermined goals. Thus, it is a goal-oriented function.

(ii) **Pervasive function** Controlling is an essential function. All managers have to perform this function at all levels of management to keep control over activities in their areas.

(iii) **Continuous function** Controlling is a never ending process as managers perform this function at all levels and at all time to ensure the conformity with plans.

(iv) **Both backward and forward looking process** Controlling is a backward looking process because it is like a postmortem of past activities to find out deviations from standard plans and it is also a forward looking process, as it seeks to improve future results by comparing the activities.

(v) **Dynamic process** Controlling involves review of standards as well as taking corrective actions, which may lead to changes in other managerial functions. The control system has to adapt to the changing conditions of the organisation.

Steps of Controlling Process

The main steps in controlling process are

(i) **Setting performance standards** The first step of the control process is to establish standards against which actual results are to be evaluated.

Standards are the criteria against which actual performance would be measured. These serves as benchmarks, towards which an organisation strives to work.

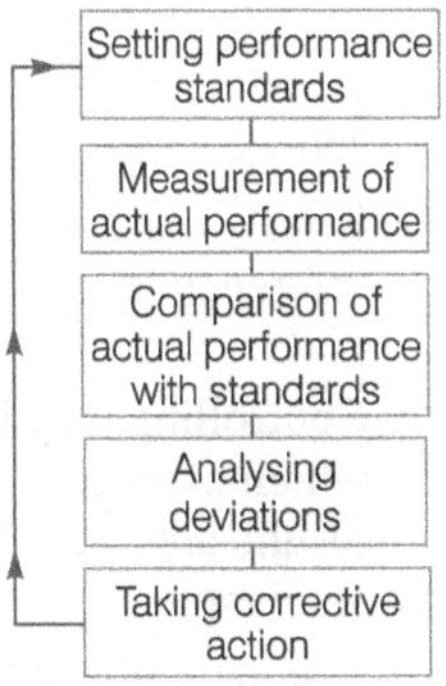

Controlling process

(ii) **Measurement of actual performance** Once the standards are fixed, the next step is to measure the actual performance. Generally, it is conducted by the managers to analyse the overall efficiency level of the employees. While measuring the performance, quantitative as well as qualitative aspects are kept in mind.

(iii) **Comparing actual performance with standards** This step involves comparison of actual performance with the standard. Such comparison helps in revealing the deviation between actual and desired results.

(iv) **Analysing deviations** Under this step, a range of deviations should be established, as the deviations in key areas of business need to be attended on urgent basis as compared to deviation in certain insignificant areas. There is a need to determine the acceptable range of deviations.

Following points should be kept in mind, while analysing deviations

(a) **Critical point control** According to this principle, control system should first focus on Key Result Areas (KRAs), which are critical for the success of the organisation.

(b) **Management/Control by exception** It suggests that, if a manager tries to control everything, he may end up in controlling nothing.

Thus, in this context, it is stated that managers should first handle the deviations which are beyond the specific range and he should not waste his time and energy in finding solutions to minor deviations.

(v) **Taking corrective measures** This is the final step in which manager takes corrective measures to bring back everything on track in the organisation i.e. according to set plans.

Importance of Controlling

A good control system helps an organisation in the following ways

(i) **Accomplishing organisational goals** The controlling function measures the accomplishment against the standards and corrects deviations. This helps in ensuring that organisation is moving on the right track to achieve the organisational goals.

(ii) **Judging accuracy of standards** A sound controlling system helps the management to verify whether the standards set are accurate and objective. It keeps a careful check on the changes which are taking place in the organisation and in the environment, thereby, helping to review and raise the standards in the light of such changes.

(iii) **Making efficient use of resources** By exercising control, a manager seeks to reduce wastage and spoilage of resources. Each activity is performed in accordance with predetermined standards and norms.

Thus, controlling ensures that resources are being used efficiently and effectively towards the attainment of organisational goals.

(iv) **Improving employee motivation** An effective control system ensures that an employee should be aware of what they are expected to do and what are the standards which are set for them, so that they will be appraised in future. Thus, it helps in motivating them to give better performance.

(v) **Ensuring order and discipline** The controlling function helps to minimise undesirable behaviour of employees by keeping a close check on their activities. Thus, it facilitates order and discipline in the organisation.

Relationship between Planning and Controlling

Planning and controlling are twins of management. They are inter-related and interdependent functions of management. Without planning, there lies no basis for controlling.

Planning and Controlling are Inter-related and Interdependent

A system of control presupposes the existence of certain standards. These standards of performance serve as the basis of controlling, which are provided by planning.

Once a plan becomes operational, controlling is necessary to monitor its progress. Thus, we can say that planning without controlling is meaningless. Similarly, controlling is blind without planning. If the standards are not set in advance, managers have nothing to control.

Planning and controlling, both are inseparable and they reinforce each other.

Both are Forward Looking as well as Backward Looking Functions

Planning and controlling are both backward and forward looking. Planning is looking ahead because all plans are prepared for future and it looks back as it is guided by past experience and feedback reports.

On the other hand, controlling is forward looking as it seeks to improve performance in future and it also looks back because it is like a postmortem of past activities to find out deviations in standard planning.

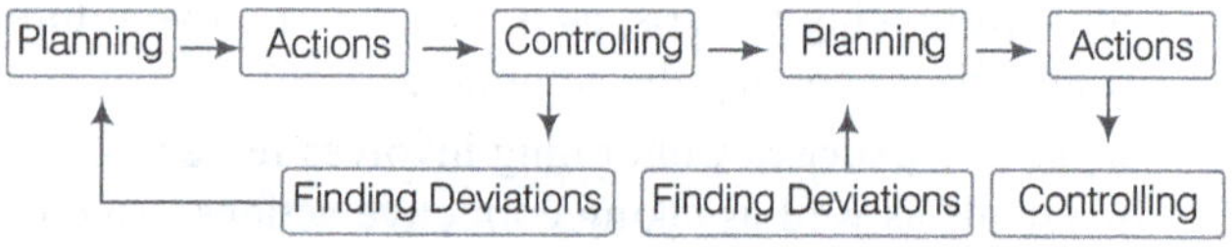

The diagram clearly depicts that planning sets action for controlling and then by finding deviations controlling provides base for planning.

PYQs Previous Years' Questions

1/2 Marks Questions

1. Explain the concept of management by exception.
ISC 2023, Sem II Specimen 2022, 16 (2M)

Ans Management by exception suggests that, if a manager tries to control everything, he may end up in controlling nothing. Thus, in this context, it is stated that managers should first handle the deviations which are beyond. A specific range and he should not waste his time and energy in finding solutions to minor deviations.

2. "The first step in the process of controlling, as a function of management, is the comparison of actual performance with standard performance."

State whether this statement is true or false.
ISC Sem II 2022 (1M)

Ans False. The first step in the process of controlling is setting performance standards.

3. Briefly discuss the meaning of controlling with reference to the functions of management.
ISC Sem II 2022 (2M)

Ans Controlling may be defined as the process, through which managers can ensure that actual activities and results are in conformity with the planned activities and results.

The main objective of this function is to check and ensure that performance of work is in accordance with plans.

4. Planning and controlling are interrelated. State true or false.
ISC Sem II Specimen 2022 (1M)

Ans True

3/4/5 Marks Questions

1. Ms. Jasdeep, the production manager in a reputed manufacturing company believes in planning to achieve the desired goals while Mr. Philips, the sales manager in the same company thinks that controlling is the best way to achieve the desired results.

Briefly explain the relationship between the two functions of management highlighted above.

ISC 2024 (4M)

Or "There is a close and reciprocal relationship between planning and controlling." Explain the statement.

ISC 2003

Ans Planning involves selecting enterprise objectives and deciding ways to achieve them.

Controlling is the process of assuring that actions are in line with the plans. Planning sets the course and control makes events conform to the chosen course. All controls imply existence of goals and plans.

No manager can ascertain whether his subordinates are operating in the desired way unless he has a plan.

Control will be much better, if the plans are clear and well coordinated. Without planning, there is no basis for controlling activities. In the absence of plans, it is not possible to evaluate performance. Similarly, without controlling, planned activities cannot be properly implemented and there cannot be improvement in future plans. Predetermined goals can be achieved only through controlling.

Planning without control is useless and control without planning is meaningless. Planning, based on facts, makes controlling easier. Thus, planning and controlling are mutually interrelated and interdependent.

Value Points

For getting maximum marks, following points can be included in the answer

- Focus on basic concept of the statement i.e. planning and controlling here.
- Connect them according to the demand of question.

2. Controlling is a systematic process involving a series of steps. Explain these steps of controlling. **ISC 2023 (5M)**

Or

Explain the various steps involved in the process of controlling, as a function of management. **ISC 2019 (5M)**

Or

Write short note on steps involved in the process of control. **ISC 2009 (4M)**

Ans Steps involved in the process of control are

(i) **Establishment of standards** The first step of the control process is to establish the standards with which the actual results are to be evaluated. A standard is the criteria against which actual performance can be compared. Standards should be set precisely in quantitative terms.

(ii) **Measurement of performance** Once the standards of desired performance are fixed, the next step is to measure the actual performance. Performance should be measured in same terms, in which standards have been established.

Steps of Controlling Process

- Establishment of standards
- Measurement of performance
- Comparison of actual performance with standards
- Analysing deviations
- Taking corrective action

(iii) **Comparison of actual performance with standards** The actual performance is then compared with the standards. Such comparison will reveal the deviations from the standards.

(iv) **Analysing deviations** Every significant deviation is analysed to find out why it has occurred. This will help in finding out causes responsible for deviations.

(v) **Taking corrective action** The final step in the control process is taking appropriate actions so that deviations may not occur again and the objectives of the organisation are achieved.

It may also necessitate reforming the process of selection and training of workers. Thus, controlling may require change in all other managerial functions.

3. State two reasons to emphasise the importance of controlling as a function of management.

ISC Sem II Specimen 2022

Or Explain any five points of importance of controlling, as a function of management. **ISC Specimen 2018, 2017 (5M)**

Ans Refer to text on page 121 and 122.

4. Explain the nature of controlling. **ISC 2002**

Ans Refer to text on page 121.

TOPIC 6

Coordination

Meaning of Coordination

Coordination is the art of achieving harmony of individual and group efforts for the accomplishment of organisational goals.

It develops a team spirit and creates an atmosphere of cooperation among the staff. It is the very essence of management, as it is inherent in all managerial functions.

According to **Koontz** and **O' Donnell**, "Coordination is the essence of managership for the achievement of harmony of individual efforts towards the accomplishment of group goals."

Features of Coordination

Following are the features of coordination

(i) **Integration of group efforts** All business activities are interdependent. Therefore, there should be coordination among them. Coordination enables the business to make efficient use of its available resources.

(ii) **Unity of action** Coordination enables the manager to secure unity of action in the realisation of common purpose.

(iii) **Continuous process** Coordination is a continuous process and not a one time task.

A manager has to continuously coordinate the activities of different departments in order to meet the targets by using the available resources efficiently.

(iv) **All pervasive function** It is an all pervasive function which runs through all managerial functions from planning till controlling. It is not only needed among different departments but also within the departments at all levels.

(v) **Deliberate function/managerial responsibility** A manager has to coordinate the efforts of different individuals working in an organisation in a conscious and deliberate manner, i.e. with cooperation.

Coordination without cooperation may lead to wastage of efforts and cooperation without coordination may lead to dissatisfaction among employees. Thus, both should be followed side-by-side.

(vi) **Dynamic process** An organisation runs smoothly with the help of coordination.

Coordination as an Essence of Management

Coordination is a systematic and orderly arrangement of individual and group efforts to provide unity of action in the pursuit of a common purpose. It is not considered as a separate function, but it is the essence of management.

Coordination is the force that binds all the other functions of management. It is a common thread that runs through the activities of management within the organisation.

According to **George Terry**, "Coordination deals with the task of binding efforts in order to ensure successful attainment of an objective. It is accomplished by means of planning, organising, actuating and controlling."

For effective coordination, a manager has to create balance and unity among all activities of his subordinates. For this purpose, he performs managerial functions.

Coordination is considered as the essence of management because of the following reasons

(i) **Coordination is Needed to Perform all the Functions of Management**

(a) In **planning**, coordination is required between the main plan and supportive plans of different departments.

(b) **Organising**, is ineffective, if there is a lack of coordination between different departments and divisions.

(c) In **staffing**, coordination is required between the required skills and abilities of an individual who is selected to perform a job.

(d) **Directing**, is of no use, if there is lack of coordination between superiors and subordinates.

(e) In **controlling**, coordination is required between standards and actual performance.

(ii) **Coordination is Needed at all Levels of Management**

(a) **Top Level** The top level coordinates the activities of the whole organisation keeping in view the desired goals.

(b) **Middle Level** The middle level managers coordinate the activities of different departments.

(c) **Lower Level** The lower level coordinates the activities of the workers for achieving goals.

Thus, we can say that coordination is the essence of management.

PYQs Previous Years' Questions

1/2 Marks Questions

1. .... is not a separate function but the essence of management. *ISC 2023 (1M)*

Ans Coordination

2. .... is the hidden force that links all the functions of management. *ISC Specimen 2023 (1M)*

Ans Coordination

3. Which function of management is often referred to as the essence of management and binds all the other functions?

   Justify its significance in the function of planning. *ISC Sem II Specimen 2022 (2M)*

Ans 'Coordination' function is the essence of management. Without coordination between employees and management, it is not possible for the organisation to achieve organisational goals. The employees are required to understand and follow the directions of the management properly.

In **planning**, coordination is required between the main plan and supportive plans of different departments.

4. Explain the meaning of coordination, as a function of management. *ISC 2016 (2M)*

Ans Coordination is the art of achieving harmony of individual and group efforts for the accomplishment of organisational goals. It develops a team spirit and creates an atmosphere of cooperation among the staff. It is the very essence of management, as it is inherent in all managerial functions.

According to **Koontz** and **O'Donnell**, "Coordination is the essence of managership for the achievement of harmony of individual efforts towards the accomplishment of group goals."

5. Explain the features of coordination. *ISC 2001 (2M)*

Ans Refer to text on page 124.

4/5 Marks Question

1. Comment briefly on 'coordination is the essence of management'. *ISC 2018, 05*

Or 'Coordination is the essence of management'. Explain. *ISC 2015*

Ans Refer to text on page 124.

Case Based Question

Case I

After pursuing a course in gemology from Australia, Raj started a workshop in Surat to support his father's jewellery business in Delhi. He was used to speaking in English, but the local skilled workers could understand only Hindi and Gujarati. As a result, Raj started facing problems in the work due to miscommunications between him and the workers. He was not able to get the jewellery designs made in the desired manner. *ISC Specimen 2023*

(i) Define the term communication.

Ans Communication is a two-way process which involves transferring of information or messages from one person or group to another.

(ii) Identify the type of communication barrier between Raj and his workers.

Ans Semantic barrier of communication

(iii) Suggest any three measures by which Raj can make his communication effective.

Ans Being clear, specific and straightforward are sometimes the easiest ways to overcome semantic barriers. But this isn't always possible. Here are some ways to achieve it

(a) **Be explicit** Hold the sarcasm and the coded messages. Express expectations clearly to eliminate the chance of misinterpretation.

(b) **Uses systems** Communication can be improved by establishing standards for meetings, documentation and training so that everyone knows what is going on. Putting things down in writing is often the best way to avoid uncertainty. Make it a part of project management and reporting structures.

(c) **Practice active listening** When it comes to deciphering meaning, context is king. The best way to establish context is to listen carefully. This involves acknowledging the fact that the other person is talking or expressing how they're feeling.

(iv) With reference to planning as a function of management, explain the term programme as a type of a plan.

Ans Programme is "a comprehensive plan that includes future use of different resources in an integrated pattern and establishes a sequence of required and time schedules for each in order to achieve stated objectives". Thus, a programme includes objective, policies, procedures, methods, standards and budgets.

CHAPTER TEST

01 Mark Questions

1. Which of the following is not a type of communication barrier?
(a) Semantic barriers
(b) Psychological barriers
(c) Rational barriers
(d) Organisational barriers

2. ……… is the process of influencing the behaviour of people by making them strive voluntarily towards the achievement of organisational goals.
(a) Supervision (b) Communication
(c) Leadership (d) Motivation

3. Identify the correct sequence of the steps involved in the staffing process.
(a) Recruitment, Estimating the Manpower Requirements, Placement and Orientation, Selection
(b) Estimating the Manpower Requirements, Selection, Placement and Orientation, Recruitment
(c) Selection, Estimating the Manpower Requirements, Recruitment, Placement and Orientation
(d) Estimating the Manpower Requirements, Recruitment, Selection, Placement and Orientation

4. "Motivation is a result of an interaction between a person and a situation." State true or false.

5. "Planning is theoretical whereas controlling is practical." State true or false.

6. ……… describes one of the concepts that are crucial for the smooth running of an organisation.

7. The plan which includes objective, policy, procedure and rule is called ……… .

8. What is span of control?

9. What is management by exception?

10. **Assertion** (A) Delegation is an optional policy decision and is done at the discretion of top management.

Reason (R) No individual can perform all tasks on his own.

Alternatives
(a) Both Assertion (A) and Reason (R) are true and Reason (R) is the correct explanation of Assertion (A)
(b) Both Assertion (A) and Reason (R) are true, but Reason (R) is not the correct explanation of Assertion (A)
(c) Assertion (A) is true, but Reason (R) is false
(d) Assertion (A) is false, but Reason (R) is true

02 Marks Questions

11. Which function of management is also called 'management in action'?

12. State two disadvantages of planning.

13. What is 'PODSCORB' and who has given this idea?

14. State two objectives of communication.

15. How does planning facilitate control?

16. Write two points of distinction between delegation and decentralisation.

17. Explain 'management by exception'.

03/04/05 Marks Questions

18. "Coordination is the essence of management." Comment.

19. Why is planning important in an organisation?

20. Discuss any five types of plans.

21. How does training help the employers?

22. What are the organisational and psychological barriers to communication?

23. "Planning and controlling are mutually interdependent and interrelated". Explain.

24. Explain the meaning of formal and informal communication. Explain, how informal communication can also facilitate formal communication?

25. How can ideal communication be achieved?

Answers

1. (c) Rational barriers
2. (c) Leadership
3. (d) Estimating the Manpower Requirements, Recruitment, Selection, Placement and Orientation
4. True *5.* True
6. Planning *7.* programme
10. (d) Assertion (A) is false, but Reason (R) is true

09

Marketing Concept and Functions

TREND ANALYSIS 5 YEARS

			Average No. of Questions Across all Sets				
		Types of Questions	2024	2023	2020	2019	2018
TOPIC 01	Market and Marketing	1 Mark	1	2	—	—	—
		2 Marks	—	—	2	1	1
		3/4/5 Marks	—	—	1	1	—
TOPIC 02	Functions of Marketing	1 Mark	1	—	—	—	—
		2 Marks	—	—	—	1	—
		3/4/5 Marks	1	—	1	—	1

Meaning and Definition of Market

In the traditional sense, market refers to a place where buyers and sellers come together to effect exchange of goods and services. In the modern sense, it is a much wider term and it does not refer to a 'place' but includes all potential buyers of a product or a service.

A market is the environment of the region where forces of demand and supply operate directly or by means of any kind of communication.

According to **Philip Kotler**, ''A market is the set of actual and potential buyers of a product.''

According to **Professor Chapman**, ''The term market refers not necessarily to a place, but always to the buyers and sellers who are in direct contact with one another.''

Classification of Market/Types of Market

Markets can be classified on the following basis

1. On the Basis of Geographical Area

(i) **Local market** Buying and selling in a limited area, in a town or a village.

(ii) **Regional market** Trading activities in a particular region.

(iii) **National market** Related to activities of buying and selling within boundaries of a country.

(iv) **International market** Where buyers and sellers of two or more nations are involved.

2. On the Basis of Volume of Business

(i) **Wholesale market** Where goods are sold in bulk to the retailers.

(ii) **Retail market** Where small quantities of goods are sold by retailers to the consumers directly.

3. On the Basis of Position of Buyers and Sellers

(i) **Primary market** Primary producers sell their agricultural output to wholesalers or their agents.

(ii) **Secondary market** Market in which wholesalers sell their products to retailers.

(iii) **Terminal market** Market where retailers sell their products to final consumers.

4. On the Basis of Nature of Transaction

(i) **Spot market** Goods are transferred from sellers to buyers on the spot at the time of purchase.

(ii) **Future market** Buyers and sellers enter into a contract to buy/sell goods at a future date.

5. On the Basis of Nature of Consumption

(i) **Consumers market** When goods are produced for direct consumption of consumers, it is a consumers market.

(ii) **Producers market** When goods are produced to be used further in the process of production, then it is a producers market.

6. On the Basis of Subject of Exchange

(i) **Commodity market** Organised market for sale and purchase of commodities is referred to as commodities market.

(ii) **Money market** Short-term finance market, which provides financing to business enterprises through a network of banking system is referred to as money market.

(iii) **Capital market** Specialised market for providing long-term finance through a network of financial institutions, stock exchanges, investment trusts and insurance companies is known as 'capital market'.

Meaning of Marketing

Marketing is an operative function of management. Merchandising, selling and distribution, etc. are all parts of a large number of activities undertaken by a firm, collectively called 'marketing'.

Features of Marketing

Following are the features of marketing

(i) The focus of marketing process is on the satisfaction of the needs and wants of individuals and organisations.

(ii) Marketing is a dynamic process as it adapts to changes in the environment on a regular basis.

(iii) Marketing makes use of knowledge from several fields of study such as economics, sociology, law, statistics, etc.

(iv) Marketing includes coordinating a number of interconnected and interdependent tasks.

(v) Marketing is a pervasive function.

Concepts of Marketing

Marketing concepts can be studied under the following two heads

I. Traditional or Production Oriented Marketing Concept

Traditionally, marketing was viewed as the process of directing the flow of goods and services from the producers to the consumers.

According to **Dudley** and **Rawzan**, "Marketing is the economic process by means of which, goods and services are exchanged and their values are determined in terms of money prices."

According to **Huegey** and **Mitchell**, "Marketing includes all activities involved in the creation of a place, time and possession utility."

Thus, the traditional concept believed in maximising profits by selling goods and services.

The following are important traditional marketing concepts

(i) **Production concept** According to this concept, the key to success was availability and affordability of a product. It believed that profits can be maximised through mass production.

(ii) **Product concept** The theorists of this concept believed good quality goods will sell for themselves.

(iii) **Selling concept** In this concept, it is believed that until the consumers are pushed, they will not purchase the goods. Thus, the focus is on selling through intensive marketing and advertising.

Features of Traditional Marketing Concept

Following are the features of this concept

(i) Marketing begins after the commodities are produced and ends with their sale.

(ii) This marketing concept is incompatible with the present business world, which is characterised by cut throat competition, consumer awareness and a dynamic environment.

(iii) This marketing strategy emphasises exclusively on one-way traffic, i.e the flow of commodities from the producer to the customer.

As a result, it focuses solely on the physical process of delivering products and services.

(iv) It focuses solely on the product rather than on customer satisfaction.

II. Modern Concept of Marketing/ Consumer Oriented Marketing

The focus of modern concept is on consumers.

The modern marketing concept emphasises that firms can achieve the objective of profit maximisation by finding out needs and requirements of customers and satisfying them in an effective manner, better than its competitors.

According to **Philip Kotler**, ''Marketing is the process of planning and executing the conception, pricing, promotion and distribution of goods and services and ideas to create exchanges with target groups that satisfy customer and organisational objectives.''

According to **Geoffrey F Francis**, ''Marketing is directed towards the satisfaction of consumers and in this context, the consumer is the attraction for which marketing is carried out.''

Thus, this concept, also known as the 'marketing concept' is wider and focuses on customer orientation.

Features of Modern Marketing Concept

The features of this concept are

(i) It is customer oriented.
(ii) It is an integrated approach.
(iii) Marketing research is an important element.
(iv) Marketing planning and control are crucial.
(v) This technique focuses on two-way traffic, in which the marketer offers satisfaction and the consumer provides response to the marketer's efforts.

Difference between Selling and Marketing

Basis	Selling	Marketing
Scope	It has a limited scope. It is concerned with transfer of ownership of goods from the sellers to the buyers through promotion and salesmanship. Thus, it is just a part of marketing.	It has a wider scope. It is concerned with identifying customer's needs, developing the product, pricing, selling and providing after sales services to satisfy the customers.
Focus	It focuses on transferring the title and ownership of goods from sellers to the buyers.	It focuses on maximum satisfaction of customer's needs and wants.
Aim	Selling aims at maximising the profit by increasing sales.	Marketing aims at increasing profit by satisfying the consumer.
Start and end	Selling activities starts after the production of products and ends with their sale.	Marketing activities start much before the production of products and continue even after their sale.
Emphasis	Under selling, the emphasis is on 'bend the customer according to the product'.	Under marketing, the emphasis is on 'developing the product and other strategies according to the need of the customers'.
Strategies	Promotion and persuasion are the main strategies under selling.	It involves strategies related to product, promotion, pricing and physical distribution.

Objectives of Marketing

The major objectives of marketing are

(i) **Consumer satisfaction** The primary objective of marketing is to satisfy the needs and wants of the customer, from identifying the need, to product planning, its pricing, labelling, packaging and distribution in a manner, which provides maximum satisfaction to the consumer.
(ii) **Creating demand and capturing the market** After identifying the needs of consumers and developing the product, the main objective is to create a demand for the product by advertising and promotion and then try to capture a reasonable share in the market.
(iii) **Promoting reputation** Creating a goodwill for the organisation and its products, is necessary for sustaining in the market and for further growth and development.
(iv) **Coordination and integration** Marketing function tries to integrate other functions of management and tries to achieve coordination among various departments, *viz* production, finance, personnel, etc.
(v) **Maximise profit** All activities will be in vain, if the profits are not maximised, as profits are necessary for survival and growth of business.
(vi) **Serving the society** Marketing system creates demand, improves the standard of living by bringing in quality products, creating employment opportunity and thus, is oriented towards service to the society.

Importance of Marketing

The importance of marketing can be viewed in following points

(i) It is a source of revenue for the business, as the production can translate into sale, on the basis of how effectively this function is performed.
(ii) Satisfying consumer needs.
(iii) Basis of decision-making, regarding what, how, when and where to produce.

(iv) Achieve coordination between production and consumption activities.

(v) Benefits the nation and society at large in the following ways

(a) Marketing stimulates the aggregate demand thereby, enlarging the size of market.

(b) Marketing in basic industries, agriculture, mining and plantation industries helps in distribution of output without which, there is no possibility of mobilisation of goods and services, which is the key point for economic growth.

(c) It also accelerates the process of monetising the economy, which in turn, facilitates the transfer of investable resources.

(d) It helps in the discovery of entrepreneurial talent.

(e) Intermediate industrial goods and semi-industrial products etc, essentially marketed for industrial purpose, in order to develop the industrial sector, accelerate economic growth.

(f) In external trade, services like tourism, banking and marketing plays an eminent role in order to facilitate growth in the economy.

Functions of Marketing

Marketing involves performance of a series of a specialised functions to meet the objectives of marketing. These functions are as follows

1. Exchange Functions

(i) **Buying and assembling** Buying means purchase of raw material for production process or purchase of finished goods for the purpose of resale.

Assembling means buying and collecting different items from various places and keeping them under one roof for the purpose of resale.

(ii) **Selling and distribution** It means finding the customers, creating demand and transferring goods for value.

The selling involves various activities to be performed, such as

(a) Product planning and development
(b) Contact the buyers
(c) Create demand
(d) Negotiation of terms of sale
(e) Contract of sale
(f) After sales support

Distribution covers all the activities required to physically move the goods from manufacturers to the ultimate customers.

2. Supply Functions

(i) **Transportation** There is a place gap between production and consumption. To cover this place gap, the marketer makes use of various modes of transport, so that goods can be transferred to different corners of the country. It removes the hindrance of place.

(ii) **Storage or Warehousing** There is a time gap between production and consumption. Thus, marketers often maintain their own warehouses to store the products or they make use of public warehouses to keep the goods safe and fresh, till they are demanded in the market. This function reduces the hindrance of time.

3. Facilitating Functions

(i) **Product planning and development** It includes the introduction and development of new products, as well as the improvement of existing products and the elimination of unprofitable products from the product line.

(ii) **Standardisation and grading** Standardisation provides quality assurance and consistency to consumers. Consumers are assured about the quality of product, packing, etc. Grading means classifying the product on some basis such as quality, size, etc. Through grading, marketer can get higher price for quality product. Grading is generally used in agricultural products, e.g. Wheat, rice, pulses, etc.

(iii) **Packaging** It is the process of designing and producing suitable packages for a product. A package is a wrapper or container, in which a product is enclosed or sealed. Packaging protects the product during storage and transportation.

(iv) **Branding and labelling** It is the process of giving a separate identity to a product with the help of brands.

A brand is a name, sign, symbol, design or a combination thereof, used to distinguish the product of one enterprise from those of others, e.g. Tata steel, Britannia biscuits, Amul butter, etc. Labelling refers to designing and developing the label to be put on the package.

(v) **Pricing of products** Price means the money, which a customer has to pay to buy a product or service. It is the most crucial element of marketing, as customer is highly price sensitive. A little variation in price may take your customer nearer to the competitor's product.

(vi) **Promotion** In marketing, promotion includes all the activities which are designed to influence the behaviour of the buyers. It involves informing and persuading customers, so as to make the products and services known and acceptable to them.
For this, several techniques are used for promotion, e.g. Advertising, personal selling, publicity and sales promotion.

(vii) **Financing** In terms of marketing, the financing need is for meeting the expenses of getting merchandise into the hands of the buyer. A large amount is required for keeping stock and for other needs.

(viii) **Risk taking** There are many unforeseen risks inherent in any business activity. Insurance provides a security against risk. Insurance helps a businessman to carry on business with confidence.

(ix) **Market research** It is a systematic investigation of facts relevant to marketing. Several techniques are followed for market research. Marketing research is necessary for knowing the needs of the consumers, demand and other dynamics of market. It provides a sound basis for formulating marketing strategies and policies.

PYQs Previous Years' Questions

1 Mark Questions

1. As a function of marketing, warehousing creates time utility. State true or false. *ISC 2024*

Ans True

2. Customer orientation is a modern approach to marketing. State true or false. *ISC 2024*

Ans True

3. A market where products are transferred immediately from seller to buyer is called a future market. State true or false. *ISC 2023*

Ans False. A market where products are transferred immediately from seller to buyer is called spot market.

4. **Assertion** (A) Marketing and selling are not synonymous with each other.

Reason (R) Selling is narrow in scope, where as marketing is wide. *ISC 2023*

Alternatives

(a) Both Assertion (A) and Reason (R) are true and Reason (R) is the correct explanation of Assertion (A)
(b) Both Assertion (A) and Reason (R) are true, but Reason (R) is not the correct explanation of Assertion (A)
(c) Assertion (A) is true, but Reason (R) is false
(d) Assertion (A) is false, but Reason (R) is true

Ans (a) Both Assertion (A) and Reason (R) are true and Reason (R) is the correct explanation of Assertion (A)

5. **Assertion** (A) Marketing research serves as the intelligence wing of the business.

Reason (R) Marketing research provides a strong basis for formulating marketing strategies and policies. *ISC Sem II 2022*

Alternatives

(a) Both Assertion (A) and Reason (R) are true and Reason (R) is the correct explanation for Assertion (A)
(b) Both Assertion and Reason (R) are true, but Reason (R) is not the correct explanation for Assertion (A)
(c) Assertion is true, but Reason (R) is false
(d) Assertion is false, but Reason (R) is true

Ans (a) Both Assertion (A) and Reason (R) are true and Reason (R) is the correct explanation for Assertion (A)

2 Marks Questions

1. Briefly explain commodity market with the help of an example. *ISC Sem II 2022*

Ans Organised market for sale and purchase of commodities is referred to as commodities market.
It is according to the prescribed rules and regulations.
e.g. A market for wheat, natural gas, precious metals, etc.

2. Marketing and selling are synonymous terms. Do you agree? Give reasons. *ISC Sem II Specimen 2022*

Ans No, marketing and selling are not synonymous, these two are different concepts. **Marketing** The main aim of marketing is to earn profits through maximum customer satisfaction. **Selling** Selling aims at earning maximum profit by increasing the volume of sales.

3. Name two types of markets on the basis of subject of exchange. *ISC 2020, Specimen 2018*

Ans On the basis of subject of exchange, market can be classified as (any two)
(i) Commodity market
(ii) Capital market
(iii) Money market

4. Mention any two facilitating functions of marketing. **ISC 2019**

Ans Facilitating functions of marketing are (any two)

(i) Product planning and development
(ii) Standardisation and grading
(iii) Packaging (iv) Branding and labelling

5. Name two types of markets on the basis of nature of transactions. **ISC 2019**

Ans Two types of markets on the basis of nature of transactions are

(i) Spot market (ii) Future market

6. Mention two types of markets on the basis of the position of buyers and sellers. **ISC 2018**

Ans Two types of markets on the basis of position of buyers and sellers are as follows

(i) Primary market (ii) Secondary market

7. State any two features of marketing. **ISC Specimen 2018**

Ans Features of marketing are

(i) The focus of marketing process is on the satisfaction of the needs and wants of individual and organisation.
(ii) Marketing is a pervasive function.

8. Mention two physical functions of marketing. **ISC 2017**

Ans Two physical functions of marketing are

(i) **Transportation** The goods are not necessarily consumed at the same place, where they are produced. There is a place gap between production and consumption. To cover this place gap, the marketer makes use of various modes of transport, so that goods can be transferred to different corners of the country. It removes hindrance of place.
(ii) **Storage and warehousing** The goods are not consumed immediately after they are produced. There is a time gap between production and consumption. Thus, marketers often maintain their own warehouses to store the products or they make use of public warehouses to keep the goods safe and fresh, till they are demanded in the market. This function reduces the hindrance of time.

9. Define the term 'market'. **ISC 2013**

Ans Market in common parlance, is referred to a place where buyers and sellers meet and effect a sale. But, according to the modern concept, it is a wider term and it is not just a place.

Philip Kotler has rightly put it, "A market is the set of actual and potential buyers of a product."

10. Name two physical supply functions of marketing. **ISC 2012**

Ans Physical supply functions of marketing are

(i) Transportation (ii) Storage

11. State two functions of exchange with reference to marketing. **ISC 2010**

Ans Functions of exchange with reference to marketing are

(i) **Buying and assembling** Buying is related to buying of raw material or finished goods for the purpose of sale. Assembling is collection of various items under one roof for the purpose of sale.
(ii) **Selling** Transferring of goods from seller to buyer for value is referred to as selling.

12. Why is buying an important function of marketing? **ISC 2007**

Ans Buying the raw materials or finished goods for the purpose of sale is considered as an important function because profitability is dependent on cost of goods purchased. If the cost of goods purchased is more than profitability will be less. So, it is important to execute the buying function carefully.

13. Define marketing. **ISC 2005**

Ans According to American Management Association, "Marketing is the process of planning and executing the conception, pricing, promotion and distribution of ideas, goods and services to create exchanges that satisfy individual and organisational goals."

14. Explain, how modern marketing concept is distinct from traditional selling concept? **ISC 2001**

Ans Modern concept of marketing is a wider concept and focuses attention on the consumers and satisfaction of their needs. It starts even before the production begins and continues even after the sale has been made.

Whereas, traditional concept of marketing emphasises on mere transfer of goods from producers to sellers and does not lay emphasis on consumer satisfaction.

More importance is given to product and selling efforts rather than analysing the needs of consumers and their satisfaction.

Value Points

For getting maximum marks, following points can be included in the answer

- Modern concept is wider and focuses attention on consumers needs.
- Traditional concept focuses on product and selling efforts.

3/4/5 Marks Questions

1. Write short note on marketing research. *ISC 2024, 20, 16, 12, 10 (4M)*

Or Explain marketing research as a function of marketing. *ISC 2009 (4M)*

Ans Marketing research is the systematic gathering, recording and analysis of qualitative and quantitative data about issues relating to marketing of products and services.

The goal of marketing research is to identify and assess how changing elements of marketing mix, i.e. price, promotion, place and product impacts consumer behaviour.

Need and importance of marketing research is as follows

(i) It provides valuable data.
(ii) It studies consumer behaviour.
(iii) It helps to select suitable sales promotional technique.
(iv) It supplies market related information and provides competitors assessment.
(v) It helps to evaluate marketing performance.
(vi) SWOT analysis is facilitated.
(vii) Identifies trends, decides price, location and target market analysis.

2. State any two points of difference between marketing and selling. *ISC 2020*

Or

Distinguish between marketing and selling. *ISC Specimen 2018, 17 (3M)*

Ans Differences between marketing and selling are

Basis	Marketing	Selling
Focus	Marketing focuses on the need of customer.	Selling focuses on the need of seller.
Objective	Main objective of marketing is earning optimum profit with customer satisfaction.	Main objective of selling is to maximise the profit and sale.
Scope	Scope of marketing is very wide. It includes activities like creation of demand, designing of product according to demand, using promotional techniques and after sale survey to find out customer satisfaction.	Scope of selling is limited to exchange of goods or services for some consideration.

3. Define marketing. Briefly explain any three features of marketing. *ISC 2020 (5M)*

Ans **Marketing** It can be defined as a social process by which individual groups obtain what they need and want through creating offerings and freely exchanging products and services of value with others.

Following are the features of marketing

(i) **Needs and wants** The focus of marketing process is on the satisfaction of the needs and wants of individuals and organisations. A need is a state of felt deprivation or feeling of being deprived of something. Wants are culturally defined products that are potential satisfiers of needs. Wants are demands for specific goods.

> **Features of Marketing**
> - Needs and wants
> - Creating a market offering
> - Customer value

(ii) **Creating a market offering** Market offering refers to a complete offer for a product or service, having certain features like size, quality, taste, etc. at a certain price, available at a given outlet or location.

(iii) **Customer value** A product is purchased only when it is perceived to be giving greatest benefit or value for money to the buyers. Therefore, the job of a marketer is to add value to the product, so that the customers prefer it in relation to the competing products present in the market.

> **Concept Enhancer** Marketing is a dynamic process as it adapts to changes in the environment on a regular basis and includes coordinating a number of interconnected and interdependent tasks.

4. Explain any three objectives of marketing. *ISC 2019 (3M)*

Or Explain the objectives of marketing. *ISC 2015 (4M)*

Or Explain any four objectives of marketing. *ISC 2012 (4M)*

Ans Refer to text on page 129.

5. Discuss any five functions of marketing. *ISC 2018 (5M)*

Or Discuss the key functions of marketing. *ISC 2004 (5M)*

Ans In the marketing of goods and services, several specialised functions are needed to be performed. Important functions of marketing are

(i) **Buying and assembling** Buying is related to buying of raw material or finished good for the purpose of resale. Assembling is collection of various items under one roof for the purpose of sale.

(ii) **Selling** Transferring of goods from producer to seller for a value is referred to as selling.

(iii) **Transportation** It involves physical movement of goods from one place to another. Marketing function analysis its transportation needs after taking into consideration, various factors like nature of product, cost and locations of target market.

Functions of Marketing
- Buying and assembling
- Selling
- Transportation
- Storage and warehousing
- Marketing research

(iv) **Storage or Warehousing** There is a time gap between production and consumption. Thus, marketers often maintain their own warehouses to store the products or they make use of public warehouses to keep the goods safe and fresh, till they are demanded in the market. This function reduces the hindrance of time.

(v) **Marketing research** It is the process of gathering, recording and analysing all facts about problems relating to marketing. It is a systematic and intensive investigation of all phases of the marketing process, with a view to obtain relevant knowledge. Marketing research helps managers in making appropriate decisions.

6. Discuss any five points of importance of marketing. ***ISC Specimen 2018, 17 (5M)***

Ans Five points highlighting the importance of marketing are discussed below

(i) **Earning profit** It provides source of revenue for an organisation for its survival and growth.

(ii) **Improves standard of living** Marketing improves the standard of living by making available products and services that satisfy the needs of consumers.

(iii) **Economic development of nation** Marketing inspire people to take up new activities and give impetus to entrepreneurship.

(iv) **Basis of decision-making** Marketing helps in finding right type of product to be manufactured, place of production and places where product should be made available, pricing and other decisions related to marketing.

Importance of Marketing
- Earning profit
- Improves standard of living
- Economic development of nation
- Basis of decision-making
- To create good image

(v) **To create good image** Marketing helps to build up the public image of firm over a period. The marketing department provides quality products to customers at reasonable prices and thus, creates its impact on the customers. This helps to enhance the reputation of the business.

7. Explain buying and assembling, as functions of marketing. ***ISC 2017 (3M)***

Ans **Buying** It is one of the important functions of marketing. It is the first step in the process of marketing. A manufacture is required to buy raw materials for the production process. Similarly, a wholesaler and retailer have to buy goods to sell. Thus, in all functions of exchange, one aspect is buying.

Assembling Assembling starts after the goods have already been purchased. It is a function separate from buying. Assembling involve creation and maintenance of the stock of goods purchased from different sources at one place.

Common Mistake Number of students have no clarity regarding the meaning of 'assembling'. The terms buying and assembling were integrated with each other. Students are advised to explain them separately.

8. What is marketing? State two features of the modern concept of marketing. ***ISC 2016 (4M)***

Ans Traditionally, marketing refers to the performance of business activities that direct the flow of goods and services from producers to consumers.

In the modern sense, marketing refers to a social process, whereby people exchange goods and services for money or for something of value to them.

The focus of modern concept is on consumers. Consumers are regarded as the king of market and all activities are directed to maximise consumer satisfaction. The features of this concept are as follows

(i) It is customer oriented.

(ii) It is an integrated approach.

9. What is market? Explain the meaning of capital market and money market. ***ISC 2015 (3M)***

Ans Market is referred to a place where buyers and sellers meet and effect a sale. But it is a wider term and it is not just a place. Philip Kotler has rightly put it, "A market is the set of actual and potential buyers of a product."

(i) **Capital market** This is a specialised market for providing long-term finance to business enterprises.

It comprises of specialised financial institutions, stock exchanges, investment trusts and insurance companies.

(ii) **Money market** This is a specialised market for providing short-term finance to business enterprises. It consists of various types of banks.

Concept Enhancer
- Instruments involved in money market are commercial papers, treasury bills, trade credit, etc.
- Instrument involved in capital market are bonds, debentures, shares, assets, etc.

10. Differentiate between traditional concept of marketing and modern concept. *ISC 2015 (4M)*

Ans Difference between traditional approach and modern approach to marketing

Basis	Traditional approach to marketing	Modern approach to marketing
Focus	On production, product and selling efforts.	On consumer satisfaction.
Objective	Profit maximisation through availability/ product quality/sales volume.	Profit maximisation through consumer satisfaction.
Means to attain objective	Through mass production/product quality/selling efforts.	Through marketing techniques.
Starting point	It starts from factory.	It starts from market, i.e, by identifying the needs of consumers and then developing a product.

11. Explain any four facilitating functions of marketing. *ISC 2015, 2011 (4M)*

Ans Facilitating functions of marketing are

(i) **Marketing research** It is the process of gathering, recording and analysing all facts about problems relating to marketing.

It is a systematic and intensive investigation of all phases of the marketing process, with a view to obtain relevant knowledge. Marketing research helps managers in making appropriate decisions.

(ii) **Product planning and development** It includes the introduction and development of new products, as well as the improvement of existing products and the elimination of unprofitable products from the product line.

(iii) **Standardisation and grading** The term 'standardisation' is derived from the word standard which means the presence of certain desirable qualities like durability, safety, purity and other features like design, weight, colour, etc. in a product.

Facilitating Functions of Marketing
- Marketing research
- Product planning and development
- Standardisation and grading
- Branding and labelling

Standardisation refers to the process of setting certain standards for a commodity on the basis of its desired qualities. It implies that the different units of the commodity are of a specified and uniform quality.

It facilitates sale of goods through description and increases the confidence of consumers. Grading refers to the process of dividing products into classes, made up of units possessing similar characteristics.

It involves division of products into classes, lots or groups in accordance with predetermined grades of quality. Grading helps in fixing and securing remunerative prices for the products.

(iv) **Branding and labelling** Branding is a name or design of a product used to differentiate it from competitors. It helps in establishing a separate identity of the product. Labelling is designing the label of a product to be put on the product. A label describes the product, its usage, manufacturing, expiry date, etc.

12. Write short note on modern concept of marketing. *ISC 2014 (4M)*

Ans Refer to text on page 129.

13. What is consumer oriented concept of marketing? State its main features. *ISC 2005*

Ans Consumer oriented concept is the modern concept of marketing which lays emphasis on determination of consumers' needs and then satisfying them by developing the required product or services. It is also known as the marketing concept.

For features, refer to text on page 129.

Value Points

For getting maximum marks, following points can be included in the answer
- Corelate keywords of features with the meaning of concepts.
- Customers needs and wants, customer satisfaction and systematic approach.

CHAPTER TEST

01 Mark Questions

1. What is identifying consumer needs in functions of marketing?
(a) Gather information and analyse the needs of the market
(b) Objectives of the company
(c) The product that suits the needs of the consumer
(d) Ensuring uniformity in the product

2. Which of these is true about marketing?
(a) Marketing is used to promote the product and services
(b) Marketing is concerned about the sales only
(c) Marketing is the activity, set of institutions, and processes for creating, communicating, delivering, and exchanging offerings that have value for customers, clients, partners, and society at large
(d) Marketing considers only the needs of the organisation and not the society

3. Who is the father of modern marketing?
(a) Philip Kotler (b) Peter F Drucker
(c) Abraham Maslow (d) Raymond Kroc

4. In the evolution of marketing, the production period ended in
(a) Late 1800s (b) After the second world war
(c) 1920s (d) Early 20th century

5. Marketing is basically selling and advertising. State true or false.

6. According to Philip Kotler, marketing is …… .

7. Marketing and selling are ……… .

8. What is modern concept of marketing?

9. What is traditional concept of marketing?

10. **Assertion** (A) Customer satisfaction is the extent to which a firm fulfills a consumer's needs, desires and expectations.

Reason (R) If a firm produces the right goods or services, marketing has little role in creating customer satisfaction.

Alternatives
(a) Both Assertion (A) and Reason (R) are true and Reason (R) is the correct explanation of Assertion (A)
(b) Both Assertion (A) and Reason (R) are true, but Reason (R) is not the correct explanation of Assertion (A)
(c) Assertion (A) is true, but Reason (R) is false
(d) Assertion (A) is false, but Reason (R) is true

02 Marks Questions

11. Give a definition of market.

12. Write the types of market on the basis of volume of business.

13. Explain the buying and assembling functions of marketing.

14. Write any two features of traditional marketing concept.

15. Define consumer oriented marketing concept.

03/04/05 Marks Questions

16. What is the importance of marketing in the modern world?

17. What are the exchange and supply functions?

18. Write short notes on
(i) Branding
(ii) Market research

19. 'Market' is a wide term and can be classified on various basis. Classify 'market' on any two basis.

20. Explain the exchange and physical/supply functions of marketing.

Answers

1. (a) Gather information and analyse the needs of the market
2. (c) Marketing is the activity, set of institutions, and processes for creating, communicating, delivering, and exchanging offerings that have value for customers, clients, partners, and society at large
3. (a) Philip Kotler
4. (c) 1920s
5. False
6. both science and art
7. different
10. (b) Both Assertion (A) and Reason (R) are true, but Reason (R) is not the correct explanation of Assertion (A)

10

Marketing Mix

TREND ANALYSIS 5 YEARS

		Average No. of Questions Across all Sets					
		Types of Questions	2024	2023	2020	2019	2018
TOPIC 01	Product Mix	1 Mark	2	—	—	—	—
		2 Marks	1	—	—	—	—
		3/4/5 Marks	1	—	1	1	5
TOPIC 02	Price Mix	1 Mark	—	—	—	—	—
		2 Marks	—	—	—	—	—
		3/4/5 Marks	—	—	—	1	—
TOPIC 03	Place Mix	1 Mark	1	2	—	—	—
		2 Marks	—	1	1	—	—
		3/4/5 Marks	—	—	1	1	—
TOPIC 04	Promotion Mix	1 Mark	—	1	—	—	—
		2 Marks	—	2	—	—	1
		3/4/5 Marks	1	1	2	2	1

Meaning and Definition of Marketing Mix

Marketing mix represents the total marketing programme of an enterprise, as it refers to the tools or methods which a marketer uses in order to interact with a particular market.

According to **Philip Kotler**, ''Marketing mix are the set of marketing tools that firm uses to pursue its marketing objectives in the target market.''

Elements of Marketing Mix

To effectively market a product or service, there are four things you need to get right, Product, Price, Place and Promotion. These four are known as the elements of marketing mix or the 4Ps.

The 4Ps of the marketing mix are

(i) **Product mix** It involves planning, developing and producing the right type of products and services to be marketed by the firm.

(ii) **Price mix** It refers to the decisions relating to the strategy, policy and method of pricing. A marketing manager has to consider a number of factors while determining the price of the product e.g. Cost of production, middlemen's margin, cost of physical distribution, etc.

(iii) **Promotion mix** It deals with informing and persuading the customers regarding the firm's products. Promotion mix involves decisions with respect to advertising, personal selling, publicity and sales promotion.

(iv) **Place or distribution mix** It consists of two things i.e. physical distribution and channels of distribution.

Physical distribution includes all those activities involved in moving products or services from producer to consumer, while channels of distribution refer to the intermediaries that facilitate transfer of goods from producers to consumers.

Importance of Marketing Mix

Marketing mix offers the following benefits

(i) It helps in pursuing customer-oriented marketing because it concentrates on the satisfaction of customers.

(ii) It emphasises an integrated approach to marketing as all the four elements are interrelated and interdependent.

(iii) It is helpful in meeting the requirements of different types of customers because a different marketing mix can be developed for each target market.

(iv) Marketing mix helps in increasing sales and earning higher profits through customer satisfaction.

(v) It enables a firm to face competition in the market.

Product Mix

Product mix refers to a combination of several features related to the product or service to be offered for sale. The tangible and intangible aspects supplied to the customer in order to satisfy his need are represented by the product element of the marketing mix.

Due to the wide variety of needs of consumers, different types of products are offered to them, such as

(i) **Physical items** Cars, televisions, shirts and soaps.

(ii) **Services** Education, healthcare, banking and insurance.

(iii) **Places of tourism** Singapore, Dubai and Kerala.

(iv) **Experiences** Cinema, meditation and multiplex.

(v) **Ideas** 'Don't kill the girl child'.

(vi) **Information** Internet surfing.

Meaning of Goods

Goods are tangible commodities which can either be consumed directly or used in the production of other goods. Items like soap, television, shirts, vehicles, etc are examples of goods.

Features of Goods

The features of goods are given below

(i) Goods are tangible. They are made of certain physical attributes such as shape, size, etc. They can be seen, touched and felt.

(ii) In addition to physical features, goods have certain attributes, which help customers to distinguish them from other goods. Package, brand name, warranty, etc are such associated attributes.

(iii) Goods have some value, which can be measured in terms of money.

(iv) Every good is meant to satisfy some human need.

Types of Goods

Goods can be classified as

1. Consumer Goods

Goods which are meant for direct consumption or which require no further processing are known as consumer goods. These goods are offered to households and ultimate consumers. e.g. Shirts, cars, watches, etc.

These can be further classified into following categories

(i) **On the Basis of Durability**

(a) **Durable** These are not consumed in single use. They last for sometime and permit many uses, therefore are bought infrequently like electric iron, television, refrigerator.

(b) **Non-durable** These are consumed in one or a few uses. They are consumed fast and bought frequently like soap, toothpaste.

(ii) **On the Basis of Buying Behaviour/ Shopping Efforts Involved**

(a) **Convenience goods** These goods are purchased frequently and with minimum efforts. They are meant for personal convenience. Newspapers, cigarettes, toothpaste, soaps, tea, etc are examples of convenience products.

(b) **Shopping goods** These goods are purchased after a comparative analysis of quality, price, warranty, etc of competitive brands. Furniture, TV, fridge, washing machine, scooters, cars are examples of such products.

(c) **Speciality goods** These goods are purchased with special efforts. Jewellery, fancy items, etc are examples of these products.

2. Industrial Goods

Industrial goods are classified into the following categories

(i) **Materials and parts** These refer to the goods that completely enter into the manufacturing process of a product. These are of two types

(a) **Raw material** These are also of two types

- Agricultural goods like sugarcane, wood, rubber, etc.
- Natural goods like iron ore, crude petroleum, etc.

(b) **Manufactured material and parts** These are also of two types

- Component materials like glass, iron, plastic, etc.
- Component parts like steering, battery, bulb, etc.

(ii) **Capital items** These goods are used in producing finished goods. They include tools, machines, computer, etc.
Capital items are classified into
(a) Installations like elevators, mainframe computers, etc.
(b) Equipments like hand tools, fax machine, etc.

(iii) **Supplies and business services** These include goods like paints, lubricants, computer stationery, etc, which are required for developing or managing the finished products.
These are classified into
(a) Maintenance and repair items like paints, nails, solutions, etc.
(b) Operating supplies like oils, lubricants, ink, etc.

Meaning of Services

The activities, benefits and satisfactions that are offered for sale are referred to as service. In other words, a service is any activity or benefit that one party can offer to another, which is essentially intangible and does not result in the ownership of anything. e.g. Dry cleaning, hair cutting, postal services, etc.

Features of Services

Following are the important features of services
(i) Services are intangible.
(ii) A service is inseparable from its source.
(iii) Services cannot be stored.
(iv) Services are highly variable as their type and quality depend on the person providing them.

Difference between Goods and Service

Basis	Goods/Products	Service
Meaning	A good is a tangible physical product, capable of being delivered to a buyer and involves the transfer of ownership from seller to the buyer.	A service is any activity or benefit that one party can offer to another, that is essentially intangible and does not result in the ownership of anything.
Nature	A physical object, e.g. Video cassette of movie.	An activity or process, e.g. Watching a movie in a cinema hall.
Type	Homogeneous, i.e. standardised goods.	Heterogeneous, i.e. difficult to standardise quality of services.
Intangibility	Tangible, e.g. Medicine	Intangible, e.g. Doctor treatment
Inseparability	Separation of production and consumption, e.g. Purchasing ice-cream from a store.	Simultaneous production and consumption, e.g. Eating ice-cream in a restaurant.
Ownership	Ownership is transferred to the buyer.	Customer has access to, but not ownership of service, e.g. When you buy a service, as a seat in an aircraft, you do not become its owner.
Time lag	Products can be bought in advance.	Services cannot be bought in advance.
Replacement	A product can be replaced.	A service delivered cannot be replaced.

Components of Product Mix

The product mix refers to important decisions related to the product such as quality of product, it's design, packaging, etc.
Various components of product mix are described below
1. Branding 2. Labelling 3. Packaging

1. Branding

Branding refers to the process of giving a name, sign, symbol or identification mark to a product.

A brand is the identification of a product. It can be in the form of a name, symbol or design, etc. Branding is not only done to identify the seller or producer, but also to make a product superior than the competitor's product.

Also it is a seller's promise to deliver quality and satisfaction of buyer's expectations.

So, it is a general term covering various activities, such as giving a brand name to a product, designing a brand mark and popularising it.

Terms Related to Brand

Various terms related to brand are
(i) **Brand name** The part of brand, which can be spoken is called brand name. In other words, we can say, it is the verbal part of a brand. e.g. Maggi, Lux, Ambuja Cement.
(ii) **Brand mark** The part of brand, which cannot be spoken, but can only be recognised is known as brand mark, e.g. Maharaja sign of Air India, red and blue ball of Pepsi, arrow sign of Nike, etc.
(iii) **Trademark** A part of brand, which is given legal protection is called trademark. No other firm can use the name or sign, for which a company gets legal protection. e.g. Maruti Suzuki sign on Maruti cars.

Characteristics of a Good Brand Name

Characteristics of good brand name are

(i) A brand name should be short, simple, easy to pronounce, spell, recognise and remember, e.g. LG, Nano, etc.

(ii) A brand name should be suggestive, i.e. it must suggest the product's benefit, e.g. Hajmola, Hair and Care Oil, etc.

(iii) A brand name should be distinctive, e.g. Google, Zodiac, etc.

(iv) A brand name should be sufficiently versatile to accomodate new products, which are added to the product line, e.g. Maggi, Vicco, etc.

Advantages/Merits of Branding

Following are the benefits of branding

(i) **Helps in product differentiation** With branding, marketer can differentiate his products from the competitor's product.

(ii) **Helps in advertising** With the brand name, advertising becomes more effective, as it not only makes people aware about the features of product, but also about the brand which can provide these benefits.

(iii) **Helps in identification of product** Branding helps the customers to buy the products easily, as the brand which is giving them satisfaction, can be selected easily over the competitor's product.

(iv) **Ensures quality** Brand name gives quality assurance and customers can buy branded goods with no doubt about the quality of product.

2. Labelling

The term 'labelling' means designing a label to be put on the package. A label is a small slip placed on the product to denote its nature, contents, ownership, destination, etc.

A label describes the product, its usage and specifies its contents. It is a medium, through which the manufacturer gives necessary information to the user or consumer.
A label plays an important role in making the packaging and branding meaningful.

Functions of Labelling

Following are the functions of labelling

(i) It gives a definite identity to the product or brand and therefore, the identification of a product is easy. e.g. the name Pears printed on toilet soaps helps us to know which soap out of several soaps is Pears.

(ii) It specifies the contents and other features of the product. It enables the manufacturer to give clear instructions to the consumer about the proper use of the product.

(iii) It provides information required under law, e.g. statutory warning, 'Smoking is injurious to health', must be stated on the package of cigarettes.

(iv) A good label can attract attention, describe the product and stimulate the buyer to buy the product. It helps in the promotion of the product.

Advantages/Merits of Labelling

Advantages of labelling are as follows

(i) It is a social service to customers.

(ii) It avoids price variations by publishing the price on the label.

(iii) It facilitates advertising activity of the organisation.

(iv) It helps the customers to assess the superiority of a product.

3. Packaging

It refers to covering, wrapping, crating, filling or compressing of goods to protect them from spoilage, pilferage, breakage, leakage, etc. Various kinds of goods are placed or packed into appropriate containers for protection and convenient handling.

For example, bulky materials like cotton and jute are compressed into bales, liquid materials like oil and wine are put into bottles, barrels and cans, etc.

Thus, packing implies placing products in suitable packages for delivery of the product to customer or for the purpose of storage and transport.

Levels of Packaging

Various levels of packaging are

(i) **Primary packaging** It means the immediate container of a product. It may be kept till the customer is ready to use the product, e.g. Plastic package for socks.

(ii) **Secondary packaging** It means additional layer of protection for the product, e.g. A toothpaste tube is packed in a cardboard box. When the consumer begins to use the product, the box is disposed-off.

(iii) **Transportation packaging** It means packaging done to protect the product in the process of transportation and storage, e.g. toothpaste boxes are sent to retailers in corrugated boxes, each containing 50 or 100 units.

Functions of Packaging

Packaging is an essential function of marketer because of following reasons

(i) **Protection** The fundamental function of packaging is that it protects the product from damage. Appropriate packaging protects the product from the sun, rain, moisture, breakage, insects, etc.

e.g. Airtight containers and packets are used for chips, biscuits, jams, cola, etc, which need protection from atmospheric contacts.

(ii) **Identification** With the help of packaging, the product can be easily identified, e.g. With the yellow and black packing and alphabet K, we can recognise from far off that it is a Kodak product.

(iii) **Convenience** The handling of the product becomes more convenient with appropriate packing.

It makes it convenient to store and convenient to shift from one place to other.

e.g. New pet bottles of cold drink has made it very convenient for middlemen to transport it, supply it and store it.

(iv) **Promotion** Packaging plays the role of silent salesman because it promotes or enhances the sale of the product. The attractive colourful and innovative packing attracts the customers, specially if the product is children's product.

Features of a Good Packaging

A good package should have following features

(i) It should be convenient to handle and use. It should be easy to open and close and should fit well into the cupboard, drawer, refrigerator, etc.

(ii) The package should provide aesthetic satisfaction in terms of design, neatness and beauty. It should be pleasing and eye-catching which can attract immediate attention.

(iii) It should be safe and should be capable of protecting the product.

(iv) It should build customer's confidence by telling the true story of the product.

(v) The package should establish its own identity appropriate to the product in terms of user's expectations. In other words, it should provide a distinct personality and status to the product.

Price Mix

The term 'price' is the monetary expression of value of a product or service. It is an important factor affecting the success of a firm, as customer is very sensitive to this element.

Little variation in the price may shift your customer to the competitor's product. e.g. If the price of Pepsi is changed from ₹ 18 to ₹ 18.50, then the customer will start demanding Coke, which is still available at ₹ 18. It is therefore important that the pricing decisions are taken with care and caution. Price must match the utility offered by the product or service.

Factors Affecting Determination of Price

The following factors affect determination of price

(i) **Pricing objectives** It is a very important factor, which helps in deciding the price. If the objective of company is profit maximisation, then generally high price is fixed, whereas the companies having the objective of sales maximisation, prefer low price to increase the sale.

(ii) **Product cost** Another important factor, which should be considered, is the cost of product or service. The price of the product must be able to cover the total cost of product. Total cost means fixed cost and variable cost.

Fixed costs are fixed irrespective of production level e.g. rent of factory, cost of machinery, etc. The variable costs vary with production e.g. Cost of raw materials, wages of labour, etc.

(iii) **Extent of competition in the market** Extent of competition is necessary to be considered, while fixing the price of a product, as competitor's price and their anticipated reactions badly affect the reputation and sale of a product.

(iv) **The utility and demand** It is necessary to anticipate the utility and demand of a product while fixing the price. If a product is offering higher utility, one can easily charge high price. Whereas, if utility is low, then high price cannot be charged.

(v) **Government and legal regulations** In order to protect the interest of general public, the government has the right to control the prices of various products and services by including the products in the category of essential commodities. The common commodities in essential commodities are drugs, some food items, LPG, etc.

(vi) **Marketing methods used** The price of the product also gets affected by various techniques or methods of marketing used to promote the products.

If the company is using intensive advertising to promote the sale of product, then it will charge high price. Other marketing methods, which affect price of a product are type of packaging, distribution system, salesmen employed, customer support services, etc.

(vii) **Risks** Seasonal and fashionable items have some inherent risk and therefore, are sold at prices out of line of costs i.e. they are sold even below the cost price, in case there is a danger of products getting out of fashion.

(viii) **Buying motives** Products which assign high prestige value to consumers may be priced high.

Place (Distribution) Mix

It consists of all the activities involved in transferring ownership and physical possession of the product to consumers. Its purpose is to make the product or service available to customers at the right time and at the right place. Distribution includes

1. Channels of distribution
2. Physical distribution

1. Channels of Distribution

The route or path through which goods move from the producer to consumers is known as distribution channel. A firm has to decide whether to sell directly or to sell through middlemen. The number and type of middlemen have also to be decided.

Types of Channels of Distribution

Channels of distribution may be classified as below

(i) **Direct channel** (Zero level) The most simple mode of distribution is direct distribution, where the goods are directly made available to consumers from the manufacturers, without the use of any intermediary. e.g. Bata selling through its own retail outlets.

Manufacturer → Customer

(ii) **Indirect channels** When one or more intermediary is involved in the distribution network, then it is referred as indirect channels. These channels can be of the following types

(a) **Manufacturer–Retailer–Consumer** (One level channel) Here, manufacturer sells the goods directly to the retailer who then sells them to the final consumer. This method is used for expensive products or for selling Fast Moving Consumer Goods (FMCG).

Manufacturer → Retailer → Consumer

(b) **Manufacturer–Wholesaler–Retailer–Consumer** (Two level channel) In this method, manufacturer sells the material to the wholesaler, wholesaler to the retailer and then retailer to the consumer.
This medium is mainly used to sell goods like soap, tea, salt, sugar, ghee, etc.

Manufacturer → Wholesaler → Retailer → Consumer

(c) **Manufacturer–Agent–Wholesaler–Retailer–Consumer** (Three level channel) In this case, manufacturers use their own agents or brokers who connect them with wholesalers and then to the retailer. Retailer then sells the goods to consumers.
This is done when the line of product is limited and wide coverage is required.

Manufacturer → Agent → Wholesaler → Retailer → Consumer

Choice of Channels of Distribution

An organisation decides channel of distribution for its product on the basis of following factors

(i) **Market related factors** Market factors such as size of market, geographical concentration of potential buyers and size of order influence the decision of choosing the channel of distribution.

(ii) **Product related factors** Product related factors such as nature of product (perishable or non-perishable product), unit value of product (when goods are costly, shorter channel is preferred) and product complexity (for products which require technical details, shorter channel is preferred) are considered, while deciding the channel of distribution.

(iii) **Company characteristics** Characteristics of the company such as financial strength (for starting a retail outlet, a company needs to be financially strong, as it requires huge funds to be invested in fixed assets) and degree of control (if the management wants to have greater control on the channel members, short channel are used) are to be considered while deciding the channel of distribution.

(iv) **Competitive factors** The choice of channel is also affected by the channel selected by the competitors in the same industry.

(v) **Environmental factors** Environmental factors such as economic conditions and legal constraints also affect the choice of channel. e.g. In a depressed economy, marketers use shorter channels to distribute their goods.

(vi) **Efficiency of middlemen** Distribution also depends on location and financial status of middlemen. If the middlemen in a channel are efficient and dependable, that channel may be selected.

2. Physical Distribution

The physical handling and movement of goods from place of production to the place of distribution, is called 'physical distribution'. It covers all the activities required to physically move the goods from the manufacturers to the customers.

Components of Physical Distribution

The main components of the process of physical distribution are

(i) **Order processing** A good physical distribution system should provide for an accurate and speedy processing of orders. In the absence of this, goods would reach the customers in wrong quality or quantity, resulting in dissatisfaction of customers.

(ii) **Transportation** It means carrying raw materials and finished goods from one place to another. It helps in creating 'place utility', by making available the goods where they are required.

(iii) **Warehousing** It refers to the act of storing and assorting products in order to create 'time utility'. It helps in proper placement of goods and providing facilities to store them, so that they can be made available as and when demanded by the market.

(iv) **Inventory control** An important decision in physical distribution is deciding about the level of inventory. Higher the level of inventory, higher will be level of service and cost of carrying the inventory and *vice-versa*. Various factors which are considered for determining inventory levels are

(a) Firm's policy regarding level of customer service.

(b) Degree of accuracy of sales forecast.

(c) Responsiveness of distribution system.

(d) Cost of holding inventory.

A good inventory decision aims at timely fulfilment of demand at minimum cost.

Promotion Mix

It refers to the use of communication with the twin objective of informing potential customers about a product and persuading them to buy it. Promotion mix consists of all the activities aimed at persuading customers to buy the product. It includes communication activities undertaken to inform and convince customers.

Elements of Promotion Mix

The various elements of promotion mix are as follows

(i) **Advertising** It includes activities concerned with providing product information to customers through newspapers, radio, television and other media. It is paid for by the seller and is a non-personal form of communication.

(ii) **Personal selling** It refers to face-to-face communication between a seller or his representative and the buyer. Salespersons of an enterprise assist and persuade the prospective buyers to buy the product.

(iii) **Sales promotion** It means increasing immediate sales through short-term incentives such as samples, special discount, offers, prize contests, coupons, etc.

(iv) **Publicity** It means promoting the name of a company or its product in newspapers, journals, radio, etc. Publicity is not paid by the seller and it is a non-personal form of communication.

Meaning of Advertising

Advertising involves dissemination of information about a product, service or enterprise to induce people to take actions beneficial to the advertiser. The message, which is disseminated is known as advertisement.

American Marketing Association has defined advertising as 'Any paid form of non-personal presentation of ideas, goods and services by an identified sponsor.'

Features of Advertising

Features of advertising are given below

(i) **Mass communication** Advertising is a form of mass communication. Advertisement can address to masses and it is a non-personal form of communication.

(ii) **Paid form of communication** It is a paid form, as the advertiser has to pay the advertising media for the space or time used to communicate the message to the user.

(iii) **Identified sponsor** Sponsor may be an individual or a firm, who pays for the advertisement. The name or identity of the advertiser is mentioned in the advertisement.

(iv) **Profit maximisation** Advertising maximises profits, not by increasing the price, but by promoting the sales. Thus, advertising follows higher sales approach, rather than the higher cost approach.

(v) **Non-personal presentation** Advertising presents the information regarding a product, service or idea in a non-personal form, as no face-to-face contact is involved between the buyer and the customers.

Objectives of Advertising

Following are the objectives of advertising

(i) To build brand loyalty for a specific product.

(ii) To improve the company's reputation.

(iii) To bring a new product to market by creating awareness among potential customers.

(iv) To warn consumers about forgeries or counterfeit goods.

(v) To inform customers about the product's numerous uses.

(vi) To combat competition in the market.

Meaning of Sales Promotion

Sales promotion refers to all the activities, which are undertaken for the purpose of increasing sales. These activities mainly include lowering the price, distributing discount coupons, conducting contests, giving away of gifts, etc.

Sales promotion refers to short-term incentives to boost sales and it supplements other promotional efforts such as advertising, personal selling and publicity, aimed at stimulating market demand for products.

According to **AHR Delers**, "Sales promotion means any steps that are taken for the purpose of obtaining or increasing sales."

Features of Sales Promotion

Following are the features of sales promotion

(i) It covers actions that are not repeated on a regular basis.
(ii) It provide incentives that are only available for a limited time.
(iii) It is aimed at both buyers and sellers.
(iv) It is intended to be used in conjunction with advertising and personal selling.

Objectives of Sales Promotion

Following are the objectives of sales promotion

(i) Creation of demand.
(ii) Attracting new customers.
(iii) Useful in new product launch.
(iv) Deals with seasonal decline.
(v) Encounter competitor's sales promotion campaign.
(vi) Induce middlemen.

Sales Promotion Techniques

To increase the sales, the company can adopt any or combination of following sales promotion methods

(i) **Samples** Many business firms distribute free samples of their products to selected consumers in order to make the products popular. This method is generally used for products of daily use, e.g. soaps, detergents, toothpaste, cosmetics, tea, etc. It is an expensive method.
(ii) **Prize contests** Contests may be held for customers, salesman and dealers. Customers are required to write a slogan or complete a sentence about the utility of the product. It provides new ideas for advertising the product. Contests for salesmen and dealers are also held to encourage them to increase the sale of the product.
(iii) **Exchange offers** Sometimes, manufacturers of household gadgets and other products make an offer 'exchange of old products with new ones'. e.g. An old iron can be exchanged with a new iron after payment of a specified amount.
Such offers are also made for refrigerators, television sets, gas stoves, scooters, air conditioners, washing machines, sewing machines, etc.
(iv) **Discount** When products are offered to customers at a price, less than the list price, the difference between the list price and offered price is known as discount. e.g. A shoe company's offer 'discount upto 50%'.
(v) **Lucky draw** A firm on purchases of a fixed amount gives a coupon to a customer, which entitles them for a lucky draw, e.g. Bikaner restaurant in particular season gives lucky draw coupon on purchase of ₹ 200 or more, to its customers, which entitles them to win exciting prizes like car, etc.
(vi) **Quantity deals** Seller devise special packages, which gives extra quantity of the product to the buyers at less price or no price, e.g. 'Buy one get one free'.

Meaning of Personal Selling

Personal selling or salesmanship is the process of informing, assisting and persuading people to buy a product or service through direct personal contact. It involves face-to-face communication between a seller and a buyer. In this technique of promotion, salesperson make oral presentation to one or more customers for the purpose of making sales.

Features of Personal Selling

Following are the features of personal selling

(i) Personal selling is a personal form of communication, which involves an interactive relationship between the seller and the buyer.
(ii) It ensures development of relationship between the salesperson and the prospective customer.
(iii) It facilitates two-way communication process. The seller and the buyer both can talk to each other.
(iv) It is used in all types of businesses.

Objectives/Importance of Personal Selling

It offers the advantages/objectives to following sections

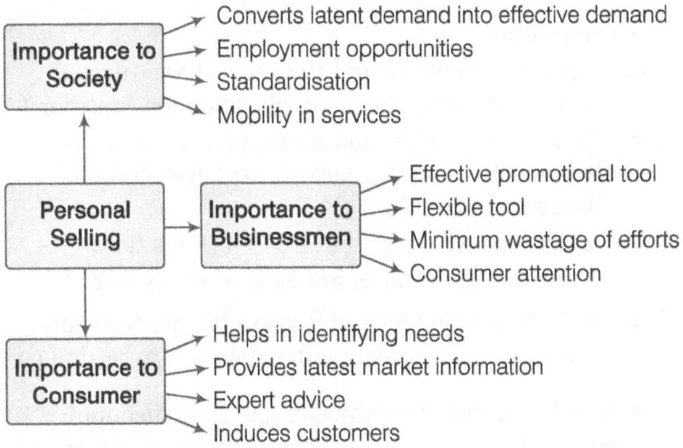

Qualities of a Good Salesman

The persons, who do the job of selling through face-to-face interaction are called salespersons or sales representatives.

If a salesman wants to become successful, he should possess the below mentioned qualities

1. **Physical qualities** A salesman should possess the following physical qualities
   (i) Good appearance and posture
   (ii) Smartness and well groomed
   (iii) Healthy physique
   (iv) Confidence
2. **Mental qualities** The following mental qualities should also be possessed by the salesman
   (i) A good salesman must have the power of observation and a sound memory.
   (ii) A successful salesman also requires wide knowledge about his company and its products.
   (iii) He must possess presence of mind, self-confidence and sense of responsibility, creativity, good judgement, etc.
3. **Social qualities** The following social qualities should also be possessed by a salesman
   (i) A good salesman must have good manners, courtesy, empathy and he must be having a strong convincing power.
   (ii) He should be a man of sound character.
   (iii) He should be loyal and honest.
   (iv) He should be enthusiastic.
   (v) He must possess good communication skills and also should be a good listener.

Meaning of Publicity

Publicity is a non-personal form of communication, which reaches the consumers in the form of a news article or news through a news agency or news channel. It can be positive or negative. The organisation does not always have control over publicity.

Features of Publicity

The important features of publicity are

(i) It is an unpaid form of communication.
(ii) It is an impersonal communication, where there is no direct face-to-face contact between the buyer and the seller.
(iii) There is no identified sponsor of the message.

Objectives of Publicity

The main objectives of publicity are

(i) It aims to reach out those consumers who do not pay attention to advertising.
(ii) Message communicated to the consumers through publicity has greater reliability.
(iii) It is a more reliable and trustworthy source of information than other sources of promotion.
(iv) It is not affected by the biasness and prejudice of the marketer.

Comparative Analysis of Various Components of Promotion Mix

Basis	Advertising	Sales promotion	Personal selling	Publicity
Form	It is an impersonal form of communication.	It refers to the incentives offered to boost the sales.	It is a personal form of communication	It is an impersonal form of communication.
Flexibility	Message is inflexible and cannot be changed according to the customers' needs.	Techniques are flexible and change from time-to-time.	Message is flexible and not be changed according to the customers' needs.	Message is inflexible and cannot be changed according to the customers' needs.
Feedback	Feedback and obtaining response is not possible.	Feedback can be observed through analysis of increase in sales.	Quick and immediate feedback is possible.	Feedback is not possible.
Medium	Newspapers, TV, radio, magazines, internet, etc.	Incentives like discount, rebate, free samples, etc.	Salesman and sales force.	News agency and news channels.

PYQs Previous Years' Questions

1/2 Marks Questions

1. **Assertion** (A) Services cannot be standardised.
Reason (R) Services are homogeneous in nature. *ISC 2024 (1M)*

Alternatives

(a) Both Assertion (A) and Reason (R) are true and Reason (R) is the correct explanation of Assertion (A)
(b) Both Assertion (R) and Reason (R) are true, but Reason (R) is not the correct explanation of Assertion (A)
(c) Assertion (A) is true, but Reason (R) is false
(d) Assertion (A) is false, but Reason (R) is true

Ans (c) Services are heterogeneous in nature.

2. State whether the following are true or false. *ISC 2023 (1M)*
"Inventory control is not an element of physical distribution."

Ans False. Elements of physical distribution include
(i) Material handling (ii) Order processing
(iii) Inventory planning and control (iv) Transportation
(v) Communication (vi) Organisational structure

3. **Assertion** (A) Advertising costs are extracted from the consumers in the form of higher prices.
Reason (R) Advertising helps in increasing sales and thereby in reducing cost. *ISC Specimen 2023 (1M)*

Alternatives

(a) Both Assertion (A) and Reason (R) are true and Reason (R) is the correct explanation for Assertion (A)
(b) Both Assertion (A) and Reason (R) are true, but Reason (R) is not the correct explanation for Assertion (A)
(c) Assertion (A) is true, but Reason (R) is false
(d) Assertion (A) is false, but Reason (R) is true

Ans (c) Assertion (A) is true, but Reason (R) is false

4. Name the element of promotion mix which involves a direct personal contact between the buyer and the seller. *ISC Sem II 2022 (1M)*

Ans Personal selling

5. **Assertion** (A) Labelling, as a function of marketing, acts as a silent salesman.
Reason (R) Labelling helps in the promotion of the products by attracting the attention of customers and providing required information. *ISC Sem II Specimen 2022 (1M)*

Alternatives

(a) Both Assertion (A) and Reason (R) are true and Reason (R) is the correct explanation for Assertion (A)
(b) Both Assertion (A) and Reason (R) are true, but Reason (R) is not the correct explanation for Assertion (A)
(c) Assertion (A) is true, but Reason (R) is false
(d) Assertion (A) is false, but Reason (R) is true

Ans (a) Both Assertion (A) and Reason (R) are true and Reason (R) is the correct explanation for Assertion (A)

6. A popular brand of toothpaste has 20% discount mentioned on the package. Name the element of promotion. *ISC Sem II Specimen 2022 (1M)*

Ans Sales promotion

7. What is meant by physical distribution? *ISC 2020 (2M)*

Ans The physical handling and movement of goods from place of production to the place of distribution is called physical distribution. It covers all the activities required to physically move the goods from the manufacturers to customers.

8. The producer of 'Lime Fresh' tea introduces 'Buy one get one free' scheme on all the products of 'Lime Fresh'. Identify the promotional strategy used by the producer. State any one objective that could be met by this strategy. *ISC 2018 (2M)*

Ans The promotional strategy used by them is 'Quantity deals'. Objective that could be met by this is that it helps to clear unwanted stocks.

9. Name the elements of physical distribution. *ISC Specimen 2018 (1M)*

Ans Transportation and warehousing.

10. State two types of products. *ISC Specimen 2018 (2M)*

Ans Products are broadly classified into two categories namely, consumer products and industrial products.

11. State any two features of advertising. *ISC 2017 (2M)*

Ans Two features of advertising are given below
(i) **Mass communication** Advertising is a form of mass communication. Advertisement can address to masses and it is a non-personal form of communication.
(ii) **Paid form of communication** It is a paid form, as the advertiser has to pay the advertising media for the space and time used to communicate the message to the user.

12. What is meant by a product? *ISC 2016 (2M)*

Ans A product is any good or service that a consumer wants. It is a bundle of utilities or a cluster of tangible and intangible attributes. It is made up of certain physical attributes such as shape, size, etc. It can be seen, touched and felt.

13. What is meant by the term 'place' in marketing mix? *ISC 2015 (2M)*

Ans Place (in marketing mix) consists of all the activities involved in transferring ownership and physical possession of the product to consumers. Its purpose is to make the product or service available to customers at the right time and at the right place.

14. Explain branding. *ISC 2015 (2M)*

Ans Branding refers to the process of giving a name, sign, symbol or identification mark to a product. A brand is the identification of a product. It can be in the form of a name, symbol or design, etc.

Branding is not only done to identify the seller or producer, but also to make a product superior than the competitor's product.

15. State any two features of 'labelling' in relation to marketing. *ISC 2013 (2M)*

Ans Two features of labelling in relation to marketing are

(i) It provides accurate information about the product and its usage.

(ii) A label plays an important role in making the packaging and branding functions meaningful.

Concept Enhancer Labelling gives a definite identity to the product or brand and therefore, the identification ofa product is easy. It also helps in promotion of product.

16. Give any two factors that influence price determination of a product. *2013 (2M)*

Ans Factors influencing price determination of product

(i) **Product cost** It is the most important factor affecting price. It includes the cost of production, distribution and selling the product. This cost sets the minimum base price at which the product may be sold.

(ii) **Extent of competition** If competition is high, lower price has to be set and if competition is low, higher price may be set.

Also before fixing a price, competitors' prices and their anticipated reaction must be considered.

17. Briefly describe any two aims of sales promotion. *ISC 2011 (2M)*

Ans Two aims of sales promotion are

(i) **Creation of demand** Its main aim is to create demand and increase sales by influencing the purchase decisions of consumers.

(ii) **Attracting new customers** Its aim is to attract new buyers with the help of the attractive benefits and freebies. The consumers of other brands are induced to buy the company's product.

18. State any two differences between packing and packaging. *ISC 2009 (2M)*

Ans Difference between packing and packaging

Basis	Packing	Packaging
Meaning	Packing implies putting the product in wrappers/ containers for protecting the product.	Packaging is concerned with designing and producing a package for products storage, convenience, functionality or re-usability.
Function	Packing provides safety to the product from breakage or spoilage.	It facilitates marketing of product by communicating brand, features, image, etc.

19. Mention any two objectives of advertising. *ISC 2009 (2M)*

Ans Objectives purpose of advertising are

(i) To introduce a new product by creating interest for it among the prospective customers, through emphasis on features and utility of the product in advertisements.

(ii) To support personal selling efforts by reaching people inaccessible to salesman, entering new markets, attracting a new group of customers, opening doors for salesman by informing people about the product.

20. How is trademark different from a brand? *ISC 2008, 01 (2M)*

Ans Difference between trademark and brand

Basis	Trademark	Brand
Meaning	When a brand is registered under the Trademarks Act, 1999, it become a trademark.	It is a name, term, symbol or design or a combination, thereof to identify the goods and services, e.g. Pepsi, Lux, etc.
Function/Role	It protects the brand from duplication.	It serves to differentiate a product from the competitors and gives a prestige value to the user of the product.

21. What is sales promotion? *ISC 2006, 04 (2M)*

Ans Sales promotion refers to short-term incentives, which are offered to encourage the buyers to make immediate purchase of a product or a service. Sales promotion is usually undertaken by a company to boost its sales.

It supplements other promotional efforts such as advertising and personal selling. Some example of sales promotion techniques are offering discounts, rebates, scratch cards, contests, etc.

22. Enumerate two vocational qualities of a good salesman. *ISC 2004 (2M)*

Ans Vocational qualities of a good salesman are

(i) **Selling techniques** He should be conversant with the knowledge of persuading the customers and how to present himself and the product in front of the prospective buyer.

(ii) **Product and producer's knowledge** The subject knowledge of product, its features, its usage, advantages and disadvantages, comparison with competitor's product should be on the tips of the salesman. The knowledge of the producer is also important for whom he is selling the product.

23. Identify two advantages of personal selling. *ISC 2004 (2M)*

Ans Two advantages of personal selling are

(i) **Links with customers** By personal selling, there is a direct contact between the salesman and the prospective buyer, which helps in reducing the chances of diffusion and distortion in the desired message.

(ii) **Acts as a flexible tool** Since, it is personal in nature, it gives the advantage to the salesperson to adjust as per the needs of the prospective buyer.

24. Give two points of distinction between advertising and salesmanship. *ISC 2001 (2M)*

KEY IDEA

Distinguish between should always be given in comparative and tabular form with basis of difference.

Ans Difference between advertising and salesmanship

Basis	Advertising	Salesmanship
Form	Advertising is a means of indirect and impersonal communication.	Personal selling is a means of direct or face-to-face communication.
Message	There is uniformity of message which means that the message is the same for all the customers.	The message has no uniformity which means it can be changed, keeping in view the behaviour of the customers.

3/4/5 Marks Questions

1. What is branding? State any two merits of branding. *ISC 2024 (4M)*

Or Branding adds to the cost of the product, yet it has several benefits. State any four advantages of branding. *ISC Specimen 2023 (4M)*

Or What is branding? Give any three advantages of branding to the marketer. *ISC 2018 (4M)*

Ans **Meaning of branding** Branding refers to the process of giving a name, sign, symbol or identification mark to a product. A brand is the identification of a product. It can be in the form of a name, symbol or design, etc. Branding is not only done to identify the seller or producer, but also to make a product superior than the competitor's product.

Advantages of branding Following are the benefits of branding

(i) **Helps in product differentiation** With branding, marketer can differentiate his products from the competitor's product.

(ii) **Helps in advertising** With the brand name, advertising become more effective, as it not only makes people aware about the features of product, but also about the brand which can provide these benefits.

Advantages of Branding
- Helps in product differentiation
- Helps in advertising
- Helps in identification of product
- Ensures quality

(iii) **Helps in identification of product** Branding helps the customers to buy the products easily, as the brand which is giving them satisfaction, can be selected easily over the competitor's product.

(iv) **Ensures quality** Brand name gives quality assurance and customers can buy branded goods with no doubt about the quality of product.

2. Explain any four features of advertising. *ISC 2023 (5M)*

Or Define advertising. Explain any four features of advertising. *ISC 2020 (5M)*

Ans **Advertising** It involves dissemination of information about a product, service or enterprise to induce people to take actions beneficial to the advertiser. The message, which is disseminated is known as advertisement. Features of advertising are given below

(i) **Mass communication** Advertising is a form of mass communication. Advertisement can address to masses and it is a non-personal form of communication.

(ii) **Paid form of communication** It is a paid form, as the advertiser has to pay the advertising media for the space or time used to communicate the message to the user.

(iii) **Identified sponsor** Sponsor may be an individual or a firm, who pays for the advertisement. The name or identity of the advertiser is mentioned in the advertisement.

(iv) **Profit maximisation** Advertising maximises profits, not by increasing the price, but by promoting the sales. Thus, advertising follows higher sales approach, rather than the higher cost approach.

Features of Advertising
- Mass communication
- Paid form of communication
- Identified sponsor
- Profit maximisation

3. A number of factors affect the fixation of the price of a product. Explain any four such factors. *ISC Specimen 2023 (4M)*

Or Explain five factors that should be taken into consideration while determining the price of a product or service. *ISC 2019 (5M)*

Or Explain five factors that affect the pricing decision of a product. *ISC 2016 (5M)*

Ans The following factors affect determination of price

(i) **Pricing objectives** It is a very important factor, which helps in deciding the price. If the objective of company is profit maximisation, then generally high price is fixed, whereas the companies having the objective of sales maximisation, prefer low price to increase the sale.

(ii) **Product cost** Another important factor, which should be considered, is the cost of product or service. The price of the product must be able to cover the total cost of product. Total cost means fixed cost and variable cost.

Fixed costs are fixed irrespective of production level e.g. rent of factory, cost of machinery, etc. The variable costs vary with production e.g. Cost of raw materials, wages of labour, etc.

(iii) **Extent of competition in the market** Extent of competition is necessary to be considered, while fixing the price of a product, as competitor's price and their anticipated reactions badly affect the reputation and sale of a product.

(iv) **The utility and demand** It is necessary to anticipate the utility and demand of a product while fixing the price. If a product is offering higher utility, one can easily charge high price. Whereas, if utility is low, then high price cannot be charged.

(v) **Government and legal regulations** In order to protect the interest of general public, the government has the right to control the prices of various products and services by including the products in the category of essential commodities. The common commodities in essential commodities are drugs, some food items, LPG, etc.

4. Vehicle Ltd. is an automobile manufacturer in India. It makes one million cars every year and has a sales network of company approved retailers who sell cars across cities.

Identify and briefly explain the type of channel of distribution adopted by the company. State any two factors that are considered while choosing the channel of distribution. *ISC Sem II 2022 (4M)*

Ans Indirect channel of distribution is adopted by the company

Manufacturer → Retailer → Consumer (One level channel)

In this method, manufacturer sells the goods to one or more retailers who in turn sell to the ultimate consumers. This method is used for expensive products and selling Fast Moving Consumer Goods (FMCG).

Two factors that are considered while choosing the channel of distribution are

(i) Product related factors

(ii) Company related factors

5. A small company produces herbal products like tooth powder, bathing soap, etc. The company packs these products in thin wrapping papers which often results in the products getting damaged in transit. The customers have complained about the products being damaged due to the delicate packaging.

They have also suggested that the company should label its products properly.

(i) Mention any two features of good packaging.

(ii) In the above context, briefly explain any two merits of labelling. *ISC Sem II 2022 (4M)*

Ans (i) The features of good packaging are (any two)

(a) **Protection** The fundamental function of packaging is that it protects the product from damage. Appropriate packaging protects the product from the sun, rain, moisture, breakage, insects, etc, e.g. Airtight containers and packets are used for chips, biscuits, jams, cola, etc, which need protection from atmospheric contacts.

(b) **Identification** With the help of packaging, the product can be easily identified, e.g. With the yellow and black packing and alphabet K, we can recognise from far off that it is a Kodak product, from red colour and unique shape of Coke bottle, we can identify it from a distance.

Features of Good Packaging
- Protection
- Identification

(ii) The merits of labelling are

(a) It is a social service to customers, who very often do not know anything about the product's characteristics or features. False claims are prevented by using labels.

(b) It avoids price variations by publishing the price on the label.

> **Concept Enhancer** Labelling facilitates advertising activity of the organisation and helps the customers to assess the superiority of a product.

6. The demand for leather will be derived from the demand for leather purses and other leather items in the market.

The above statement brings forth the characteristics of one of the categories of the products. Name the category and state three other characteristics of this category of product. **ISC Sem II Specimen 2022 (4M)**

Or Explain any three features of industrial products. **ISC 2020 (3M)**

Ans Category of products discussed is industrial products.

Other characteristics of this category are

(i) **Semi-finished goods** These are the goods which are finished for one unit and raw material for another unit.

(ii) **Fabricating parts** These are manufactured by one industrial unit and used by another without any further processing in producing the production of consumer goods.

(iii) **Production supplies** These are the products necessary for the operation of industrial units but do not become a part of finished goods.

7. Explain any three objectives of publicity, as an element of promotion mix. **ISC 2020 (3M)**

Or

Write short note on publicity. **ISC 2017 (4M)**

Ans Publicity is a non-personal form of communication, which reaches the consumers in the form of a news article or news through a news agency or news channel.

The main objectives of publicity are

(i) It aims to reach out those consumers who do not pay attention to advertising.

(ii) Message communicated to the consumers through publicity has greater reliability.

(iii) It is a more reliable and trustworthy source of information than other sources of promotion.

(iv) It is not affected by the biasness and prejudice of the marketer.

8. What are the various channels of distribution available to a manufacturer in the process of distribution? **ISC 2020 (4M)**

Ans Refer to text on page 142.

9. Distinguish between advertising and sales promotion. **ISC 2019 (3M)**

Ans Difference between advertisement and sales promotion

Basis	Advertisement	Sales promotion
Objective	It aims to attract customer towards a particular brand.	It aims to convince customers to actually purchase the product.
Usefulness	It is useful in creating demand and goodwill.	It is useful in increasing immediate sales.
Medium	TV, newspapers, internet, etc.	Rebates, free samples, discount, etc.

> **Concept Enhancer** Advertisement is done to build brand image and increase sales while promotion is used to push short-term sales.

10. Explain three features of goods, as an element of product mix. **ISC 2019 (3M)**

Ans Features of goods are

(i) A good has some value which can be measured in terms of money.

(ii) Every good is meant to satisfy some human need.

(iii) Goods can be seen and touched i.e. they are tangible. They have attributes such as shape, size etc.

11. Write short note on channels of distribution. **ISC 2019 (4M)**

Ans Refer to text on page 142.

12. What is meant by promotion mix? Briefly explain the elements of promotion mix. **ISC 2019 (5M)**

Or

Explain any three elements of promotion mix. **ISC 2014 (3M)**

Ans Promotion mix refers to use of communication with the twin objective of informing potential customers about a product and persuading them to buy it.

Various elements of promotion mix are

(i) **Advertising** Advertising is the paid form of non-personal presentation and promotion of idea, goods or services by an identified sponsor. It is generally done through newspaper, radio, television and social media platforms.

> **Elements of Promotion Mix**
> - Advertising
> - Personal selling
> - Sales promotion
> - Publicity

(ii) **Personal selling** Personal selling refers to face-to-face communication between a seller or his representative and buyer. Sales persons assist and persuade prospective buyers to buy the product.

(iii) **Sales promotion** Sales promotions refers to use of short-term incentives such as samples, special discount, offers, coupons etc to increase immediate sales.

(iv) **Publicity** Publicity means promoting the name of a company or its product in newspapers, journals, radio, etc. It is non-personal form of communication.

13. Give three points of difference between a product and a service. **ISC 2018 (3M)**

Or Mention any two specific differences between product and service. **ISC 2014**

Ans Difference between goods/product and service

Basis	Goods/Product	Service
Meaning	A product is a tangible physical product, capable of being delivered to a buyer and involves the transfer of ownership from seller to the buyer.	A service is any activity or benefit that one party can offer to another, that is essentially intangible and does not result in the ownership of anything.
Nature	A physical object, e.g. Video cassette of movie.	An activity or process, e.g. Watching a movie in a cinema hall.
Type	Homogeneous, i.e. standardised products.	Heterogeneous, i.e. difficult to standardise quality of services.

14. Discuss the features of good packaging. **ISC 2018 (3M)**

Ans A good package should have following features

(i) It should be convenient to handle and use. It should be easy to open and close and should fit well into the cupboard, drawer, refrigerator, etc.

(ii) The package should provide aesthetic satisfaction in terms of design, neatness and beauty. It should be pleasing and eye-catching which can attract immediate attention.

(iii) It should be safe and should be capable of protecting the product.

(iv) It should build customer's confidence by telling the true story of the product.

(v) The package should establish its own identity appropriate to the product in terms of user's expectations. In other words, it should provide a distinct personality and status to the product.

15. Write short note on meaning and elements of product mix. **ISC 2018 (4M)**

Ans **Meaning of product mix** Product mix means a group of closely related elements of a product which give it a unique identity.

Elements of product mix The following are the elements of product mix

(i) **Branding** Branding is the process of assigning a distinctive name or symbol to a product by which it can be remembered.

(ii) **Labelling** Labelling means designing a label it be put on the package.

(iii) **Packaging** It refers to covering, wrapping, crating, filling or compressing of goods to protect them from spoilage, pilferages, breakage, leakage, etc.

16. Distinguish publicity from advertising. **ISC 2018**

Or Distinguish between advertisement and publicity. **ISC 2008 (4M)**

Ans Difference between advertising and publicity

Basis	Advertising	Publicity
Form	It is a non-personal, paid form of communication.	It is non-personal, non-paid form of communication.
Control	It is within the control of the marketing firm.	It is beyond the control of marketing firms.
Effect	It has a positive effect on the product's image.	It may have a positive or negative effect on the product's image.
Source	Information is provided through advertisements in TV, newspapers, magazines, etc.	Information is provided through news agencies and news channels.

17. What is labelling? Explain four advantages of labelling. **ISC 2018 (5M)**

Ans **Labelling** A simple looking, but important task in the marketing of goods relates to designing the label to be put on the packets. The label may vary from a simple tag attached to the product to complex graphics that are part of the packages. The label affixed on the package indicates the features and quality of product, brand name, grade, price, contents, cautions for use, method of use and other details.

Advantages of labelling Refer to text on page 140.

18. Give three differences between advertising and personal selling **ISC Specimen 2018, 17 (3M)**

Or

Distinguish between advertising and personal selling. **ISC 2016, 06 (4M)**

Ans The three differences between advertising and personal selling are

Basis	Advertising	Personal selling
Form	It is an impersonal form of communication.	It is a personal form of communication.

Basis	Advertising	Personal selling
Flexibility	Message is inflexible and cannot be changed according to the customers' needs.	Message is flexible and can be changed according to the customers' needs.
Feedback	Feedback and obtaining response is not possible.	Quick and immediate feedback is possible.
Medium	Newspaper, TV, radio, etc.	Salesman and sales force.

Value Points

For getting maximum marks, following points can be included in the answer

- Advertising is an impersonal form of communication.
- Message under personal selling, is flexible and can be changed according to customers' needs.

19. What are the objectives of personal selling? ***ISC 2017 (3M)***

Ans Following are the objectives of personal selling

(i) To induce the customer to demand the product.

(ii) To assist the customer to take wise decision regarding purchase.

(iii) To build a long lasting relationship with the customers.

(iv) To provide standardised products to the customers.

20. State three objectives of sales promotion. ***ISC 2016 (3M)***

Ans Following are the objectives of sales promotion

(i) Sales promotion incentives helps in getting new customers for the existing product.

(ii) Sales promotion helps in maintaining demand for seasonal products throughout the year.

(iii) Sales promotion proves effective for the introduction of new product in the market.

21. Explain the term 'labelling' and 'packaging'. ***ISC 2016 (3M)***

Ans **Labelling** A simple looking, but important task in the marketing of goods relates to designing the label to be put on the packets.

The label may vary from a simple tag attached to the product to complex graphics that are part of the packages.

The label affixed on the package indicates the features and quality of product, brand name, grade, price, contents, cautions for use, method of use and other details.

Packaging It refers to covering, wrapping, crating, filling or compressing of goods to protect them from spoilage, pilferage, breakage, leakage, etc.

Various kinds of goods are placed or packed into appropriate containers for protection and convenient handling.

For example, bulky materials like cotton and jute are compressed into bales, liquid materials like oil and wine are put into bottles, barrels and cans, etc.

Thus, packing implies placing products in suitable packages for delivery of the product to customer or for the purpose of storage and transport.

22. What is meant by service? Mention three features of service. ***ISC 2015 (4M)***

Ans Service means an intangible act or performance that can satisfy some need and can be offered for sale. Beauty parlour, nursing home, courier service, entertainment and repair stores are providers of service.

The three features of services are as follows

(i) **Intangibility** Services are intangible, as they cannot be seen or touched. They are abstract and invisible.

(ii) **Perishability** Services cannot be stored for future use, e.g. If a bus has ten vacant seats, these cannot be utilised in future.

(iii) **Inseparability** Services are produced and consumed at the same time. The service cannot be separated from the service provider.

23. What is meant by indirect channels of distribution? Explain the types of indirect channels of distribution. ***ISC 2015 (5M)***

Ans Refer to text on page 142.

24. What is packaging? Explain any three functions of packaging. ***ISC 2014 (5M)***

Ans **Meaning of packaging** Refer to Q. No. 21 (3/4/5 Marks) on page 152.

Functions of packaging are

(i) **Silent salesman** Packaging plays an important role in self-service outlets. It attracts the attention of customers, describes the products features, creates customer confidence and makes a favourable impression on the customers, e.g. Calcium Sandoz, Ferrero Rocher chocolates, etc. Hence, packaging is considered as a silent salesman.

Functions of Packaging

- Silent salesman
- Product differentiation
- Protection of the product

(ii) **Product differentiation** The colour, size, material, etc of packaging makes real difference in the perception of customer about the quality of the product.

(iii) **Protection of the product** Packaging is the process of designing and producing the package for a product. A package is a wrapper or container in which a product is enclosed, encased or sealed.

The purpose of packaging a product, is to reduce the risk of spoilage, breakage, leakage, etc in the process of storage and transportation.

25. What is marketing mix? Explain the elements of marketing mix. *ISC 2013 (5M)*

Ans Marketing mix refers to the combination of four basic elements known as four Ps, i.e. product, price, promotion and physical distribution.

From a number of alternatives available, firm chooses a particular combination to develop a market offering. The combination of variables chosen by a firm to prepare its marketing offering is called marketing mix.

Elements/Components of marketing mix are

(i) **Product mix** It refers to important decisions related to the products. Product mix involves product planning and development. Decisions are to be taken regarding product, range, quality, size, features, packaging, after sale services, branding, warranties, etc.

Production must satisfy consumer needs and expectations. These decisions play an important role in attracting the customers towards the product.

(ii) **Price mix** Price is the money paid by a buyer (or received by a seller) in consideration of the purchase of a product or a service.

Pricing plays an important role in the marketing of goods. It is often used as a regulator of product's demand. It is an effective tool during stiff competition. Price affects the revenue and profits of a firm.

Functions of Marketing
- Product mix
- Price mix
- Promotion mix
- Place mix

(iii) **Promotion mix** It refers to informing the customers about the product and persuading them to purchase these products.

This job is done by the company through the medium of advertisement, personal selling, sales promotion and publicity. Decisions with regard to all these factors directly influence the sale of the product.

(iv) **Place mix** (Physical distribution) It includes decisions about channels of distribution, means of transportation, warehousing, inventory control, etc. Place mix is concerned with linking the sellers and buyers.

The choice of channels of distribution depends on nature of product, competition, willingness of middlemen and producer's financial resources.

26. Explain qualities of a good salesman. *ISC 2013, 06, 02 (5M)*

Ans Refer to text on page 145.

27. Write a short note on 'branding and labelling'. *ISC 2010 (3M)*

Ans **Branding** Branding refers to the process of giving a name, sign, symbol or identification mark to a product. A brand is the identification of a product. It can be in the form of a name, symbol or design, etc. Branding is not only done to identify the seller or producer, but also to make a product superior than the competitor's product.

Labelling A simple looking, but important task in the marketing of goods relates to designing the label to be put on the packets. The label may vary from a simple tag attached to the product to complex graphics that are part of the packages.

The label affixed on the package indicates the features and quality of product, brand name, grade, price, contents, cautions for use, method of use and other details.

28. Define sales promotion as an element of promotion mix and highlight its objectives. *ISC 2008 (5M)*

Ans Sales promotion refers to short-term incentives, which are designed to encourage the buyers to make immediate purchase of a product or service. These include all promotional efforts, other than advertising, personal selling and publicity used by a company to boost its sales.

Sales promotion activities include offering cash discounts, sales contests, free gift offers and free sample distribution.

Sales promotion is usually undertaken to supplement other promotional efforts such as advertising and personal selling, e.g. 20% off on branded clothes, free samples with new products, gold coin inside the bag of tea leaves, etc.

Objectives of sales promotion are (any four)

(i) **Creation of demand** It induces the buyers buying behaviour by giving instant benefits on their purchases. Thus, increases the current demand for the product or service.

(ii) **Attracting new customers** Sales promotion activities attract attention of the people, because of the use of incentives, gifts, discounts, etc.

(iii) **Useful in new product launch** Sales promotion tools can be very effective at the time of introduction of a new product in the market. It induces people to break away from their regular buying behaviour and try new product.

(iv) **Deals with seasonal decline** It is especially helpful in off-season, when the demand decreases. e.g. Incentives are given on car purchase at the end of the year.

(v) **Encounter competitor's sales promotion campaign** To maintain the same sales turnover, it becomes necessary for the company to counter the competitors move of introducing same sales promotion technique.

(vi) **Induce middlemen** Sales promotion is equally effective for middlemen. They purchase more and maintain a regular supply for the customers throughout the year.

Objectives of Sales Promotion
- Creation of demand
- Attracting new customers
- Useful in new product launch
- Deals with seasonal decline
- Encounter competitor's sales promotion campaign
- Induce middlemen

29. A washing machine is launched in the market. Describe any five methods of sales promotion that can be used to do so. *ISC 2007 (5M)*

Ans Sales promotion is an effort to stimulate consumers to purchase more and more of a particular commodity. There are various methods of sales promotion. For sales promotion of washing machine, following techniques of sales promotion can be used

(i) **Rebates** Companies give rebate by making some kind of manipulation with the price of the product to make it attractive to buyers to buy their products on urgent basis. So, the company can offer the washing machine at 10% discount.

(ii) **Contests** In this, consumers are required to participate in some competitive event involving application of skills or luck. The winner is given some reward. The company can organise for writing a slogan and the winner will be given a new washing machine.

Techniques of Sales Promotion
- Rebates
- Contests
- Product combination
- Lucky draw
- Financing

(iii) **Product combination** Offering another product as gift alongwith the purchase of a product, is an example of product combination. With washing machine some other household item like steam iron or a mixer grinder can be given as a gift.

(iv) **Lucky draw** Under this scheme, some coupons bearing distinct numbers are issued on the purchase of some products. At the end of a day, week or month, draws are taken and the winner is awarded some gifts. e.g. The company can use this technique at a trade fair and the winner of the lucky draw will get the washing machine.

(v) **Financing** In case of consumer durable goods like electronic goods or automobiles, the seller offers easy financing schemes at 0% interest. e.g. In our case on a fully automatic machine of ₹ 25,000, payment can be done as ₹ 10,000 immediately and balance ₹ 15,000 in 5 instalments of ₹ 3,000 each.

30. Discuss the objectives and significance of salesmanship. *ISC 2002 (5M)*

Ans The main objectives of salesmanship are

(i) Inducing the customer to demand the product.

(ii) Assisting the customer to take wise decision regarding purchase.

(iii) Build a long lasting relationship with the customers.

(iv) Providing standardised products to its customers.

Significance of salesmanship is as follows

It is a process of informing customers and persuading them to purchase products through personal communication. Companies appoint salespersons to contact prospective buyers and create awareness about the product and develop product preferences with the aim of making sale. It is beneficial in following ways

(i) **Effective promotion tool** Personal selling is an effective tool to increase the sale of product. Salesman explains the merits of products to customers.

(ii) **Flexible tool** Personal selling efforts can be changed according to the type of customer, salesman are attending.

(iii) **Consumer attention** Through personal selling, it is easy to get the attention of customer as there is face-to-face interaction between customers and salesman.

Concept Enhancer Personal selling helps sellers to create lasting relationship with customers and create personal rapport among them.

Case Based Questions

Case 1

Pooja has started a small company that manufactures steel and aluminium rods used by construction firms. She has made a large capital investment in this venture and also hired an excellent sales team.

Their marketing approach is to contact the buyers directly and explain the features of their product. They have a complete control over the distribution of their products.

ISC 2024

(i) Identify the type of product manufactured by Pooja's company.

Ans Pooja's company manufactures industrial goods/ product.

(ii) Briefly explain any two features of the product identified in sub-part (i).

Ans Features of industrial product are

(a) They have longer life cycles as compared to consumer goods.

(b) They are designed for a specialised purpose.

(iii) State the channel of distribution used by the company in the above case.

Ans Direct channel of distribution is used by the company in this case.

(iv) Identify and briefly discuss any three objectives of the element of promotion mix used by the sales team in the above case.

Ans Element of promotion mix used by the sales team in the above case in 'personal selling'.

Objectives of personal selling Refer to Q.No. 19 (3/4/5 Marks) on page 152.

Case 2

Spices and Cheese Burgers has various outlets to sell burgers and deal with the customers directly. This channel of distribution was adopted by the organisation keeping in mind the nature of the product. In order to boost its sales, the management decided to introduce 'Buy one Get one Free' offer to its customers.

ISC 2023

(i) Identify the channel of distribution used by Spice and Cheese Burgers.

Ans Direct channel (Zero level)

(ii) Briefly explain the channel of distribution identified in (i) above.

Ans **Direct channel** (Zero level) It is where manufacturers or producers directly deal with customers without having any middlemen involved. Businesses catering to the low volume of consumers and targeting a narrower market place consider this zero-level channel. Perishable and expensive goods producers, such as bakers, meat and milk producers, and jewelers, opt for this route.

(iii) Which element of promotion mix is highlighted in the above case?

Ans Sales promotion

(iv) State any four objectives of the element of promotion mix identified in (iii) above.

Ans Refer to Q. No. 28 (3/4/5 Marks) on page 153 and 154.

Case 3

A reputed publishing company is planning to open new showrooms in some big cities in North India. The company wishes to invite celebrity novelists to inaugurate their new outlets. It also plans to invite other celebrities from the literary world and make new book releases before August. Introductory offers will be given in the form of price reductions, limited edition of autographed copies and discount coupons.

ISC Sem II Specimen 2022

(i) Identify the promotional tools adopted by the company.

Ans Sales promotion

(ii) In what way do the promotional tools adopted by the company generate sales?

Ans Sales promotion helps to increase the sales in the following ways

(a) **Creation of demand** It must have a clear cut pre-requirement to influence, capture and create a demand of the product for the existing and potential customers.

(b) **Creation of goodwill** Sales promotion is required to add value to the product and it can be done by communicating to the public about the superiority of the product that will effectively stimulate the prospective customers to change their attitude for linking of the product. The sum total of this will surely create goodwill for the firm's product.

CHAPTER TEST

01 Mark Questions

1. ………… are the key elements of promotion mix.
   (a) Advertising and sales promotion
   (b) Publicity and public relations
   (c) Direct marketing and personal selling
   (d) All of the above
2. ………… is not a part of marketing mix.
   (a) Product (b) Purpose (c) Place (d) Price
3. Which of the following is/are the ingredient(s) of product mix?
   (a) Advertising (b) Public relation
   (c) Personal selling (d) All of these
4. Capital goods are usually classified as consumer products. State true or false.
5. Most new products are commercial failures. State true or false.
6. Marketing mix for products consists of ………… .
7. Zero level channel has no ……… .
8. What is labelling?
9. What is publicity?
10. **Assertion** (A) Marketing discourages the development and spreading of new ideas, goods and services.
    Reason (R) Marketing does not occur unless two or more parties are willing to exchange something for something else.
    Alternatives
    (a) Both Assertion (A) and Reason (R) are true and Reason (R) is the correct explanation of Assertion (A)
    (b) Both Assertion (A) and Reason (R) are true, but Reason (R) is not the correct explanation of Assertion (A)
    (c) Assertion (A) is true, but Reason (R) is false
    (d) Assertion (A) is false, but Reason (R) is true

02 Marks Questions

11. Write any two differences between goods and services.
12. Explain the terms 'labelling' and 'packaging'.
13. Define the term 'price'.
14. What do you understand by 'promotion'?
15. State two functions performed by a package of a product.
16. Explain two factors which determine the price of a product or a service.
17. Name the four elements of promotion mix.
18. Explain any two techniques of sales promotion.

03/04/05 Marks Questions

19. Distinguish between advertising and sales promotion.
20. Explain the functions performed by the label of a product.
21. Explain any five factors which affect the pricing decision.
22. 'Advertising is a non-personal presentation or promotion of goods or services'. Explain with reference to its features.
23. Explain briefly the elements of marketing mix.
24. What is physical distribution? Explain the major types of channels of distribution involved in physical distribution of product.
25. What do you understand by sales promotion? How is it different from personal selling?

Answers

1. (d) All of the above
2. (b) Purpose
3. (d) All of these
4. False
5. True
6. 4P's
7. intermediaries
10. (d) Assertion (A) is false, but Reason (R) is true

11

Consumer Protection

TREND ANALYSIS 5 YEARS

		Average No. of Questions Across all Sets					
		Types of Questions	2024	2023	2020	2019	2018
TOPIC 01	Concept of Consumer Protection	1 Mark	—	—	—	—	—
		2 Marks	—	—	—	—	—
		3/4/5 Marks	—	1	1	—	1
TOPIC 02	Consumer Protection Act, 2019	1 Mark	1	1	—	—	—
		2 Marks	—	—	—	1	—
		3/4/5 Marks	1	1	—	1	—

Concept of Consumer Protection

Consumer protection is a very wide term. It includes providing information to the consumers about their rights and responsibilities and helping them in getting their grievances redressed.

There are various practices which misguide, mislead, cheat and harm the consumer's interests. A consumer is required to be protected from such activities.

Some examples of such practices are

(i) Black marketing
(ii) Hoarding
(iii) Adulteration
(iv) Not meeting safety standards
(v) False and misleading advertisement
(vi) Profiteering
(vii) Raising prices by restricting output
(viii) Monopolising

Need/Importance of Consumer Protection

The following points highlight the need/importance of consumer protection

1. From the Point of View of Consumers

(i) **Consumer ignorance** Consumer Protection Act provides required information related to the rights and remedies available to consumers. It spreads awareness, so that a consumer will be able to know about the redressal agencies and can approach them whenever needed.

(ii) **Unorganised consumers** Consumers need to be organised in the form of consumer organisations which would take care of their interests.

(iii) **Widespread exploitation of consumers** Consumer is the kingpin of the market, still there is a lot of exploitation of consumers, as businessmen use various unfair trade practices to cheat and exploit consumers. Consumer protection provides safety to consumers from such exploitation.

2. From the Point of View of Businessmen

(i) **Consumer is the purpose of business** It is the consumer which is the fulcrum of any business activity. They bring the business into existence and provides for its stability. Thus, business should provide quality goods at right price to the consumers.

(ii) **Long-term interest of business** Customer is the foundation of business. In order to satisfy and retain consumers for long-term, consumer protection is necessary.

(iii) **Social responsibility** Business organisations make money by selling their products to consumers. It is the social responsibility of businessman to provide satisfaction to their customers.

(iv) **Moral justification** Business exists to serve human beings. It is the moral duty of a businessman to serve their customers well and keep them away from exploitative and unfair trade practices.

(v) **Government intervention** If a business organisation is engaged in any form of exploitative trade practices, government would interfere and can tarnish the image of the company.

(vi) **Multiple objectives of business** Profit is not the only objective of doing business, but it has social responsibility to take care of all sections of the society.

Methods of Consumer Protection

Following are the methods to ensure consumer protection

(i) **Consumer awareness** (Self help) A consumer, who is well informed about his rights and the reliefs available to him, would be in a position to raise his voice against any unfair trade practices or unscrupulous exploitation. They should also be aware of their rights and responsibilities.

(ii) **Government/Legislative measures** The government can protect the interests of the consumers by enacting various legislations. The legal framework in India encompasses various legislations, which provide protection to consumers. The most important of these regulations is the Consumer Protection Act, 2019.

(iii) **Self-regulation by business** Business firms realise that it is in their long-term interest to serve the customers well. Socially responsible firms follow ethical standards and practices in dealing with their customers. Many firms have set-up their customer service and grievance cells to redress the problems and grievances of their consumers.

(iv) **Business associations** The associations of trade, commerce and business like FICCI (Federation of Indian Chambers of Commerce of India) and CII (Confederation of Indian Industries) have laid down their code of conduct, which lay down for their members the guidelines regarding their dealings with the customers.

(v) **Formation of consumer organisations/associations** The consumers need to organise themselves for the protection of their rights. Various NGO's are also working in this field, which can be contacted in case of any grievances.

Consumer organisations play an important role in educating consumers about their rights and providing protection to them.

Role of NGOs and Consumer Organisations

Consumer organisations or associations are voluntary associations of consumers. Several consumer associations have been formed in different parts of the country. However, only a few of them have become prominent.

Some of them are VOICE (Voluntary Organisation in Interest of Consumer Education) New Delhi, Common Cause (New Delhi), Consumer Guidance Society of India (Mumbai), CERC (Consumer Education and Research Centre) Ahmedabad, CUTS (Consumer Utility and Trust Society) Jaipur.

The Consumer Coordination Council had been set-up as an apex body of consumer organisations in India.

Non-Governmental Organisations (NGOs) are voluntary organisations formed to serve different sections of society in the following ways

(i) Making consumers aware of their rights and responsibilities.

(ii) Educating consumers about the remedies available to them for protecting their rights.

(iii) Collecting data on different products and testing them.

(iv) Publishing journals, brochures and monographs on consumer affairs.

(v) Arranging talks, seminars, conferences and workshops on issues concerning consumers.

(vi) Organising protests and boycotts against adulteration, underweight, price rigging, etc.

(vii) Producing films and video messages on food adulteration, drug misuse, etc.

(viii) Filing suits, complaints and writing petitions before the courts on behalf of consumers.

Role of Government

The government also works for welfare of consumers. It takes following steps in protecting the rights of consumer.

(i) **Passing Various Laws** The government has passed the following laws for consumer protection
   (a) The Weights and Measures Act, 1958
   (b) Drug Control Act, 1950
   (c) The Competition Act, 2000
   (d) Essential Commodities Act, 1955
   (e) Consumer Protection Act, 2019

(ii) **Publicity** It drives a publicity campaign 'Jago Grahak Jago', under which it has launched various advertisements to spread awareness among customers.

(iii) **Consumer welfare fund** Government of India has created a fund for consumer education, training and research, guidance and complaint handling facility and setting up product testing laboratories, etc.

(iv) **PIL** (Public Interest Litigation) This type of facility provides any individual or group to file a written petition in the larger interest of people.

(v) **Institution of awards** Awards have been instituted to encourage participation in consumer protection.

Consumer Protection Act, 2019

The Consumer Protection Act, 2019 came into effect by 20th July, 2020. It seeks to protect and promote the interests of consumers through speedy and inexpensive redressal of their grievances. It is applicable to all types of businesses whether a manufacturer or a trader and whether supplying goods or providing services including e-commerce firms.

The act confers certain rights to consumers with a view to empowering them and to protect their interests.

Rights of Consumers

The Consumer Protection Act provides the following rights to consumers

(i) **Right to safety** It means that a consumer has a right to be protected against the marketing of such goods and services that are harmful to life and health.

(ii) **Right to be informed** A consumer has the right to get true and complete information about the quality, quantity, price, contents, expiry date of the goods and services, which he intends to buy.

(iii) **Right to be assured** Consumers have the freedom to choose products of their choice. This implies that the marketers should offer a wide variety of products in terms of quality, brand, size, etc to the consumers.

(iv) **Right to be heard** The consumer has a right to file a complaint and to be heard in case of dissatisfaction with a good or a service. It is because of this reason, many enlightened business firms have set-up their own consumer service and grievance cells.

(v) **Right to seek redressal** This right assures justice to consumers against exploitation and includes compensation for any loss or injury suffered by the consumers, replacement of goods or repair of defects in the goods in order to provide satisfaction to consumers.

(vi) **Right to consumer education** Consumer should have knowledge about the various rights and reliefs provided by the legislations to protect their interest.

Consumer Responsibilities

The Consumer Protection Act lays down the following responsibilities for consumers

(i) **Exercise rights** Consumers should be aware of their own rights and should make an intelligent and wise choice, while making a purchase.

(ii) **Assert yourself** Assert yourself to get into a fair deal.

(iii) **Buy only standardised goods** Check for quality assurance and look for ISI mark on electrical goods, FPO on food products, Hallmark on jewellery, etc.

(iv) **Ask for cash memo** Whenever a purchase is made, cash memo should be taken. In case of any grievance, cash memo serves as a proof of purchase.

(v) **Read the instructions for use** Consumers should follow instructions and use the products safely.

(vi) **File a complaint** If there is a shortcoming in the product, a complaint should be filed immediately.

(vii) **Form consumer societies** This is the best way of helping themselves, by actively participating in educating consumer and safeguarding their interests by forming consumer societies.

Meaning of Consumer

Consumer means any of the following persons

(i) A person, who buys any goods or avails any service for a consideration which has been paid or promised, or partly paid and partly promised, or under any scheme of deferred payment.

(ii) The term includes any other user of such goods when such use is made with the approval of the buyer. The term 'consumer' however, does not include a person, who obtains such goods for resale or for any other commercial purpose.

Who can File a Complaint?

The following can file a complaint under the Act

(i) A consumer.
(ii) Any voluntary consumer association registered under any law for the time being in force.
(iii) The Central Government or any State Government.
(iv) One or more consumers, where there are numerous consumers having the same interest.
(v) In case of death of a consumer, his legal heir or representative.
(vi) In case of a consumer being minor, his parent or legal guardian.

Against Whom a Complaint can be Filed?

(i) A complaint can be filed against seller, manufacturer or dealer of goods, whose goods are defective.
(ii) It can be filed against the provider of services, if they are deficient in any manner.

Reliefs Available Under Consumer Protection Act, 2019

If the Consumer Court is satisfied about the genuineness of the complaint, it can issue one or more of the following directions to the defaulting party

(i) To remove the defect in goods or deficiency in service.
(ii) To replace the defective product with a new one, free from any defect.
(iii) To refund the price paid for the product or the charges paid for the service.
(iv) To pay a reasonable amount of compensation for any loss of injury suffered by the consumer due to the negligence of the opposite party.
(v) To pay punitive damages in appropriate circumstances.
(vi) To discontinue the unfair/restrictive trade practice and not to repeat it in the future.
(vii) To cease manufacture of hazardous goods and to desist from offering hazardous services.
(viii) To pay any amount (not less than 5% of the value of the defective goods or deficient services provided), to be credited to the Consumer Welfare Fund or any other organisation/person, to be utilised in the prescribed manner.

The Consumer Disputes Redressal Commissions

The Consumer Protection Act, 2019 provides for seting up a 3-tier, quasi-judicial machinery. This machinery is authorised to provide time bound relief to consumers. The reliefs can be one or combination of reliefs as discussed above.

1. District Commission

(i) The State Government is required to establish District Commission in each district.
(ii) Each District Commission shall consist of a president and not less than two and not more than such number of members as may be prescribed, in consultation with the Central Government. All members are to be appointed by the state government.
(iii) A District Commission can receive consumer complaints, where the value of goods or services and the compensation claimed does not exceed ₹ 50 lakh.
[As per Consumer Protection (Jurisdiction of the District Commission, the State Commission and the National Commission) Rules, 2021]
(iv) On receiving the complaint, the District Commission shall refer the complaint to the opposite party concerned against whom the complaint has been filed and send the sample of goods for testing in a laboratory.
(v) The District Commission, after being satisfied that the goods are defective or there is some unfair trade practices, can issue an order to the opposite party directing him to either resolve the issue or replace the goods, or return the price paid, or pay compensation to the consumer for loss or injury, etc.
(vi) An appeal against the order of the District Commission can be filed with the State Commission, within 45 days of passing of the order.

2. State Commission

(i) This is established by the State Government in each State and its jurisdiction is restricted to the boundaries of the State concerned.
(ii) Each State Commission shall consist of a president and not less than four and not more than such number of members as may be prescribed, in consultation with the Central Government. All members are to be appointed by the State Government.

(iii) Only those complaints can be filed in the State Commission, where the value of goods or services and the compensation claimed exceeds ₹ 50 lakh, but does not exceed ₹ 2 crore.
[As per Consumer Protection (Jurisdiction of the District Commission, the State Commission and the National Commission) Rules, 2021]

(iv) On receiving the complaint, the State Commission shall refer the complaint to the opposite party concerned against whom the complaint has been filed and send the sample of goods for testing in a laboratory.

(v) The State Commission, after being satisfied that the goods are defective or there is some unfair trade practices, can issue an order to the opposite party directing him to either resolve the issue or replace the goods, or return the price paid, or pay compensation to the consumer for loss or injury, etc.

(vi) An appeal against the order of the State Commission can be filed before the National Commission, within 30 days of passing of the order.

3. National Commission

(i) This is established by the Central Government.

(ii) The National Commission shall consist of a president and not less than four and not more than such number of members as may be prescribed. All members are to be appointed by the Central Government.

(iii) Only those complaints can be filed in the National Commission, where the value of goods or services and the compensation claimed is more than ₹ 2 crore.
[As per Consumer Protection (Jurisdiction of the District Commission, the State Commission and the National Commission) Rules, 2021]

(iv) On receiving the complaint, the National Commission shall refer the complaint to the opposite party concerned against whom the complaint has been filed and send the sample of goods for testing in a laboratory.

(v) The National Commission, after being satisfied that the goods are defective or there is some unfair trade practices, can issue an order to the opposite party directing him to either resolve the issue or replace the goods, or return the price paid, or pay compensation to the consumer for loss or injury, etc.

(vi) An appeal against the order of the National Commission can be filed before the Supreme Court, within 30 days of such order.

Difference between Consumer Protection Act, 1986 and Consumer Protection Act, 2019

Basis	Consumer Protection Act, 1986	Consumer Protection Act, 2019
Regulator	No central regulator.	Central Consumer Protection Authority is set-up.
Filing of complaint	A complaint needs to be filed in the consumer court under whom jurisdiction of the seller falls.	A complaint can be filed from anywhere or from where the consumer resides.
Mediation	No provision available.	Courts can work towards settlement through mediation cells.
Jurisdication	The jurisdiction at District level was complaints worth of ₹ 20 lakh.	District level authorities can take-up complaints with goods and services worth up to ₹ 50 lakh.
Product liability	No provision available.	Consumers have the right to seek compensation for any harm caused.
E-commerce	No provision available.	E-commerce transactions also come under the provisions involving direct sales.
Video conferencing	No provision available.	Consumers can seek hearing through video conference.

PYQs Previous Years' Questions

1/2 Marks Questions

1. Ms. Anamika visited a reputed dealer of electronic goods to buy a bluetooth headset. The salesman at the shop forced her to buy a particular brand of headset. Which consumer right of Anamika was violated?
ISC 2024 (1M)

Or Sushant went to a shop to buy detergent. The shopkeeper forced him to buy a particular brand of detergent out of the various available brands, irrespective of the willingness of Sushant. Which right of Sushant as a consumer, has been violated?
ISC Specimen 2023 (1M)

Ans Right to be assured

2. A wholesaler sold adulterated goods which were hazardous to the customer's health. Which customer right was violated in this case? *ISC 2023 (1M)*

Ans Right to safety

3. Publication of a magazine on consumer rights is an example of the right to .... *ISC Sem II 2022 (1M)*

Ans consumer education

4. How many rights of consumers are given in the Consumer Protection Act, 2019? *ISC Sem II Specimen 2022 (1M)*

(a) 4 (b) 3 (c) 6 (d) 5

Ans (c) 6

5. Mr. Kappa has recently purchased a refrigerator from TUTU Enterprises, paying ₹ 30,000. After using it for a day or two, he found mechanical defects in the refrigerator. Immediately, he informed the dealer about the defect but there was no response from the dealer. Mr. Kappa decided to lodge a complaint against TUTU Enterprises.

(i) Which court should Mr. Kappa approach to file a complaint?

(ii) State any one relief the concerned court may order in favour of Mr. Kappa. *ISC 2019 (2M)*

Ans (i) Mr. Kappa should approach District Commission to file the complaint as case involves amount less than ₹ 50 lakh.

(ii) The court may order replacement of good or removal of defect from good.

6. Agrim purchased a Diesel Car for ₹ 7 lakh from an automobile company and found its engine to be defective. Despite many complaints, the defect was not rectified. Suggest the appropriate authority where Agrim under his right as a consumer, could file a complaint. *ISC Specimen 2018, 17 (2M)*

Ans Agrim could file a complaint in District Commission under the Consumer Protection Act, 2019. The District Commission has the powers of a civil court for enquiring into any complaint lodged with it by the consumer.

However, the value of goods or services and the compensation claimed should not be more than ₹ 50 lakh. Since, in the given case, the car costs ₹ 7 lakh, therefore it is the most appropriate authority where Agrim should file a complaint.

7. Expand the terms 'ISI' and 'Agmark'. *ISC 2002 (2M)*

Ans **'ISI'** stands for 'Indian Standards Institute', which is now known as Bureau of Indian Standards. It checks the quality of products and gives the ISI certification.

'Agmark' stands for 'Agricultural Marketing'.

Concept Enhancer ISI is a certification mark that is used for industrial products in India while Agmark is made specially for agricultural products.

3/4/5 Marks Questions

1. Mr. Deepak purchased a washing machine from a renowned e-commerce platform for ₹ 25,000. He ensured that he received a cash memo.

Unfortunately, his clothes got damaged in the first wash due to a manufacturing defect in the machine's rotator.

(i) Mr. Deepak can be called a responsible consumer. Give one reason to support this statement.

(ii) Which provision under Consumer Protection Act, 2019 enables Mr. Deepak to claim a compensation for the manufacturing defect in the washing machine?

(iii) Mention any two points of mandatory information which e-commerce platform must provide to a consumer. *ISC 2024 (4M)*

Ans (i) Mr. Deepak is a responsible consumer as he took a cash memo while purchasing a washing machine.

(ii) 'Right to seek redressal' enables Mr. Deepak to claim a compensation for the manufacturing defect in the washing machine.

(iii) (a) Description of the product which includes features, specification, MRP, expiry date, etc.

(b) Return or replacement option.

2. A patient suffering from high fever was hospitalised for few days. During the treatment, he was given an injection which caused a permanent nerve damage resulting in paralysis. The cost of treatment was ₹ 2,00,000 which was disputed by the patient's family.

Which consumer dispute redressal authority can be approached by the patient's family? Explain any three rights of the consumers. *ISC 2023 (4M)*

Ans District Redressal Commission can be approached by the patient's family.

(i) **Right to safety** Consumers have the right to be protected against goods and services which are hazardous to life and health.

(ii) **Right to be heard** Consumers have the right to file a complaint and to be heard. Usually reputed companies have their own consumer service and grievance cell where they can file their complaints and have the right to be heard.

(iii) **Right to seek redressal** Consumers have the right to get relief in case if the product falls short of their expectations or hazardous to life or health.

The Consumer Protection Act provides a number of reliefs to the consumers including replacement of the product, removal of defect in the product etc.

Value Points

For getting maximum marks, following points can be included in the answer

- Protection against hazardous goods and services.
- File a complaint and exercise right to be heard.

3. Explain any four points on the need for consumer protection. *ISC 2023, 18, 16 (4M)*

Ans Following points highlight the need for consumer protection

(i) **Consumer ignorance** Consumer Protection Act provides required information related to the rights and remedies available to consumers.

It spreads awareness, so that a consumer will be able to know about the redressal agencies and can approach them whenever needed.

(ii) **Unorganised consumers** Consumers need to be organised in the form of consumer organisations which would take care of their interests.

Due to lack of consumer organisations in India, consumer protection becomes necessary to promote and protect the interests of consumers.

Need for Consumer Protection

- Consumer ignorance
- Unorganised consumers
- Widespread exploitation of consumers
- Social responsibility

(iii) **Widespread exploitation of consumers** Consumer is the kingpin of the market, still there is lot of exploitation of consumers as businessmen use various unfair trade practices to cheat and exploit consumers. Consumer protection provides safety to consumers from exploitations such as adulteration, black marketing, hoarding, defective and unsafe products etc.

(iv) **Social responsibility** Business organisations make money by selling their products to consumers. It is the social responsibility of businessman to provide satisfaction to their customers.

4. Manu bought an electric iron of a reputed brand for ₹ 500, but it caused an electric shock while in use. Manu wants to exercise his right as an aggrieved consumer. Identify and explain the right under which he can protect himself. Explain any two remedies available to him as an aggrieved consumer. *ISC Specimen 2023 (4M)*

Ans Manu can exercise the 'right to seek redressal'. This right assures justice to consumers against exploitation and includes compensation for any loss or injury suffered by the consumers, replacement of goods or repair of defects in the goods in order to provide satisfaction to consumers.

Remedies availabe to him are

(i) To remove the defect in goods or deficiency in service.

(ii) To replace the defective product with a new one, free from any defect.

Common Mistake Number of times, students are not able to identify the suitable right as per situation. Thus, careful reading is highly required, in order to attempt these kind of questions.

5. Rashmi went to purchase a packet of chocolates. The shopkeeper handed her a packet which did not have the MRP, date of manufacture and date of expiry printed on it. Rashmi decided not to buy the packet.

Identify and explain the right of the consumer which has been violated in the above case. Briefly explain any two points highlighting the need for consumer protection. *ISC Sem II 2022 (4M)*

Ans The right of the consumer violated in the given case is 'right to be informed'.

According to this right, a consumer has the right to get true and complete information about the quality, quantity, price, contents, expiry date of the goods and services which he intends to buy.

For points that highlight the need for consumer protection, refer to Q. No. 3 (3/4/5 Marks) on page 163.

6. Palak went to a shop to buy hair oil. The shopkeeper forced her to buy a particular brand of hair oil from various available brands, irrespective of the willingness of Palak.

Which right of Palak, as a consumer, has been violated and where can she file a case against the shopkeeper? Name the two other rights of the consumer. *ISC Sem II Specimen 2022 (3M)*

Ans Right of Palak violated here is 'right to be assured'. She can file case against the shopkeeper in District Commission.

Other rights of consumers are

(i) Right to safety

(ii) Right to be informed

7. Explain any three methods of consumer protection. *ISC 2020 (3M)*

Or Write four methods by which the objective of consumer protection can be achieved. *ISC 2014 (4M)*

Ans The objectives of consumer protection can be achieved through the following methods

(i) **Self-regulatory business** Many big business houses have realised that their long-term interests lie in the satisfaction and welfare of the customers. Thus, they follow ethical standards and practices and have also established customer service and grievance cells to attend to the problems and complaints of the customers.

(ii) **Business association** Various business associations like FICCI (Federation on Indian Chambers of Commerce of India) and CII (Confederation of Indian Industries) have set-up code of conduct for their members. This code provides guidelines for dealing with customers.

Methods of Consumer Protection
- Self-regulatory business
- Business association
- Consumer awareness
- Government

(iii) **Consumer awareness** (Self help) A consumer would be in a position to raise his voice against any kind of exploitation, if he is well aware of the rights and reliefs available to him.

Moreover, this awareness helps him to safeguard his interest. They should also form consumer association for safeguarding themselves.

(iv) **Government** The government has enacted various laws and legislations for protecting the consumers. The most important among these is the Consumer Protection Act, 2019.

Some of the government measures other than Consumer Protection Act, 2019, provides for other acts like Essential Commodities Act, 1955. The Sale of Goods Act, 1930, The Competition Act, 2000, etc.

Apart from these legislations, government also plays an important role in educating and informing the consumers.

8. Explain any four rights available to a consumer under the Consumer Protection Act, 2019. *ISC 2019 M (4M)*

Or Explain any five rights of consumers as provided under the Consumer Protection Act, 2019. *ISC 2015 M (5M)*

Ans Refer to the text on page 159.

9. Mention three remedies available to consumers under the Consumer Protection Act, 2019. *ISC 2015 M (3M)*

Ans A consumer can ask for a number of remedies in case of default in goods and services used. If the Consumer Court is satisfied about the genuineness of the complaint, it can issue one or more of the following directions to the defaulting party

(i) To remove the defect in goods or deficiency in service.

(ii) To replace the defective product with a new one, free from any defect.

(iii) To refund the price paid for the product or the charges paid for the service.

Additional Questions

2 Marks Questions

1. What is the objective of the Consumer Protection Act, 2019?

Ans The main objective of the Consumer Protection Act, 2019 is to protect the interests of consumers in India. It aims to provide a speedy and simple redressal to consumers grievances. It provides effective safeguards to consumer against various types of exploitations and unfair trade practices.

The act has created special Consumer Courts for enforcement of the Rights of Consumers. It provides a convenient and an inexpensive procedure for redressal of grievances of consumers.

2. How does consumer awareness protect consumers from exploitation?

Ans Self help is the ideal way to overcome problems. If every consumer becomes aware of his/her rights and the remedies available against exploitation, unscrupulous businessmen will not be able to exploit consumers.

Therefore, consumers should be made aware of and educated about their rights. They should know how to protect themselves against malpractices in the market.

5 Marks Question

1. Explain the redressal mechanism available to consumers under the Consumer Protection Act, 2019.

Ans The Consumer Protection Act, 2019 provides a three-tier machinery for the redressal of consumer grievances. For explanation of redressal agenices, refer to text on page 160 and 161.

CHAPTER TEST

01 Mark Questions

1. Which consumer right is not guaranteed under Consumer Protection Act, 2019?
(a) Right to be assured (b) Right to exploitation
(c) Right to be heard (d) Right to seek redressal

2. Consumer Protection Act is significant to
(a) immovable goods (b) movable goods
(c) particular goods and services
(d) all goods and services

3. Under this Act, the minimum age of forum member of a District Commission should be
(a) 30 (b) 40
(c) 35 (d) 65

4. A complaint can be made to a State Commission when the value of the goods or services in question, along with the compensation claimed, exceeds ₹ 50 lakh, but does not exceed ₹ 2 crore. State true or false.

5. ISI is the quality certification mark used in case of food products. State true or false.

6. The right to ……… refers to the right to be safeguarded from products that are harmful to one's life or health.

7. ……… is the standardised mark on jewellery.

8. What are NGOs?

9. What is the meaning of District Commission?

10. **Assertion** (A) Consumer protection has a moral justification for business.

Reason (R) Under the Consumer Protection Act, a complaint can be filed by a consumer for a defective good and also for deficiency in service.

Alternatives
(a) Both Assertion (A) and Reason (R) are true and Reason (R) is the correct explanation of Assertion (A)
(b) Both Assertion (A) and Reason (R) are true, but Reason (R) is not the correct explanation of Assertion (A)
(c) Assertion (A) is true, but Reason (R) is false
(d) Assertion (A) is false, but Reason (R) is true

02 Marks Questions

11. Who is a consumer?

12. Who can file a complaint?

13. State four activities that cheat and misleads the consumers.

14. What steps has the government taken to protect the rights of consumers?

15. State any two reliefs available under the Consumer Protection Act.

16. What are rights of consumers? Discuss any two.

17. How can consumer associations play a major role in safeguarding the interest of a consumer?

03/04/05 Marks Questions

18. Discuss the redressal agencies as provided by Consumer Protection Act.

19. Explain the rights of consumers.

20. What is the need of consumers protection?

21. Discuss briefly about Consumers Protection Act, 2019.

22. Give any five points of difference between Consumer Protection Act, 1986 and Consumer Protection Act, 2019.

Answers

1. (b) Right to exploitation
2. (d) all goods and services
3. (c) 35 *4.* True
5. False
6. safety
7. Hallmark
10. (a) Both Assertion (A) and Reason (R) are true and Reason (R) is the correct explanation of Assertion (A)

ISC

Examination Paper 2025

Time : 3 hrs
Marks : 80

Commerce XII

General Instructions

1. Candidates are allowed additional 15 minutes for only reading the paper. They must not start writing during this time.
2. There are thirteen questions in the paper. All questions are compulsory.
3. This paper is divided into three **Sections : A, B** and **C**.
4. Section A has sixteen subparts which are very short answer questions. Each question carries 1 mark.
5. Section B has eight questions which are short answer questions. Each questions carries 4 marks.
6. Section C has four questions which are long answer questions. Each question carries 8 marks.
7. Internal choices have been provided in two questions in Section B and in one question in Section C.
8. The intended marks for questions are given in brackets [ ].

Section A

(16 Marks)

1. (i) In recent years, the street vendors have begun to accept UPI as a mode of payment. The feature of business environment indicated here is **[1]**

(a) inter-relatedness (b) relativity
(c) diversity (d) dynamism

(ii) With reference to dimensions of business environment, select the odd one out from the following **[1]**

(a) Suppliers of raw materials
(b) Changes in technology
(c) Competition with other companies
(d) Change in consumer preferences

(iii) In 2021, Arun Singhal, the CEO of India's food regulator, FSSAI said, "Consumers should be aware of the food that they are consuming and that can be ensured through labelling…. From November onwards, disclosures about (sodium, sugar and fat) per serving will be mandatory."
(Source*(edited) https://m.economictimes.com)*

Which consumer rights are being protected by the new regulations of FSSAI? **[1]**

(P) Right to information
(Q) Right to be heard
(R) Right to safety
(S) Right to seek redressal

(a) Only (P) and (Q)
(b) Only (Q) and (R)
(c) Only (P) and (R)
(d) Only (R) and (S)

(iv) Paryavaran Ltd. Focuses on sustainable development by following a 'zero waste policy'. **[1]**

Which internal factor of micro environment is referred to here?

(a) Mission and objectives
(b) Human resources
(c) Power structure
(d) Customer focus

(v) Which element of directing is shown below? [1]

Source *www.googleimage.com*

(a) Leadership (b) Motivation
(c) Supervision (d) Communication

(vi) Identify the organisation and the type of structure shown below. [1]

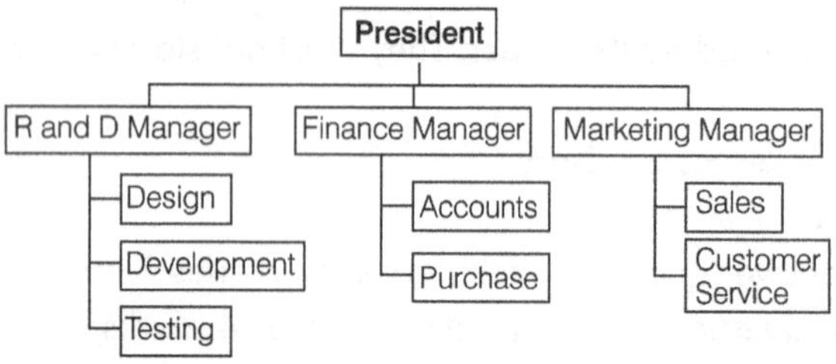

(a) Informal organisation and divisional structure
(b) Informal organisation and functional structure
(c) Formal organisation and divisional structure
(d) Formal organisation and functional structure

(vii) **Assertion** Marketing aims to earn profit through customer satisfaction.

Reason Marketing begins before production of goods and ends with sale. [1]

Alternatives

(a) Both Assertion and Reason are true and Reason is the correct explanation for Assertion.
(b) Both Assertion and Reason are true but Reason is not the correct explanation for Assertion.
(c) Assertion is true and Reason is false.
(d) Both Assertion and Reason are false.

(viii) Study the relation between the first and the second words given below and fill in the fourth word on that basis.

(a) Universal validity : Science :: Creativity : ……… [1]

(b) Positive process : Recruitment :: Negative process : ……… [1]

(ix) State whether the following are true or false.

(a) As a facilitating function of marketing, packaging helps to protect the product. [1]

(b) According to Henri Fayol, the principle of harmony not discord states that there should be healthy cooperation between employees and the employer. [1]

(x) The data given below shows that the capital structure of ABC Ltd. is ……… geared. [1]

ABC Ltd.

DEBT	EQUITY
60%	40%

(xi) The profit of Kriti Ltd. is ₹ 90,000 for the current financial year. Study the data of Kriti Ltd. given below and answer the question that follows. [1]

Security	Yield
Interest on Debenture	₹ 10,000
Dividend on Preference shares	₹ 10,000
Dividend on Equity shares	₹ 30,000

……… and equity shareholders will have a share in ₹ 40,000.

(xii) Identify the document shown in the image below. [1]

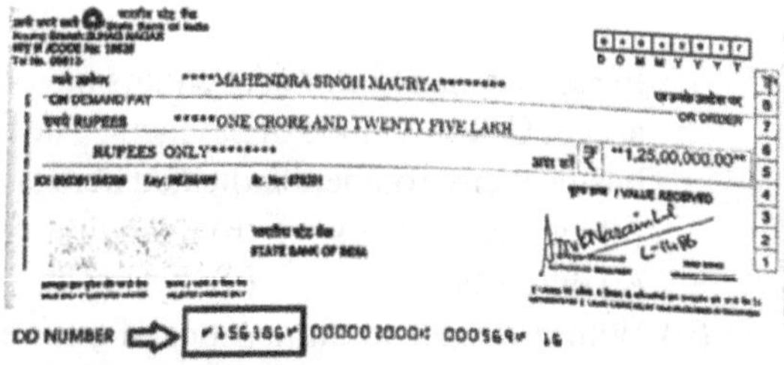

(xiii) Pizzas and Shakes, a famous fast-food chain, has been facing stagnant demand. To overcome this, the management decides to offer discounted meals during the forthcoming festival season. Which element of promotion mix has been used by Pizzas and Shakes? [1]

(xiv) Management is required in all types of organisations and at all levels. Which characteristic of management is highlighted in this statement? [1]

Section B

(32 Marks)

2. As a Finance Manager, outline any four factors you would consider while determining working capital needs of the organisation. **[4]**

3. Food and grocery delivery company, Swiggy announced a programme before its Initial Public Offering (IPO). This programme allows employees to buy a portion of their company stock option for a combined total of up to $65 million.

Source *(edited) https://www.business-standard.com*

Identify and explain the financial incentive given to the employees. **[4]**

4. Siddhi works in a private company. One of her main responsibilities is to develop the company's goals and strategies.

What managerial level is Siddhi employed at? Name three more responsibilities that she needs to fulfill at this level. **[4]**

5. (i) When employees are specialised in their tasks, their efficiency increases resulting in an increased output. Name and briefly explain the principle given by Henri Fayol that supports the above statement. **[2]**

(ii) Some employees strive to fulfill their individual goals rather than achieving the objectives of the organisation.

Which principle of Henri Fayol can be applied to change the mindset of such employees? Briefly explain this principle. **[2]**

6. Rajan has a small size business. He aims to increase his market share by 25% in the next three years.

Specify the type of plan chosen by Rajan. Illustrate any three of its features. **[4]**

Or

In an organisation, there exists a network of social relationships among employees of different departments.

Identify the type of organisation referred to here. State any three of its merits.

7. You are the Manager at Keya Pvt. Ltd. You have to select a Chartered Accountant for the company.

Explain the next four steps in the selection procedure that you will follow after receiving the application blank. **[4]**

8. Annie purchased a car for ₹ 1 crore from a showroom on 7th May, 2023. Within few days, she noticed that its speedometer was not giving accurate results.

Which consumer forum can Annie approach to file a complaint? Suggest any three remedies that the consumer forum can provide to Annie. **[4]**

9. What is Product mix? Explain any three elements of product mix.

Or

Highlight the importance of marketing by giving any four reasons.

Section C

(32 Marks)

10. (i) Name and explain the technique used by a business organisation to diagnose and analyse its micro and macro environment. **[5]**

(ii) Discuss how coordination is embedded in planning, organising and staffing functions of management. **[3]**

11. (i) Ramanpreet is a cautious investor who wants to invest ₹ 1,00,000 for ten years in a debt security offered by a company.

Which debt security should Ramanpreet invest in? Explain any four of its features. **[5]**

(ii) Differentiate between credit card and debit card on any three bases. **[3]**

Or

(i) A company's decision to retain profits for reinvestment rather than distribute them as dividends can prove to be a double-edged sword for the company. Justify this statement by discussing any three merits and any two demerits of retained earnings. **[5]**

(ii) Write a short note on digital banking. **[3]**

12. (i) Several factors influence the price of a product. Explain any five of these factors. **[5]**

(ii) Explain any three features of a service which is offered for sale. **[3]**

13. Read the passage given below and answer the questions that follow.

XYZ Company had planned to increase its profit margin by 30% in the current financial year. But it could not achieve the set target in the first quarter of the year due to cases of theft by employees.

The Board of Directors formulated a policy of 'zero tolerance' for theft. To prevent such cases, it was decided to install CCTV cameras in the rooms where the expensive products were stored.

The team of Senior Managers communicated the same to all the employees of the organisation.

The decisions were implemented and instructions were given to the concerned departments to impose a penalty if an employee was found guilty.

The Human Resource department incorporated the same in the employee handbook.

(i) Explain any two steps of controlling highlighted in the above case. **[2]**

(ii) With reference to the above case, mention any two objectives of communication. **[2]**

(iii) Provide any four points to highlight the importance of controlling. **[4]**

Answers

1. (i) (d) dynamism

(ii) (a) Suppliers of raw materials

(iii) (c) Only (P) and (R)

(iv) (a) Mission and objectives

(v) (a) Leadership

(vi) (d) Formal organisation and functional structure

(vii) (c) Marketing continues even after the sale, including after-sales service, customer feedback and relationship management.

(viii) (a) Art

(b) Selection

(ix) (a) True

(b) False. The principle of Harmony, not Discord was given by F.W. Taylor.

(x) high

(xi) Participating preference shares

(xii) Demand draft

(xiii) Sale promotion

(xiv) Pervasive

2. Following are the four factors that would be considered while determining the working capital needs of an organisation

(i) **Nature of business** Enterprises engaged in manufacturing require more working capital and enterprises engaged in trading/services require less working capital.

(ii) **Size of business** Large scale enterprises require more working capital whereas small scale enterprises require less working capital.

(iii) **Manufacturing cycle** Firms with longer manufacturing cycle require more working capital as compared to firms with shorter manufacturing cycle.

(iv) **Rapidity of turnover** Firms having rapid turnover require less working capital, whereas firms having slow turnover require more working capital.

3. The financial incentive given to employees is Employee Stock Option Plan (ESOP).

An ESOP is a type of employee benefit plan, which is intended to encourage employees to acquire stock or ownership in the company by issuing them equity shares. The shares are issued to the employees at considerable discount.

4. Siddhi is employed at the top level of management.

Following are the responsibilities that needs to be fulfilled by Siddhi

(i) To strive for welfare and survival of business.

(ii) To formulate overall organisational goals and policies of the business.

(iii) To integrate diverse elements and coordinate the activities of different departments according to the overall objectives of the organisation.

5. (i) The principle given by Henri Fayol that supports the statement is 'division of work'.

Division of work Fayol has advocated division of work. According to him, if work is divided into small tasks, then this will help in taking the advantage of specialisation.

The intent of division of work is to produce more and better work with the same effort. It is the most efficient way to use human effort.

(ii) The principle of Henri Fayol can be applied to change the mindset of such employees is 'subordination of individual interest to general interest'.

Subordination of Individual Interest to General Interest The interest of an organisation is to achieve its goals.

These goals are achieved after integrating the efforts of different individuals, who are working in the organisation to satisfy their own personal needs. Sometimes, an individual starts giving priority to his own interest, but according to Fayol in all situations, company's interest should supersede the interest of individual.

6. The type of plan chosen by Rajan is Objective.

Following are the features of objectives

(i) They are clearly and specifically defined.

(ii) They are expressed in quantitative terms.

(iii) They are time-bound.

Or

The type of organisation referred is 'informal organisation'. Various merits of informal organisation are

Faster Spread of Information Under informal organisation, fixed lines of communication are not followed. Thus, informal organisation leads to faster spread of information as well as quick feedback.

Fulfillment of Social Needs It helps to fulfill the social needs of the members of the organisation. This enhances their job satisfaction, since it gives them a sense of belongingness in the organisation.

Fills Inadequacies of Formal Structure It contributes towards fulfillment of organisational objectives by compensating for inadequacies in the formal organisation, e.g. Employees reactions towards plans and policies can be tested through informal network.

7. The next four steps that would be followed after receiving the application blank are as follows

(i) **Selection tests** Candidates are required to take tests which measures the individual's job related proficiency and skills. Various types of tests are aptitude test, personality test, interest test, intelligence tests, etc.

(ii) **Employment interview** It involves an oral face-to- face interaction with the candidate.

It helps to check the details of application blank provided and also judge certain qualities like

(a) Quickness of response

(b) Personality

(c) Suitability for the job

(iii) **Reference and background checks**

Many employers request names, addresses and telephone numbers of references for the purpose of verifying information and gaining additional information about an applicant.

(iv) **Medical examination** After reference check and before the job offer, the candidate is required to undergo a medical fitness test.

The job offer is given to the candidate, only when the examiner has declared him fit after the medical examination.

8. Annie can approach the State Commission since the value of the car is ₹ 1 crore and State Commission includes complaints where the value of goods and services and the compensation claimed exceeds ₹ 50 lakhs but does not exceed ₹ 2 crore.

Following are the remedies that the consumer forum can provide to Annie

(i) To remove the defect in goods or deficiency in service.

(ii) To replace the defective product with a new one, free from any defect.

(iii) To refund the price paid for the product or the charges paid for the service.

9. **Meaning of product mix** Product mix means a group of closely related elements of a product which give it a unique identity.

Elements of product mix The following are the elements of product mix

(i) **Branding** Branding is the process of assigning a distinctive name or symbol to a product by which it can be remembered.

(ii) **Labelling** Labelling means designing a label it be put on the package.

(iii) **Packaging** It refers to covering, wrapping, crating, filling or compressing of goods to protect them from spoilage, pilferages, breakage, leakage, etc.

Or The importance of marketing can be viewed in following points

(i) It is a source of revenue for the business, as the production can translate into sale, on the basis of how effectively this function is performed.

(ii) Satisfying consumer needs.

(iii) Basis of decision-making, regarding what, how, when and where to produce.

(iv) Achieve coordination between production and consumption activities.

10. (i) The technique used by a business organisation to diagnose and analyse its micro and macro environment is SWOT analysis.

SWOT is an acronym for Strengths (S), Weaknesses (W), Opportunities (O) and Threats (T).

This is a very important and useful tool for the marketer, entrepreneur or business person for analysing business environment.

The SWOT analysis provides information that is helpful in matching the firm's resources and capabilities to the competitive environment in which it operates.

As such, it is instrumental in strategy formulation and selection. Environmental factors internal to the firm usually can be classified as strengths or weaknesses and those external to the firm can be classified as opportunities or threats.

Strengths (S) These are the inherent competencies of the organisation which help them to have advantage over competitors.

Weaknesses (W) These are the constraints or limitations which an enterprise faces. These poses challenges to the enterprise and place them at a disadvantageous position in front of their competitors.

Opportunities (O) Opportunities refer to the positive external trends or changes which put the firm in a favourable position and help them to strengthen their foothold in the market.

Threats (T) External environment may, many a times create obstacles in the functioning of the enterprise.

These may be due to economic slowdown, political instability, natural calamity, technological advancements, etc.

SWOT Analysis Example

Strengths	Opportunities
• Innovative product offering • Affordable prices • Loyal current users	• Expand social media presence • Work with industry influencers
Weaknesses	**Threats**
• Not enough brand recognition • No resources spent on marketing	• Touch competition • Supply chain challengers • Touch job market

(ii) Coordination is needed to perform all the functions of management. It can be highlighted through following points

(a) In **planning**, coordination is required between the main plan and supportive plans of different departments.

(b) **Organising**, is ineffective, if there is a lack of coordination between different departments and divisions.

(c) In **staffing**, coordination is required between the required skills and abilities of an individual who is selected to perform a job.

11. (i) Ramanpreet should invest in debentures. Following are the features of debentures

(a) Debenture represent borrowed funds.

(b) It carries a fixed rate of interest, to be paid regularly.

(c) They do not carry voting rights and right to participate in the company's management.

(d) There are repayable after a specific time period.

(ii) Following are the differences between debit card and credit card

Basis	Debit card	Credit card
Meaning	With a debit card, one's money will get deducted to make purchase directly from his or her bank account.	With a credit card, one can take a loan to make purchases and can pay back later.
Payment	The cardholder has to pay before using the card.	The cardholder has to pay after using the card.
Interest	No interest is charged.	One has to pay back the exact amount by its due date, otherwise interest will be charged.

Or

(i) Following are the three merits of retained earnings

(a) There is no liability for repayment of funds.
(b) It helps to increase the credit worthiness of the company.
(c) It helps the company to face contingencies and uncertainties of business.

Following are the two demerits of retained earnings

(a) It may result in monoply and concentration of economic power.
(b) It is an uncertain source of finance.

(ii) In the old days, banking used to be a time-consuming business.

If you wanted cash, for instance, you had to go to the bank branch, hand over a cheque to a bank employee, get a token and wait until the cashier called your number.

In the first week for a month, when there was a scramble for cash among customers, you had to wait a long time indeed.

But with the introduction of digital banking, the process of banking has become much effective and efficient.

The digital banking refers to banking done through the digital platform, doing away with all the paperwork like cheques, pay-in slips, demand drafts and so on. It enables a bank's customers to access banking products and services *via* an electronic/online platform.

12. (i) The following factors affect determination of price

(a) **Pricing Objectives** It is a very important factor, which helps in deciding the price. If the objective of company is profit maximisation, then generally high price is fixed, whereas the companies having the objective of sales maximisation, prefer low price to increase the sale.

(b) **Product Cost** Another important factor, which should be considered, is the cost of product or service. The price of the product must be able to cover the total cost of product. Total cost means fixed cost and variable cost. Fixed costs are fixed irrespective of production level e.g. rent of factory, cost of machinery, etc.

The variable costs vary with production e.g. Cost of raw materials, wages of labour, etc.

(c) **Extent of Competition in the Market** Extent of competition is necessary to be considered, while fixing the price of a product, as competitor's price and their anticipated reactions badly affect the reputation and sale of a product.

(d) **The Utility and Demand** It is necessary to anticipate the utility and demand of a product while fixing the price. If a product is offering higher utility, one can easily charge high price. Whereas, if utility is low, then high price cannot be charged.

(e) **Government and Legal Regulations** In order to protect the interest of general public, the government has the right to control the prices of various products and services by including the products in the category of essential commodities. The common commodities in essential commodi- ties are drugs, some food items, LPG, etc.

(ii) Following are the important features of services

(a) Services are intangible.
(b) A service is inseparable from its source.
(c) Services cannot be stored.

13. (i) Following are the two steps of controlling highlighted in the case

(a) **Setting Performance Standards** The first step of the control process is to establish standards against which actual results are to be evaluated.

Standards are the criteria against which actual performance would be measured. These serves as benchmarks, towards which an organisation strives to work.

(b) **Taking Corrective Measures** This is the final step in which manager takes corrective measures to bring back everything on track in the organisation i.e. according to set plans.

(ii) Following are the objectives of communication

(a) **Acts as Basis of Coordination** Communication acts as basis of coordination. It helps in coordinating the activities of various departments and persons in an organisation.

(b) **Helps in Smooth Working of an Enterprise** Communication ensures smooth functioning of an enterprise. Existence of an organisation depends fully on communication, i.e. transmitting information.

(iii) Following points highlight the importance of controlling

(a) **Accomplishing Organisational Goals** The controlling function measures the accomplishment against the standards and corrects deviations.
This helps in ensuring that organisation is moving on the right track to achieve the organisational goals.

(b) **Judging Accuracy of Standards** A sound controlling system helps the management to verify whether the standards set are accurate and objective. It keeps a careful check on the changes which are taking place in the organisation and in the environment, thereby, helping to review and raise the standards in the light of such changes.

(c) **Making Efficient Use of Resources** By exercising control, a manager seeks to reduce wastage and spoilage of resources. Each activity is performed in accordance with predetermined standards and norms.
Thus, controlling ensures that resources are being used efficiently and effectively towards the attainment of organisational goals.

(d) **Improving Employee Motivation** An effective control system ensures that an employee should be aware of what they are expected to do and what are the standards which are set for them, so that they will be appraised in future. Thus, it helps in motivating them to give better performance.

ISC

SAMPLE PAPER 01

Time : 3 hrs
Marks : 80

Commerce XII

General Instructions

1. Candidates are allowed additional 15 minutes for only reading the paper. They must not start writing during this time.
2. There are thirteen questions in the paper. All questions are compulsory..
3. This paper is divided into three Sections : A, B and C.
4. Section A has sixteen subparts which are very short answer questions. Each question carries 1 mark.
5. Section B has eight questions which are short answer questions. Each questions carries 4 marks.
6. Section C has four questions which are long answer questions. Each question carries 8 marks.
7. Internal choices have been provided in two questions in Section B and in one question in Section C.
8. The intended marks for questions are given in brackets [ ].

Section A

(16 Marks)

1. (i) The changes in technology and the taste and preferences of the consumers cannot be predicted. Which feature of the business environment is highlighted here? **[1]**

(a) Non-controllable
(b) General and specific forces
(c) Interrelatedness
(d) Uncertainty

(ii) Manjeet Singh is considered to be in the top management of Amlof Automotive Ltd. since he **[1]**

(a) works with the actual workforce and gives them all kinds of support
(b) ensures that his department has necessary personnel
(c) implements the plans developed by his superiors
(d) analyses the strategies of other automotive companies and formulates the goals of the company

(iii) Amtek Company plans to capitalise its undistributed profits. Which one of the following shares will the company issue to its existing shareholders? **[1]**

(a) Rights Shares (b) ESOP
(c) Sweat Equity Shares (d) Bonus Shares

(iv) In 2023, Raghav Enterprises, a manufacturer of consumer electronics, faced challenges in securing bank loans due to high interest rates and lengthy approval processes. To maintain its production cycle and sustain sales, the company relied on trade credit from its suppliers. This arrangement allowed Raghav Enterprises to procure raw materials without immediate payment, ensuring smooth business operations. The management found trade credit beneficial as it provided funds without creating a charge on the company's assets and helped increase sales by maintaining a steady supply of goods. **[1]**

Source *(Adapted) from Business Finance Reports*

Which of the following are advantages of trade credit as highlighted in the case?

(P) It is a continuous and convenient source of funds.
(Q) It involves legal formalities for approval.
(R) It does not create a charge on the firm's assets.
(S) It helps in promoting sales.

Codes

(a) Only (P) and (Q) (b) Only (P) and (R)
(c) Only (P), (R) and (S) (d) Only (Q) and (S).

(v) Identify the type of card in the below picture. [1]

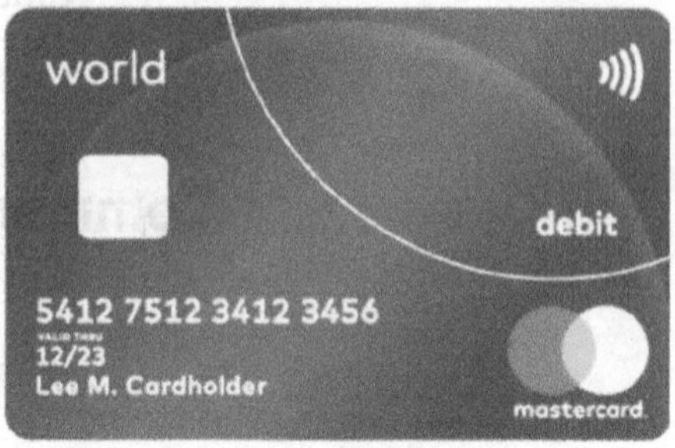

(a) Debit card (b) Credit card
(c) Prepaid card (d) None of these

(vi) Identify the factor affecting working capital requirement for candle making business during Diwali season illustrated in the below picture. [1]

(a) Credit policy (b) Seasonal factor
(c) Cyclical fluctuations (d) Nature of business

(vii) State whether the following are true or false. [2]

(a) When equity shares dominates the capital structure; the capital is considered as high geared.
(b) Bonus issue is made out of free reserves or securities premium collected in cash only.

(viii) The profit of Meenal Ltd. is ₹ 80,000 for the current financial year. Study the data of Meena Ltd. given below and answer the question that follows. [1]

Security	Yield
Interest on Debenture	₹ 5,000
Dividend on Preference Shares	₹ 5,000
Dividend on Equity Shares	₹ 25,000

……….. and equity shareholders will have a share in ₹ 45,000.

(ix) Identify the type of shares that are being discussed in the given picture. [1]

(x) The data given below shows that capital structure of XYZ Ltd is ……….. geared. [1]

XYZ Ltd.

DEBT 70%	EQUITY 30%

(xi) Sometimes, business houses fulfil their short-term financial needs through the help of commercial banks' assistance.

Identify any one type of short-term financial assistance provided by the commercial banks. [1]

(xii) The employees of MNL Co. have formed a Dramatics Club for their recreation. Name the type of organisation formed by them and state one of the features of such an organisation. [1]

(xiii) **Assertion** (A) Management of working capital refers to the management of current assets and current liabilities.

Reason (R) The major thrust of course is on the management of current assets; because current liabilities arise in the context of current assets. [1]

Alternatives

(a) Both Assertion (A) and Reason (R) are true and Reason (R) is the correct explanation of Assertion (A)
(b) Both Assertion (A) and Reason (R) are true, but Reason (R) is not the correct explanation of Assertion (A)
(c) Assertion (A) is true, but Reason (R) is false
(d) Assertion (A) is false, but Reason (R) is true

(xiv) Study the relation between the first and second words given below and fill in the fourth word on that basis. [2]

(a) Net settlement basis : NEFT :: Gross settlement basis : ……….. .
(b) Equity : Long-term source :: Public deposits : …………

Section B

(32 Marks)

2. There are number of factors which are required to be considered in devising a suitable capital plan for an industry.

In the light of this statement, explain any four factors to be considered while preparing a suitable capital plan. **[4]**

Or Based largely on his own experience, Fayol developed his own concept of administration.

As a part of his contributions, he gave certain principles of management. In the light of this statement, discuss any four principles formulated by Fayol.

3. Rajan Ltd. needs to raise funds from the financial market and hence, considers issuing equity shares. State any four reasons to explain why this source of raising funds is considered by the company. **[4]**

4. What are industrial products? How are they different from consumer products? **[4]**

Or Discuss how personal selling is important from customer's point of view.

5. Riya recently started a small bakery business and needed immediate funds to buy ingredients and equipment.

She approached different financial institutions and explored various short-term financing options to meet her working capital requirements.

Which short-term sources of finance can Priya consider to fulfill her financial needs? Explain any four such sources. **[4]**

6. As a Business Manager, outline the meaning and the three elements of delegation that are being considered for effective functioning. **[4]**

7. (i) A company decides to retain a portion of its earnings instead of distributing it as dividends to shareholders. This retained amount is reinvested into the business for expansion and modernisation. Name and briefly explain the source of finance that supports the above statement. **[2]**

(ii) A leading smartphone company has to constantly upgrade its products to keep up with rapid advancements in artificial intelligence and automation. Name and explain the dimension of the business environment being referred to in the above case. **[2]**

8. Zento Electronics, a leading smartphone manufacturer, recently introduced a new policy to strengthen consumer trust. The company now provides detailed product manuals and online tutorials to educate customers about the features and usage of their devices.

Additionally, Zento Electronics has launched a dedicated grievance redressal platform where consumers can easily file complaints and receive quick resolutions regarding product defects and after-sales services.

Source *Adapted from a business news article*

Identify and explain the two consumer rights that are taken into consideration by Zento Electronics in this case. **[4]**

9. You are the manager at Kaya Industries Ltd. You have to select a Marketing Manager for the company.

Explain any four advantages of external source of recruitment that you would consider while determining the type of source. **[4]**

Section C

(32 Marks)

10. (i) Vikram, a financial consultant, advises his client, Mehak, who wants to invest ₹ 5,00,000 in a secure long-term debt instrument offered by a reputed company. Vikram suggests an instrument that allows the company to raise long-term capital while ensuring periodic interest payments to investors.

Which long-term debt instrument should Mehak invest in? Explain any four benefits of this instrument from the company's perspective. **[5]**

(ii) State three characteristics of management. **[3]**

Or

(i) Through NEFT, an individual or company can transfer funds from any bank branch to another individual or company having an account with any other bank branch in the country. In the light of this statement, explain any five features of NEFT.

(ii) State any three advantages of branding to the companies.

11. (i) Differentiate between fixed capital and working capital. **[5]**

(ii) State the objectives of personal selling. **[3]**

12. (i) Discuss the merits and demerits of preference shares to the shareholders and the company. **[5]**

(ii) In functional structure, all functions are separated and resulting employees have little understanding or concern outside their functional area. In the light of this statement, state any three disadvantages of functional structure. **[3]**

13. Read the case given below and answers the questions that follow.

Chilly and Chocks Pizzas has various outlets to sell Pizzas and deal with the customers directly.

This channel of distribution was adopted by the organisation keeping in mind the nature of the product. In order to boost its sales, the management decided to introduce 'Buy one Get one Free' offer to its customers.

(i) Identify and explain the channel of distribution used by Chilly and Chocks Pizzas. **[2]**

(ii) Which element of promotion mix is highlighted in the above case? Explain. **[2]**

(iii) State any four objectives of the element of promotion mix identified in (ii) above. **[4]**

Answers

1. (i) (d)	(ii) (d)	(iii) (d)	(iv) (c)
(v) (a)	(vi) (b)	(vii) (a) T	(b) T
(viii) Participating preference shares		(ix) Sweat equity shares	
(x) highly	(xiii) (a)	(xiv) (a) RTGS	(b) Short-term source

ISC

SAMPLE PAPER 02

Time : 3 hrs
Marks : 80

Commerce XII

General Instructions

1. Candidates are allowed additional 15 minutes for only reading the paper. They must not start writing during this time.
2. There are thirteen questions in the paper. All questions are compulsory..
3. This paper is divided into three Sections : A, B and C.
4. Section A has sixteen subparts which are very short answer questions. Each question carries 1 mark.
5. Section B has eight questions which are short answer questions. Each questions carries 4 marks.
6. Section C has four questions which are long answer questions. Each question carries 8 marks.
7. Internal choices have been provided in two questions in Section B and in one question in Section C.
8. The intended marks for questions are given in brackets [ ].

Section A

(16 Marks)

1. (i) Small retail shops in India have increasingly started offering home delivery services through WhatsApp and other online platforms to meet changing consumer preferences. The feature of business environment indicated here is **[1]**

(a) Inter-relatedness
(b) Relativity
(c) Diversity
(d) Dynamism

(ii) Which one of the following is not counted as a current asset? **[1]**

(a) Inventory
(b) Cash
(c) Account receivable
(d) Equipment

(iii) In 2023, Raghav Mehta, the CEO of XYZ Ltd., announced, "Our company is committed to ensuring transparency and long-term sustainability in financing. As part of this commitment, we rely primarily on **equity shares**, which provide ownership rights, permanent capital, and voting rights to investors."
Source *Adapted: www.financialnews.in*

Which of the following features of equity shares are highlighted in the statement by Raghav Mehta? **[1]**

(P) Owner's Fund
(Q) Residual Owners
(R) Permanent Capital
(S) Voting Rights

Codes

(a) Only (P) and (Q) (b) Only (Q) and (R)
(c) Only (P), (R) and (S) (d) Only (P), (Q) and (S)

(iv) Rajiv's company faces rising raw material costs and slowing sales. To sustain operations and invest in new technology, he needs additional funds. Which of the following best highlights the importance of finance for Rajiv's business? **[1]**

(a) Finance is only required at the initial stage of business.
(b) Adequate finance helps in meeting contingencies and investing in innovation.
(c) Financial management is not important once the business is established.
(d) Finance is only necessary for day-to-day operations and not for expansion.

(v) Identify the type of banking service illustrated in the picture which helps in fund transfer through mobile applications. **[1]**

(a) Mobile Banking
(b) Debit Cards
(c) Online Banking
(d) Automated Teller Machine (ATM)

(vi) Identify the characteristic of management illustrated by the below picture in which the heads of all departments have contributed towards the company's growth. **[1]**

(a) Management is pervasive
(b) Management is multi-dimensional
(c) Management is a group activity
(d) Management is a dynamic function

(vii) State whether the following are true or false. **[2]**

(a) The organisational structure and the composition of the board of directors are one of the internal factors of micro environment of a business organisation.
(b) No bonus issue shall be made within 12 months of any public or right issue.

(viii) Identify the dimension of business environment highlighted in the below picture. **[1]**

(ix) .... function of management is related to placing the right person in the right job. **[1]**

(x) Business environment differs from country to country and region to region. Which feature of business environment is being referred to here? **[1]**

(xi) Kirti wants to transfer funds to another account using the services of XYZ Bank. Study the following table and answer the question that follows. **[1]**

XYZ Bank

Settlement Basis	Gross Settlement Basis
Amount	₹ 5,000,000

Kirti can transfer the funds using .... fund transfer system.

(xii) At Adtec Solutions, there is no reward or appreciation for a good suggestion. Thus, the subordinates do not want to offer any useful suggestions to their superiors. Which type of barrier to communication has been created in the firm? **[1]**

(xiii) **Assertion** (A) The business environment is the sum total of the external forces.
Reason (R) The different elements of the business environment are closely interrelated. **[1]**

Alternatives

(a) Both Assertion (A) and Reason (R) are true and Reason (R) is the correct explanation of Assertion (A)
(b) Both Assertion (A) and Reason (R) are true, but Reason (R) is not the correct explanation of Assertion (A)
(c) Assertion (A) is true, but Reason (R) is false
(d) Assertion (A) is false, but Reason (R) is true

(xiv) Study the relation between the first and second words given below and fill in the fourth word on that basis. **[2]**

(a) Gross National Product: Economic environment :: Customs : ....
(b) Free of cost : Bonus shares :: Discounted prices : ....

Section B

(32 Marks)

2. You are a financial expert and your company starts a business of manufacturing baby toys. Briefly explain any two types of working capital required by your business concern. **[4]**

3. (i) A company follows a clear chain of communication where employees receive orders from only one superior, ensuring no confusion in responsibilities.

   Name and briefly explain the principle given by Henri Fayol that supports the above statement. **[2]**

   (ii) In an organisation, there is a lack of discipline among employees, leading to delays in work and decreased productivity.

   Which principle of Henri Fayol can be applied to improve the situation? **[2]**

4. As a Marketing Manager, outline any four functions of packaging that you would consider essential for ensuring product success in the market. **[4]**

5. Aarav is a manager at an organisation where he is responsible for ensuring smooth communication between different departments. However, he often faces issues like language barriers, lack of attention, and differences in perception while conveying messages.

   State any four ways through which he can overcome the barriers to communication. **[4]**

6. Ravi urgently needed to transfer money to his friend, so he used his mobile banking app to send funds instantly, even outside banking hours.

   Identify the type of service and state its three features. **[4]**

Or A leading smartphone company has introduced AI-powered features in its latest model, keeping up with industry advancements.

At the same time, a popular food chain has modified its menu to include more plant-based and organic options due to changing consumer preferences for healthier choices.

Identify and explain the two components of the business environment being referred to here.

7. In an organisation, all the employees take things easy and are free to approach anyone for minor queries and problems. This has resulted in everyone talking to each other and thus resulting in inefficiency in the office. It has resulted in loss of secrecy.

   What system do you think the manager should adopt to improve communication? **[4]**

8. A leading smartphone company, TechNova, launched a new model with an advanced camera system and long battery life. However, soon after purchase, several customers reported that the battery drained within a few hours and the camera quality did not match the advertised features. Additionally, the company refused to accept returns or provide a replacement, stating that all sales were final.

   Source *(edited):https://www.business-standard.com*

   Identify and explain the two consumer rights that have been violated in the above case and justify your answer. **[4]**

9. Why is management considered to be a profession? **[4]**

Or Explain the importance of organising function of management.

Section C

(32 Marks)

10. (i) Explain how commercial banks help in meeting the financial needs of a firm? **[5]**

    (ii) What is economic and non-economic environment? **[3]**

11. (i) Riya Enterprises is expanding its operations and needs to hire skilled professionals for various roles. The company has decided to recruit candidates from outside the organisation to bring in fresh talent and new perspectives.

    Which external sources of recruitment can Riya Enterprises use? Explain any five of them. **[5]**

    (ii) Explain the essential elements of delegation. **[3]**

Or (i) "A country's decision to implement Real Time Gross Settlement (RTGS) for high-value transactions rather than relying solely on other payment methods can be a strategic move." Justify this statement by discussing the meaning and any four features of RTGS.

(ii) State any three features of debit card.

12. (i) Controlling is an indispensable function of management. Do you agree? Give reasons in support of your answer. **[5]**

(ii) Explain any three demerits of internal sources of recruitment. **[3]**

13. Read the case given below and answer the following questions that follow.

A reputed publishing company is planning to open new showrooms in some big cities in North India. The company wishes to invite celebrity novelists to inaugurate their new outlets. It also plans to invite other celebrities from the literary world and make new book releases before August. Introductory offers will be given in the form of price reductions, limited edition of autographed copies and discount coupons.

(i) Identify and explain the promotional tool adopted by the company. **[2]**

(ii) State any two benefits of promotional tool identified in (i) above. **[2]**

(iii) Briefly state any four sales promotion techniques. **[4]**

Answers

1. (i) (d) (ii) (d) (iii) (c)

(iv) (b) (v) (a) (vi) (c)

(vii) (a) T (b) T (viii) Technological environment (ix) Staffing

(xi) Real Time Gross Settlement (RTGS) (xiii) (b)

(xiv) (a) Social environment (b) Right Shares

ISC

SAMPLE PAPER 03

Time : 3 hrs
Marks : 80

Commerce XII

General Instructions

1. Candidates are allowed additional 15 minutes for only reading the paper. They must not start writing during this time.
2. There are thirteen questions in the paper. All questions are compulsory..
3. This paper is divided into three Sections : A, B and C.
4. Section A has sixteen subparts which are very short answer questions. Each question carries 1 mark.
5. Section B has eight questions which are short answer questions. Each questions carries 4 marks.
6. Section C has four questions which are long answer questions. Each question carries 8 marks.
7. Internal choices have been provided in two questions in Section B and in one question in Section C.
8. The intended marks for questions are given in brackets [ ].

Section A

(16 Marks)

1. (i) Select and write the odd one out of the following. **[1]**

(a) Different elements of business environment are closely interrelated.
(b) Business environment is rigid in nature.
(c) Business environment is difficult to predict.
(d) Social and cultural forces exercise significant influence on business.

(ii) When Sheetal Company acquired a toy manufacturing company; it paid a large amount for the goodwill. Which source of business funds of Sheetal Company was impacted? **[1]**

(a) Fixed Capital
(b) Special Working Capital
(c) Circulating Capital
(d) Gross Working Capital

(iii) In 2023, ABC Ltd., a well-established company, decided to issue bonus shares to its existing shareholders instead of distributing profits as dividends. The company followed the necessary conditions, including ensuring adequate undistributed earnings, complying with the Articles of Association, and passing a resolution in the Board of Directors' meeting. Additionally, since its articles required shareholder approval, the company sought approval in the general meeting. SEBI regulations were also adhered to during the process.

Source *Adapted from SEBI Guidelines on Bonus Shares, 2023*

Which of the following is a mandatory condition for issuing bonus shares? **[1]**

(P) The company must have adequate undistributed earnings.
(Q) The Board of Directors must pass a resolution.
(R) The company must take prior approval from SEBI for issuing bonus shares.
(S) SEBI guidelines regarding bonus shares must be followed.

Codes

(a) Only (P) and (Q)
(b) Only (Q) and (R)
(c) Only (P) (Q) and (R)
(d) Only (R) and (S)

(iv) EcoFin Ltd. ensures seamless and instant transfer of funds for its suppliers and stakeholders, enhancing financial efficiency. Which type of facility is being used by the company. **[1]**

(a) Debit Card
(b) Payment mechanism
(c) RTGS
(d) Financial instrument

(v) Identify the characteristic of management illustrated in the below picture where all the heads have contributed towards company's growth. [1]

(a) Management is multi-dimensional
(b) Management is all pervasive
(c) Management is a group activity
(d) Management is a dynamic function

(vi) Shift towards Packaged Food industry as represented in below picture is related to which dimension of business environment? [1]

(a) Social environment
(b) Legal environment
(c) Political environment
(d) Technological environment

(vii) State whether the following are true or false. [4]

(a) During the Covid-19 pandemic, many businesses started selling goods online and flourished. For such firms, the pandemic situation was an opportunity.

(b) Publication of a magazine on consumer rights is an example of the right to consumer education.

(viii) Study the data given below and answer the question that follows.

ABC Ltd

Current Assets	₹ 1,00,000
Current Liabilities	₹ 5,00,000

The gross working capital of ABC Ltd is .... [1]

(ix) The data given below shows that the capital structure of Kirti Enterprises is .... geared. [1]

Kirti Enterprises

Debt – 30%	Equity – 70%

(x) ITG Pharmacy planned to sell 1 crore 'Covicare' tablets in a year. The company received good response from the market and sold 1.5 crore tablets in a year.

Seeing the progress, the company decided to increase sales target to 2 crore tablets in a year. Which major benefit of planning has the company achieved? [1]

(xi) The symbol which appears on all 'Audi' cards and cannot be spoken but is a term related to brand is known as its [1]

(xii) Sushant went to a shop to buy detergent. The shopkeeper forced him to buy a particular brand of detergent out of the various available brands, irrespective of the willingness of Sushant.

Which right of Sushant, as a consumer, has been violated? [1]

(xiii) **Assertion** (A) In a balance sheet, the sum of retained earnings and common stock is known as common equity.

Reason (R) Common equity is nothing but just a poughing back of profit in business. [1]

Alternatives

(a) Both Assertion (A) and Reason (R) are true and Reason (R) is the correct explanation of Assertion (A)

(b) Both Assertion (A) and Reason (R) are true, but Reason (R) is not the correct explanation of Assertion (A)

(c) Both Assertion (A) and Reason (R) are true

(d) Both Assertion (A) and Reason (R) are false

(xiv) Study the relation between the first and second words given below and fill in the fourth word on that basis. **[2]**

(a) Security : Safety needs :: Recognition : ....

(b) Forward looking : Planning :: Backward looking ....

Section B **(32 Marks)**

2. Ravi is a business studies student who learned that the term 'market' is broad and can be classified based on different criteria. In this context, classify the market on any two basis. **[4]**

Or The pros and cons of each alternative needs to be weighed. Name and briefly explain the logical steps in the process of planning which are followed by manager before performing the step highlighted in the above statement.

3. (i) In an organisation, it is important that work-related decisions and instructions flow from a single source to avoid confusion and conflict among employees. Name and briefly explain the principle given by Henri Fayol that supports the above statement. **[2]**

(ii) A manager ensures that all employees are treated fairly and paid suitable compensation for their work. Which principle of Henri Fayol is being followed? **[2]**

4. Aman purchased a defective mobile phone of ₹ 15,000 from a reputed store. When the seller refused to replace it, he decided to file a complaint. He approached the appropriate authority that handles consumer disputes based on the value of the claim.

Which redressal authority is Aman approaching under the Consumer Protection Act, 2019? Explain. **[4]**

5. As a Regional Manager of a company, outline the four limitations of planning that you would consider while formulating plans. **[4]**

6. TechGadgets Ltd., a smartphone manufacturing company, is set to launch its latest budget-friendly model. The company has heavily invested in large-scale production facilities to lower costs, ensuring the phone is widely available at an affordable price. Simultaneously, the company is focusing on enhancing the product's features, such as battery life and camera quality, believing that customers prioritise superior product performance.

Source *(edited): https://www.economictimes.indiatimes.com*

Identify and explain the two marketing concepts being followed by TechGadgets Ltd. **[4]**

7. Manav, a manager of Acro Ltd., does not distribute the work amongst his subordinates, according to the capabilities. He has given the work on the basis of favouritism. Which principle is overlooked? Give some of its violating effects. **[4]**

8. You are a consumer rights activist. Explain the four rights of consumers that you will emphasise while educating people about their consumer rights. **[4]**

9. Explain the process of communication. **[4]**

Or Discuss the exchange functions of marketing.

Section C **(32 Marks)**

10. (i) The demand for leather will be derived from the demand for leather purses and other leather items in the market. This statement brings forth the characteristics of one of the categories of products. Identify the category and state four other characteristics of this category of product. **[5]**

(ii) Discuss the two concepts of management. **[3]**

Or

(i) Management is the dynamic, life giving element in every business. In the context of this statement, explain the importance of management in modern times.

(ii) Management is getting things done by people. Discuss.

11. (i) Explain how is coordination required in each function of management. **[5]**

(ii) Management is a systematised body of knowledge which explain certain general truths. Identify the nature of management highlighted in the given statement and state other two features of the nature so identified. **[3]**

12. (i) 'Find wants and fill them', 'create products and sell them' are the two important concepts of marketing. Identify them and differentiate between them on any five basis. **[5]**

(ii) Which function of management is also called 'management in action'? Discuss any two points of its importance. **[3]**

13. Read the case given below and answer the questions that follow.

After pursuing a course in Gemology from Australia, Raj started a workshop in Surat to support his father's jewellery business in Delhi. He was used to speaking in English, but the local skilled workers could understand only Hindi and Gujarati. As a result, Raj started facing problems in the work due to miscommunication between him and the workers. He was not able to get the jewellery designs made in the desired manner.

(i) Define the term communication. **[2]**

(ii) Suggest any four measures by which Raj can make his communication effective. **[4]**

(iii) With reference to planning as a function of management, explain the term programme and objective as a type of a plan. **[2]**

Answers

1. (i) (c) (ii) (a) (iii) (c) (iv) (c) (v) (c)
(vi) (a) (vii) (a) T (b) T
(viii) ₹ 1,00,000 (Gross Working Capital = Current Assets) (ix) low geared
(xi) Brand mark (xiii) (b) (xiv) (a) Self-esteem needs (b) Controlling

ISC

Latest ISC Specimen Paper

Time : 3 hrs
Marks : 80

Commerce XII

General Instructions

1. Candidates are allowed additional 15 minutes for only reading the paper. They must not start writing during this time.
2. There are thirteen questions in the paper. All questions are compulsory..
3. This paper is divided into three Sections : A, B and C.
4. Section A has sixteen subparts which are very short answer questions. Each question carries 1 mark.
5. Section B has eight questions which are short answer questions. Each questions carries 4 marks.
6. Section C has four questions which are long answer questions. Each question carries 8 marks.
7. Internal choices have been provided in two questions in Section B and in one question in Section C.
8. The intended marks for questions are given in brackets [ ].

Section A

(16 Marks)

1. (i) A company is facing liquidity crunch, hence offers relatively higher interest rates for upfront borrowing in comparison to commercial banks.

Which source of short-term finance would be suitable in the above case? **(Understanding) [1]**

(a) Factoring
(b) Customer advances
(c) Public deposits
(d) Instalment credit

(ii) The Supreme Court clarified that its firecracker restrictions are applicable not only to Delhi-NCR but to all states. It directed State Governments to control air and noise pollution, addressing petitions seeking a nationwide ban on the sale and use of firecracker.

The court emphasised the importance of raising awareness and noted its previous orders must be implemented.

Source *(edited) Economic Times-7th Nov, 2023, 12:22:00 PM IST*

How does the decision of the Supreme Court affect the businesses? **(Analysis) [1]**

P – Changes in preference of people affect consumer spending.

Q – Political changes influence the decisions of the business.

R – Judicial decisions impact business.

S – Social concerns change the mindset of consumer.

Codes

(a) P, Q and R are correct
(b) P, R and S are correct
(c) Q, R and S are correct
(d) P, Q and S are correct

(iii) Which one of the following is a disadvantage of e-banking? **(Recall) [1]**

(a) It gives a 24 × 7 access to customers
(b) Monitoring of each transaction by the customer inculcates financial discipline
(c) It reduces the load on the branch of the bank
(d) It requires technological proficiency on the part of bank and customer

(iv) Criya Automobiles Ltd. plans to increase its production services in India, hence they want to analyse the economic environment of the business.
Which one of the following factors should the company focus on? **(Application) [1]**
(a) Increase in the disposable income of the people
(b) Facilities available for usage of automation in the production process
(c) Modification in the foreign policy of the government
(d) The age composition of potential buyers

(v) Analyse the organisation chart given below carefully and identify the principle of management, as given by Henri Fayol, that is being violated here. **(Analysis) [1]**

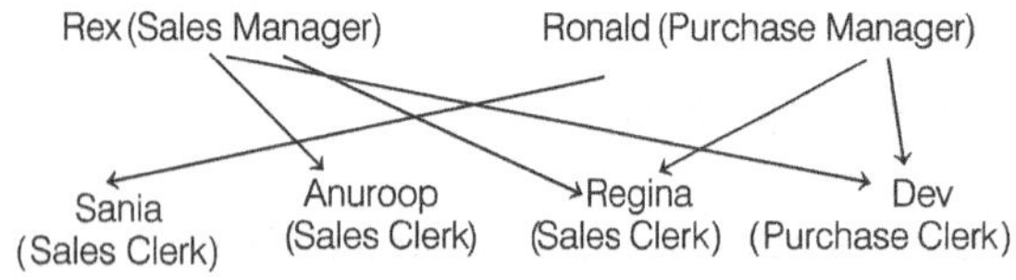

(a) Unity of direction
(b) Equity
(c) Unity of command
(d) Discipline

(vi) Identify the element of promotion mix used in the image shown below. **(Understanding) [1]**

Source *Yahoo Images*
(a) Sales promotion (b) Publicity
(c) Advertising (d) Personal selling

(vii) Study the relation between first and the second words given below and fill in the fourth word on that basis. **(Analysis) [2]**
(a) Commodity Market : Gold :: Capital Market : ....
(b) Advertiser : Advertising :: Publicity ....

(viii) State whether the following are true or false. **(Recall)**
(a) A company can identify its strengths by analysing its external environment. **[1]**
(b) Planning helps in identifying deviations and taking corrective actions. **[1]**

(ix) The diagram below shows that ....
is inherent in all the functions of management **(Understanding) [1]**

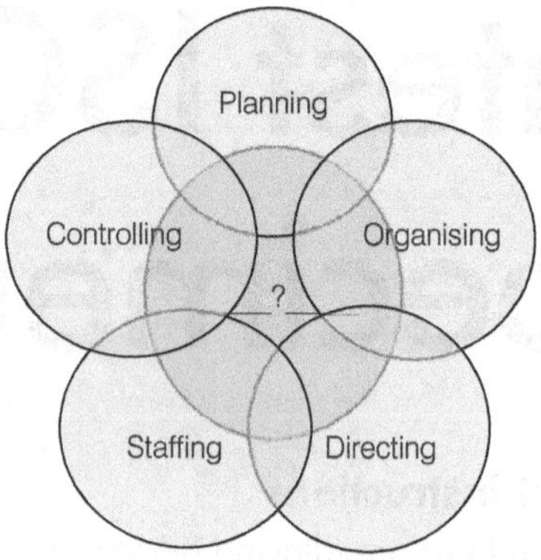

(x) Which element of directing is responsible for preparing the following chart in an organisation? **(Analysis) [1]**

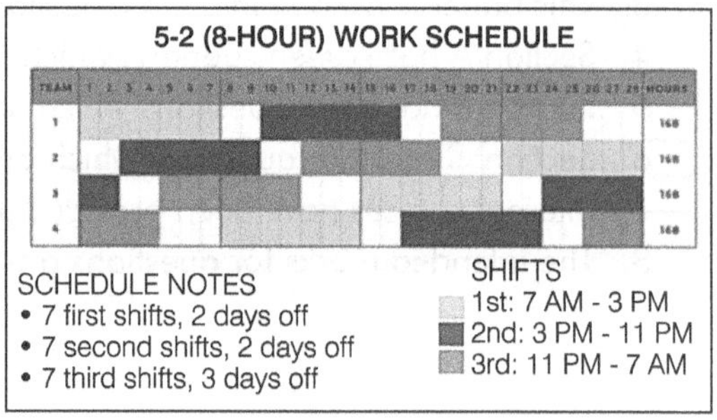

Source *buildremote.com*

(xi) Aradhya bought a tricycle online, but upon delivery found that its dimensions were not as big as she had expected.
When attempting to return it, she realised that the item was non-returnable.
Which consumer responsibility was overlooked by her? **(Understanding) [1]**

(xii) Fretta Tech Ltd. has expanded and opened multiple branches. To cope with the situation, the CEO starts transferring some of his authority to the general manager. The general manager feels over burdened and with the approval of the CEO disperses a part of his authority to different levels of management throughout the organisation.
Which concept of management has made Fretta Tech Ltd. a decentralised organisation? **(Understanding) [1]**

(xiii) Mohan, the manager of a business organisation, is very lax with his employees and subordinates. He does not give them parameters or rules for reporting to work and deadlines for completion of assignments.

Which principle of management given by Henri Fayol is not being followed by Mohan? **(Understanding) [1]**

(xiv) **Assertion** (A) Consumers must always be conscious of quality certification marks.

Reason (R) Quality certification marks act as a proof of purchase while filing a case in the consumer court. **(Analysis) [1]**

Alternatives

(a) Both Assertion (A) and Reason (R) are true and Reason (R) is the correct explanation of Assertion (A)

(b) Both Assertion (A) and Reason (R) are true, but Reason (R) is not the correct explanation of Assertion (A)

(c) Assertion (A) is true, but Reason (R) is false

(d) Both Assertion (A) and Reason (R) are false

Section B

(32 Marks)

2. Illustrate any four ways by which comprehensive planning contributes to goal alignment within different levels of a business organisation. **(Understanding) [4]**

Or Outline any four benefits of decentralisation that enhance the overall resilience of an organisation in the face of unforeseen challenges. **(Understanding)**

3. Elucidate any four factors affecting the capital structure of a joint stock company. **(Understanding) [4]**

4. Background Tech Solutions, a rapidly growing start-up company, faced the challenge of attracting and retaining 'top talent' in a competitive market. To address this, the company decided to implement a shares programme aimed at rewarding and incentivising key employees and directors.

Name and explain the type of shares that can be issued by the company. **(Understanding) [4]**

5. Outline any four fundamental characteristics of effective management in a modern business organisation. **(Understanding) [4]**

6. XYZ manufacturing company faced challenges related to the following issues

(i) The communication channels within the organisation were not clearly defined by the management, causing delays and misunderstandings.

(ii) The workplace was disorganised for both employees and material resources, affecting the overall efficiency.

Which principles of Henri Fayol can be applied to overcome the above challenges? Explain. **(Application) [4]**

7. Discuss the interplay between the goal setting during planning phase and the use of these goals as benchmarks for performance evaluation in controlling phase. **(Understanding) [4]**

8. Enumerate any four distinctions between marketing and selling. **(Recall) [4]**

9. (i) As packaging manager of a leading manufacturing company, provide four specific features which you would take into consideration while designing the packaging for a smart phone. **(Understanding) [4]**

Or

(ii) As a marketing manager, explain any four objectives of advertising you will familiarise a new sales team with, during their training and orientation sessions. **(Understanding)**

Section C

(32 Marks)

10. (i) What are the five key points that highlight the significance of environmental scanning in guiding organisations to adapt to rapidly changing business environment? **(Recall) [5]**

(ii) Explain any three fundamental differences between recruitment and selection. **(Understanding) [3]**

11. (i) As a financial manager for a growing Tech Start-up, evaluate three advantages and two disadvantages of choosing debt financing for your long-term capital needs. **(Evaluate) [5]**

(ii) Identify and explain two features of a plastic money having an overdraft facility which is issued by the commercial bank to its customers. **(Understanding) [3]**

Or (i) Anjum is a first time investor wanting to invest ₹ 10 lakhs in long-term capital appreciation. She is willing to take risks in return for high growth.

Which type of security should she invest in? Suggest any four features of this type of security. **(Application)**

(ii) Identify an electronic fund transferred in batches and state any two of its features. **(Recall)**

12. (i) The concept of marketing is customer centric which aims to achieve long-term business growth. Justify the statement by explaining any five objectives of marketing. **(Understanding) [5]**

(ii) TeeJay sales, a popular electronic retailer, sold a batch of smartphones with malfunctioning batteries to its customers. The manufacturing company misrepresented the products specifications in its advertisement.

On being approached by the grieving customers, TeeJay sales refused to entertain any complaints from the customers or replace or refund the products.

State and explain any three rights of the consumers which were violated in this case, as per the Consumer Protection Act, 2019. **(Understanding) [3]**

13. Read the passage given below and answer the questions that follow.

By applying Maslow's Hierarchy of needs, the human resources department in organisations strive to make the workplace a second home for the employees.

The professional employees who studied psychology and organisational behaviour create good working conditions in the workplaces.

In offices, one can find comfortable places, places to rest and nap, kitchen and plenty of food and drinks and transportation facility. Training programmes are conducted for employees on principles and ethics of workplace and respect for fellow employees.

Some organisations also have rewarding systems club membership, profit shares and promotion, retirement plan and social insurance, medical insurance and annual paid vacations. All these conditions and benefits have a great impact on the behaviour of employees which eventually impacts the work environment and business of the organisation.

Source *Alaa Etman (edited): Egypt case: How companies can use Maslow's Hierarchy of needs to enhance the motivation of their workforce?*

(i) Discuss how each need, as given by Maslow, is satisfied in the above case. **(Analysis) [5]**

(ii) To which level of management, does the human resource manager belong? Mention any two functions performed by her. **(Recall) [3]**

Answers

1. (i) (*c*) Public deposits (ii) (*b*) P, R and S are correct

(iii) (*d*) It requires technological proficiency on the part of bank and customer

(iv) (*a*) Increase in the disposable income of the people

(v) (*c*) Unity of command (vi) (*a*) Sales promotion

(vii) (a) Stock Exchange/Financial Institutions

(b) Media

(viii) (a) True

(b) False. Controlling helps in identifying deviations and taking corrective actions.

(ix) coordination (x) Supervision

(xi) Asking for full information

(xii) Delegation of authority (xiii) Discipline

(xiv) (*c*) Quality certification marks do not primarily act as proof of purchase while filing a case in the consumer court. Proof of purchase is typically provided through receipts or other documentation, not the quality certification marks themselves.

2. Comprehensive planning contributes to goal alignment within different levels of a business organisation in the following ways

(i) **Planning provides Directions** Planning sets out standards for controlling in an organisation. It ensures that the objectives are certainly asserted so that they serve as a model for determining what action should be taken and in which direction. If objects are well established, employees are informed of what the company has to do and what they need do to accomplish those purposes.

(ii) **Planning Decreases the Chances of Risk** Planning is an activity which permits a manager to look forward and predict changes. By determining in prior the tasks to be completed, planning considers the way to deal with changes and unpredictable effects.

(iii) **Planning Decreases Overlapping and Wasteful Activities** Planning works as the foundation of organising the activities and purposes of distinct branches, departments and people. It assists in avoiding chaos and confusion. Since planning guarantees precision in understanding and action, work is conducted easily without delays.

(iv) **Planning Encourages Innovative Ideas** As the primary function of management, planning allows new approaches to be developed into actionable plans. This is one of the most challenging aspects for management, as it directs all planned actions towards the growth and development of the business.

Or Following are the benefits of decentralisation that enhance the overall resilience of an organisation in the face of unforeseen challenges

(i) **Growth and Diversification** Decentralisation allows different parts of the company to explore new markets and products, leading to overall growth and variety in business operations.

(ii) **Quick Decision-making** With decision- making power closer to the operational level, responses to challenges are faster and more effective.

(iii) **Efficient Communication** Information flows more smoothly and quickly within smaller, decentralised units, improving coordination and understanding.

(iv) **Ease of Expansion** It's easier to expand into new areas or markets because local managers can make decisions that fit their specific situations.

3. Factors affecting the capital structure of a joint stock company are as follows (any four)

(i) **Position of Cash Flow** It is important to consider the size of projected cash flow before raising debt. Cash flow must not only cover fixed cash payment obligations, but there must be sufficient cash for smooth working of the business.

(ii) **Cost of Financing** It may be defined as the payment made by the company to obtain capital. Thus, interest is the cost of debentures or loan and dividend paid by the company is the cost of equity and preference share capital. The rate of dividend or preference shares is fixed which is generally lower than that of equity shares. The cost of debentures is generally lower and tax deductible.

(iii) **Period and Purpose** It also affect the capital structure. For long-term funds, equity shares are preferable while for medium-term, preference shares and debentures help in fulfilling the needs of modernisation and growth.

(iv) **Flexibility** The capital structure should be flexible. Since, debentures and preference shares are redeemable, they help in making the capital structure flexible. Equity shares are not redeemable and hence they make the capital structure rigid.

(v) **Control Consideration** If the company wants to retain control, then debt financing should be preferred. Equity shares can result in dilution of control because of existence of voting rights and ability to participate in management activities.

4. Sweat equity shares can be issued by the company. These are a type of equity shares that a company issues to its employees or directors. The shares are issued at a discount or for consideration other than cash. The purpose of issuing sweat equity shares is to motivate employees to work harder and contribute to the company's success. Sweat equity shares can be issued for providing know-how or for making intellectual property rights available.

The sweat equity shares issued to employees or directors must be subject to a lock in period of three years from the date of allotment. During the lock-in period, the shares cannot be transferred or sold by the employee or director who has been issued the shares.

5. Following are the fundamental characteristics of effective management (any four)

(i) **Management is Goal-oriented** There are some basic goals which become the reason for existence of all organisations.

(ii) **Management is a Group Activity** Management helps in uniting the efforts of diverse individuals towards fulfilling the common organisational goal.

(iii) **Management is Universal** It exists in all organisations whether big or small, business or non-business.

(iv) **Management is a Dynamic Function** An organisation interacts with external environment which keeps on changing. Management strives to adapt to the changing environment.

(v) **Management is an Intangible Force** Its presence can only be felt by orderliness and accomplishment of targets, as it is an invisible force.

6. (i) According to principle of **Scalar Chain**, formal lines of authority should be established from the highest to the lowest ranks in the organisational structure. As per the scalar chain, communication from top to bottom should follow official lines of command. This principle by Henri Fayol needs to be implemented in XYZ company as it would help in establishing the chain of authority and communication from top to bottom and would be followed by managers and subordinates.

(ii) As per the principle of **order**, there should be an orderly arrangement for both men and material. It implies that there should be a fixed place for all the things and for everyone in the organisation. The implementation of the principle of order would help in ensuring the proper use of resources in a structured manner.

7. The interplay between goal setting during the planning phase and using these goals as benchmarks for performance evaluation in the controlling phase is critical for ensuring organisational effectiveness and achieving desired outcomes.

Planning and controlling are intertwined and complementary functions. They co-exist in an organisation. Planning specifies the goals for an organisation, while controlling ensures the accomplishments of these goals.

Planning also determines the process of control while controlling provides the basis for planning. Once a plan becomes operational, controlling is necessary to monitor its progress.

Thus, we can say that planning without controlling is meaningless. Similarly, controlling is blind without planning. If the standards are not set in advance, managers have nothing to control. Planning and controlling, both are inseparable and they reinforce each other.

As a process, planning involves creative thinking and judgement. Controlling ensures that these thoughts and decisions are converted into desired actions.

Planning and controlling are both backward looking and forward-looking functions. Planning is prescriptive, while controlling is evaluative. Controlling provides feedback to planning by identifying areas for improvement. By assessing the performance against the plans, it provides a review and thus ensures that future performance matches the planned performance.

8. Differences between marketing and selling are (any four)

Basis	Marketing	Selling
Meaning	Marketing implies understanding the customers' needs and introducing a product accordingly.	It is a transfer of product from the manufacturer to the customer in exchange for the money.
Approach	Customer-oriented approach is followed.	Product-oriented approach is followed.
Strategy	Marketing adopts pull strategy.	Selling follows push strategy.
Target Audience	The targets audience for marketing is the general public.	It targets specific individuals and companies.
Tenure	It involves planning and is long-term.	It is immediate and hence considered as short-term.
Primary Aim	Its main aim is to create products that provide fulfill customers' requirements and provide them maximum satisfaction.	It aims at attracting the buyers to influence the target audience to become buyers of the product.
Scope	The scope of marketing is varied and includes advertisement, customer support, after sales service, etc.	Sales is narrow and limited only to selling of a product.

9. (i) Features that would be taken into consideration while designing the packaging for a smartphone are as follows (any four)

(a) The package should be convenient to handle and use. It is important that package should be easy to open and close and should fit well into the cupboard, drawer, refrigerator, etc.

(b) The package should aim to provide aesthetic satisfaction in terms of design, neatness and beauty. Package should be attractive and eye-catching that can gather the attention immediately.

(c) It should be safe and should be able to protect the contents of the product.

(d) It should build customer's confidence by telling the true story of the product.

(e) The package should establish its own identity appropriate to the product in terms of user's expectations. In other words, it should provide a distinct personality and status to the product.

Or (ii) Following are the objectives of advertising that should be familiarised with the new sales team (any four)

(a) **To Build Brand Loyalty for a Specific Product** Advertising aims to create a strong emotional connection with customers, encouraging repeated purchases and long-term commitment to the brand.

(b) **To Improve the Company's Reputation** By highlighting positive attributes and achievements, advertising can enhance the public image of a company, fostering trust and goodwill among consumers.

(c) **To Bring a New Product to Market by Creating Awareness among Potential Customers** Advertising generates buzz and interest about a new product, informing potential customers of its existence and benefits.

(d) **To Warn Consumers about Forgeries or Counterfeit Goods** Advertisements can alert consumers to the presence of counterfeit products, educating them on how to identify and avoid fake items.

(e) **To Inform Customers about the Product's Numerous uses** Through advertising, companies can demonstrate the versatility and various applications of their products.

10. (i) Environmental scanning plays a significant role in guiding organisations to adapt to rapidly changing business environment in the following ways (any five)

(a) It helps a firm in attaining the first mover advantage by identifying opportunities and using them for the growth of the business.

(b) It provides early warning signals by identifying various threats and helps the enterprise to take measures to reduce their adverse effects on business.

(c) It helps to improve efficiency and performance of the enterprise.

(d) It guides in formulation of policies and strategies so as to deal effectively with changing conditions, for the benefit of the organisation.

(e) It prepares the firm to cope-up with rapid changes that are occurring in the environment. If the firm is not able to cope-up with the changes, then it may adversely affect the organisation's efficiency.

(f) It helps in tapping useful resources, that are present in its environment such as efficient labour, natural resources, etc.

(g) It helps the organisation to understand customers' needs and focus on fulfilling them, in order to increase turnover and profitability.

(ii) Following are the differences between recruitment and selection (any three)

Basis	Recruitment	Selection
Meaning	Recruitment can be defined as the process of searching and motivating candidates to apply for a job.	Selection is that process of staffing, which eliminates the unsuitable candidates and chooses the suitable candidates.
Sequence	Recruitment is the process which ends with staffing and precedes selection in the process of staffing.	Selection is the last step of recruitment in the process of staffing.
Purpose	The basic purpose is to create a large pool of applicants for the jobs.	The basic purpose is to eliminate as many candidates as possible until the most suitable person gets finalised.
Scope	Recruitment relates to the extent of receiving applications and selection from within them.	Selection involves sorting of the candidates.

11. (i) Advantages of debentures from company's point of view (any three)

(a) The company's control remains in the hands of its shareholders, even the profit sharing ratio remains the same.

(b) Debentureholders are paid-off first, as it is treated as a liability to the business.

(c) The use of debentures can encourage long- term funding to grow a business. It is also cost-effective when compared with other forms of lending.

(d) Benefit of trading on equity.

Disadvantages from company's point of view (any two)

(a) The interest payment is a financial burden on a company because it must pay the interest dues to the debentureholders even if it faces monetary loss.

(b) Issuing debentures assists a company in trading on equity. However, such debt instruments make it reliant on debt. Often, an imbalanced debt-equity ratio hampers the financial viability of a company.

(c) Redeeming debentures causes a huge cash outflow which may imbalance a company's liquidity.

(ii) Credit card facility is issued by the bank to its customers.

Features of credit card are as follows (any two)

(a) A credit card comes with a bank approved credit limit. This limit defines the amount that the credit holder can spend using that card.

(b) The credit amount must be paid back by the holder to the bank on the due date, which is mostly after 30 days of making the purchase.

(c) The limit on the credit card is decided by the bank, depending on the customer's credit score and credit history.

Or (i) Anjum should invest in equity shares as she wants to invest in long-term capital appreciation and is also willing to take risks.

Following are the features of equity shares

(a) **Owner's Fund** The equity shareholders provide fixed capital for initialising the business. Therefore, they are a part of owner's fund.

(b) **Permanent Capital** The equity share capital is not redeemable during the lifetime of the company.

Hence, it is a permanent capital. In case of winding-up of the company, they are the last one to receive repayment of capital.

(c) **Residual Owners** Returns are uncertain as the rate of dividend is not fixed. Once all the claims on the income of the company and assets have been settled, the equity shareholders receive their share.

(d) **Voting Rights** Equity shareholders can participate in the company's affairs and management. The equity shareholders can exercise their voting rights.

(ii) NEFT stands for National Electronic Funds Transfer. It is an electronic payment system that allows individuals, companies and organisations to transfer funds between bank accounts. NEFT transactions are processed in batches and settled in hourly intervals throughout the day.

Following are the features of NEFT (any two)

(a) NEFT is an electronic payment system that uses a secure mode of transferring funds from one bank branch to another bank branch.

(b) It uses the Public Key Infrastructure (PKI) technology to ensure end-to-end security and rides on the Indian Financial Network (INFINET).

(c) Fund transfer generally takes place on the same day, depending upon the time of requesting such funds transfer.

12. (i) Marketing is a crucial function in any business, focusing on understanding and meeting customer needs to achieve sustainable growth. Following are the five objectives of marketing

(a) **Customer Satisfaction** The primary objective of marketing is to satisfy the needs of consumers by producing the right products and services at the right time, right place and right price.

All marketing activities are guided by information concerning what customers expect from business. No business enterprise can survive and grow in the long-run unless it provides full satisfaction to consumers.

(b) **Profitability** A business enterprise is an economic institution. It must earn profits otherwise it cannot survive and prosper.
But profits should be achieved through customer satisfaction.

(c) **Coordination and Integration** Marketing must aim at bringing about an effective coordination and integration between product, price, promotion and distribution.
It must also ensure coordination between marketing and business activities such as manufacturing, finance, personnel, etc.

(d) **Service to Society** Marketing should focus on improving the quality of living of people by providing a wide variety of quality products and services at reasonable prices. According to Malcom McNair, "Marketing is the creation and delivery of a standard of living to society." Marketing should also be oriented towards conservation of national resources and protection of environment.

(e) **Creation of Demand** A business firm can sell goods and services only when there are customers willing to buy them, therefore, the first purpose of marketing is to create demand for goods and services. For this purpose, marketing finds out the needs and preferences of customers.

(ii) Three rights of the consumers which were violated in this case, as per the Consumer Protection Act, 2019 are as follows

(a) **Right to be Heard** The consumer has a right to file a complaint and to be heard in case of dissatisfaction with a good or a service.
The interests and complaints of the customers were not heard by the retailer. Hence, right to be heard was violated.

(b) **Right to Seek Redressal** This right assures justice to consumers against exploitation and includes compensation for any loss or injury suffered by the consumers, replacement of goods or repair of defects in the goods in order to provide satisfaction to consumers. The electronic retailer refused to accept any complaints. Hence, the right to seek redressal was violated.

(c) **Right to be Informed** Consumers have the right to be informed about the quality, quantity, potency, purity, standard and price of goods and services that he intends to buy.
The customers were not informed about the accurate product specifications in its advertisement. Hence, right to be informed was violated.

13. (i) Maslow's hierarchy of needs is a theory about what motivates and fulfills humans. It states that five categories of human needs dictate an individual's behaviour.
Following are the five categories of needs that are satisfied in the case

(a) **Physiological Needs** These needs are the basic needs for food, water, sleep, etc. They are also called survival needs. In the given passage, the organisation fulfills the physiological needs of its employees by providing them comfortable working conditions, places to rest, kitchen facility.

(b) **Safety Needs** These needs include physical safety against accidents, fire, etc. and economic security against sickness, old age, etc. With reference to the given case, the organisation takes care of the safety needs by providing its employees with social insurance and medical insurance schemes.

(c) **Love and Belonging Needs** These needs are the need for association and friendship with others.
The organisation ensures the fulfillment of these needs by giving certain opportunities to its employees outside workplace and gives them club memberships, annual paid vacations, etc.

(d) **Esteem Needs** These needs include self-esteem and esteem for others which is self-confidence, power, prestige, etc.
The organisation has a rewarding system, profit shares and promotion opportunities for its employees to ensure the fulfilment of esteemed needs.

(e) **Self-actualisation Needs** These needs refer to the employees' needs for growth and self-fulfillment. The organisation provides its employees with training programmes on principles and ethics of workplace for employees to grow and learn.

(ii) **Middle Level** Human resources manager belongs to the middle level.
Following are the two functions performed by human resource manager (any two)

(a) Interpret the policies to lower management.

(b) Taking decisions regarding the number of personnel in the department.

(c) Assigning duties and responsibilities to employees in their departments.

Newly Added Topics

Chapter 1 Business Environment

Environmental Scanning

It refers to the process by which an organisation gathers, analyses and interprets information from the external environment to identify opportunities and threats that can impact its business.

It is an important part of understanding the business environment, as it helps managers to

(i) Understand the changing trends in the market, (ii) Anticipate future challenges and (iii) Make informed and strategic decisions.

It involves monitoring factors like political, economic, social, technological, legal and environmental conditions that influence business operations.

Chapter 3 Long-term Sources of Finance for a Joint Stock Company

Qualified Institutional Placement (QIP)

Qualified Institutional Placement (QIP) is a method through which a listed company can raise capital by issuing equity shares, fully and partly convertible debentures or any other securities (other than warrants) to Qualified Institutional Buyers (QIBs) without the need to submit any pre-issue filings to the Securities and Exchange Board of India (SEBI).

It is a faster and simpler way of raising funds compared to public offerings and is used primarily to avoid long regulatory procedures.

Features of Qualified Institutional Placement (QIP)

1. **Lower legal and compliance costs** It eliminates the high legal fees associated with listing overseas or conducting a public offering.
2. **SEBI-regulated pricing** It's pricing is based on the company's average stock price over the last six months to protect investors and the issuing company.
3. **Quick capital access** The setup and subscription process is significantly faster.
4. **Minimal ownership dilution** Qualified Institutional Placement allows companies to raise funds without significantly diluting promoter stakes.

Chapter 5 Banking Latest Trends

Digital Banking

In the old days, banking used to be a time-consuming business. If you wanted cash, for instance, you had to go to the bank branch, hand over a cheque to a bank employee, get a token and wait until the cashier called your number. In the first week for a month, when there was a scramble for cash among customers, you had to wait a long time indeed. But with the introduction of digital banking, the process of banking has become much effective and efficient. The digital banking refers to banking done through the digital platform, doing away with all the paperwork like cheques, pay-in slips, demand drafts and so on. It enables a bank's customers to access banking products and services via an electronic/online platform.

UPI

Unified Payment Interface (UPI) is a popular mobile payment method that allows you to transfer funds from one bank account to the other, instantly and free of charge. Ever since its inception, UPI has made financial transactions much easier for account holders.

E-wallet

E-wallet is a type of electronic card which is used for transactions made online through a computer or a smartphone. Its utility is same as a credit or debit card. An e-wallet needs to be linked with the individual's bank account to make payments.

Chapter 6 Management : An Introduction

Levels of Management

There are three levels in the hierarchy of an organisation. These levels of management determines the amount of authority and status enjoyed by an employee.

1. Top Level Management

Top level consist of senior most executives of organisation. This level includes Board of Directors, Chief Executive Officer (CEO), Managing Director, Chairman, President, Vice-President, Chief Financial Advisor (CFO) etc. The people working at this level have maximum authority.

Main functions of top level management

(i) To strive for welfare and survival of business.

(ii) To formulate overall organisational goals and policies of the business.

(iii) To integrate diverse elements and coordinate the activities of different departments according to the overall objectives of the organisation.

(iv) To analyse the business environment and its implications for the survival of the firm.

(v) They are responsible for all the activities of business and their impact on society.

2. Middle Level Management

Middle level management acts as a link between top and lower level management. This level includes division heads, such as Finance Manager, Marketing Manager, Branch and Regional Managers, Departmental and Divisional Heads, Plant Superintendent, etc.

Main functions of middle level management

(i) To interpret the policies framed by top management.

(ii) To select and appoint employees for middle and supervisory level and evaluate their performance.

(iii) To assign duties and responsibilities to lower level managers.

(iv) To motivate them to achieve desired objectives.

(v) To cooperate with other departments for smooth functioning of organisation.

3. Operational or Supervisory Level Management

This management level includes the groups or members, who are concerned with execution of the work. They are also known as first line managers and relates to the lower level in the hierarchy of the organisation.

Main functions of lower level management

(i) To directly oversee the efforts of the workforce.

(ii) To interact with actual workforce and pass on middle level manager's instructions to the workers.

(iii) To ensure that wastage of materials is minimised, output quality and safety standards are maintained. The quality and quantity of output depends on the hardwork, discipline and loyalty of workers.

(iv) To represent workers' grievances and suggestions before the management.

(v) To ensure safe and proper working conditions for workers.

Chapter 8 Functions of Management

Strategy (As a Type of Plan)

A strategy is a comprehensive plan, which includes three dimensions *viz.* determining long-term objectives, adopting a particular course of action and allocating resources necessary to achieve objectives.

Following are the **features** of strategy

(i) It is implied for a long period of time.

(ii) It is formed by top level management.

(iii) It may be changeable according to changes in environment.

(iv) It is formed usually after SWOT analysis.

(v) It helps to cope up with environmental issues and changes.

Styles of Leadership

Leadership style refers to a leader's behavioural pattern reflected by him/her in his/her role.

Following are the different leadership styles

1. Democratic Leadership

A democratic leader involves the team in making decisions and values their opinions. A democratic leader provides freedom of thinking and listens to suggestions, grievances and opinions of the subordinates.

This style is of mutual benefit which help subordinates to become part of team and help leaders (seniors) to make better decisions. A democratic leader exercises more control by using forces within the group.

2. Autocratic Leadership

An autocratic leader makes all the decisions and expects everyone to follow orders without question. This leadership style is very effective in getting productivity in many situations. It also facilitates quick decision-making.

3. Laissez-Faire Leadership

A laissez-faire leader gives team members a lot of freedom to do their work as they see fit. The group members work on their own tasks resolving issues themselves. The manager is there only to support them and supply them the required information to complete the task assigned. At the same time, the subordinate assumes responsibility for the work to be performed.

4. Bureaucratic Leadership

Bureaucratic leadership relies on a clear chain of command, strict regulations and conformation by its followers. A bureaucratic leadership style is a management style that follows a hierarchical structure and adheres to established procedures. Bureaucratic leadership relies more on the entire line of authority versus a single leader. Organisations that follow a bureaucratic leadership style include government agencies such as the military, rescue services or a government research team.

Chapter 10 Marketing Mix

Pricing Strategies

1. **Cost plus pricing method** In this method of pricing, price of a product is equal to its cost plus margin of profit. It ensures that the business covers its cost and earns a reasonable profit.
2. **Competitive pricing** In this method, prices are set based on what competitors are charging for similar products. The business may charge the same, slightly lower or slightly higher depending on its brand and market strategy.

   It is useful in markets with intense competition. This strategy helps the firm stay relevant and attract price-sensitive customers.
3. **Price-skimming** Under this method, at the beginning, business charges a very high price for its product and later on reduces the price.
4. **Penetration pricing** Under this method, prices are set very low, so as to capture maximum market share and later on the price is increased.
5. **Value-based pricing** Value-based pricing is decided by estimating how much value the customer places on a product. Instead of focusing on production cost or competition, it focuses on the customer's perception. If customers see the product as highly valuable, they are willing to pay more. This strategy is common for luxury items, brands, or unique services.

Chapter 11 Consumer Protection

Punishment for False or Misleading Advertisement (The Consumer Protection Act, 2023)

Any manufacturer, service provider, advertiser, advertising agency or endorser who causes a false or misleading or surrogate advertisement to be made, which is prejudicial to the interest of consumers, shall be punished with imprisonment for a term which may extend to **two years** and with fine which may extend to **ten lakh rupees**; and for every subsequent offence, be punished with imprisonment for a term which may extend to **five years** and with fine which may extend to **fifty lakh rupees**.

Relief Available under Consumer Protection Act

As per Consumer Protection Act, 2023, to issue corrective advertisement to neutralize the effect of misleading advertisement at the cost of the supplier responsible for issuing such misleading advertisement.

